Fourth Grade Math with Confidence

Student Workbook
Part A

Fourth Grade Math with Confidence

Student Workbook

Part A

KATE SNOW

WELL-TRAINED MIND PRESS

Names: Snow, Kate (Teacher), author.

Title: Fourth grade math with confidence. Student workbook part A / Kate Snow.

Other titles: Student workbook part A

Description: [Charles City, Virginia] : Well-Trained Mind Press, [2024] | Series: Math with confidence | Interest age level: 009-010.

Identifiers: ISBN: 978-1-944481-52-0 (paperback)

Subjects: LCSH: Mathematics--Study and teaching (Elementary) | LCGFT: Problems and exercises. | BISAC: JUVENILE NONFICTION / MATHEMATICS / Arithmetic.

Classification: LCC: QA107.2 .S664 2024 | DDC: 372.7--dc23

4 5 6 7 8 9 10   Versa   30 29 28 27 26 25 | J25-10801

Table of Contents

Author's Note

You'll need three books to teach *Fourth Grade Math with Confidence*. All three books are essential for the program.

- The Instructor Guide contains the scripted lesson plans for the entire year (Units 1-16).
- Student Workbook Part A contains the workbook pages for the first half of the year (Units 1-8).
- Student Workbook Part B contains the workbook pages for the second half of the year (Units 9-16).

The Student Workbooks are not meant to be used as stand-alone workbooks. The hands-on teaching activities in the Instructor Guide are an essential part of the program. You'll need the directions in the Instructor Guide to guide your child through the Lesson Activities pages. The icon with two heads means that your child should complete these pages with you, and that she is not expected to complete these pages on her own.

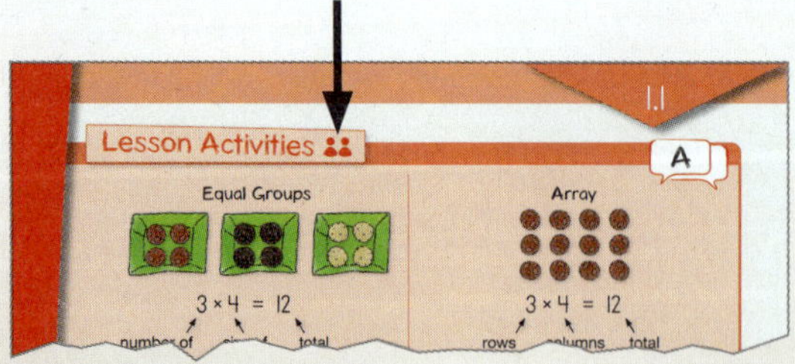

The Practice and Review pages give your child practice with new concepts and review previously-learned skills. The icon with one head means that your child may complete these pages on his own. Most fourth-graders will be able to complete these workbook pages independently, but some may need help reading and interpreting the directions.

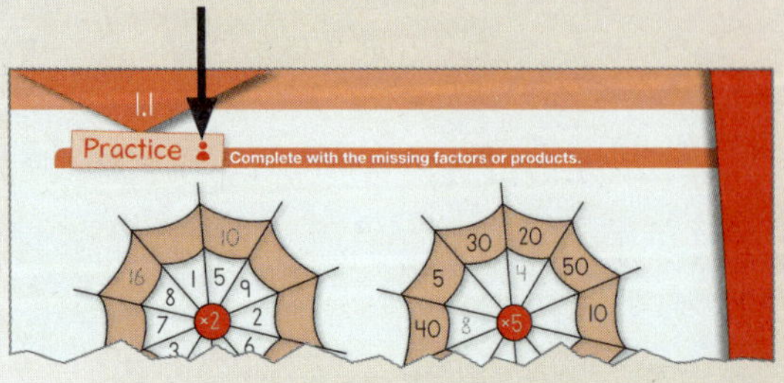 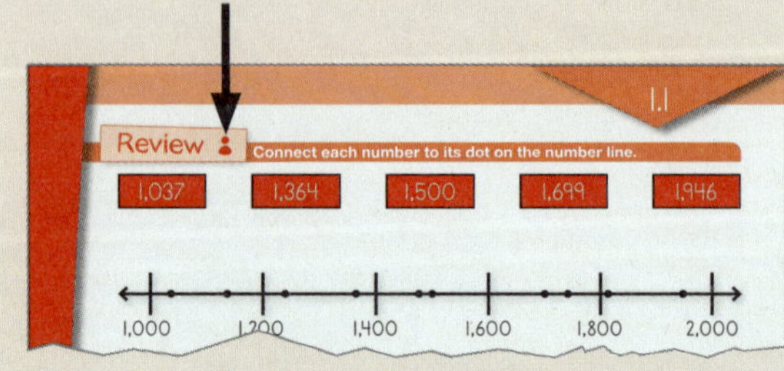

Lesson Activities 

A

Equal Groups

$$3 \times 4 = 12$$

number of groups   size of each group   total

Array

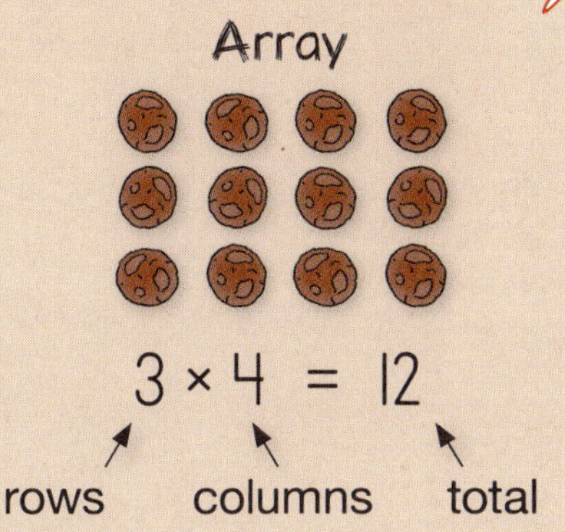

$$3 \times 4 = 12$$

rows   columns   total

B

$$3 \times 4 = 12$$

factors   product

C

Climb and Slide

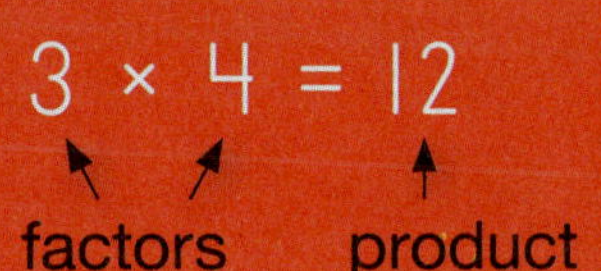

Practice

Complete with the missing factors or products.

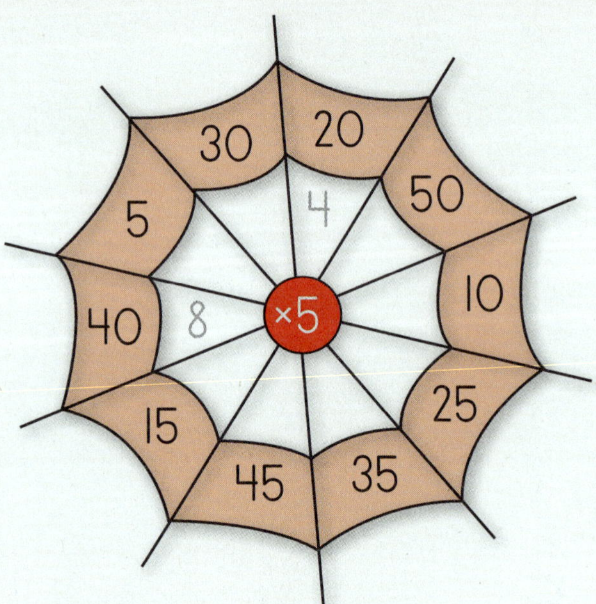

Complete.

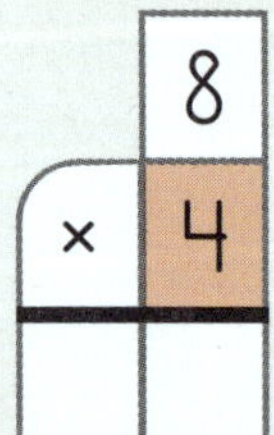

	8			9			2			3			4
×	4		×	5		×	7		×	8		×	9

Review

Connect each number to its dot on the number line.

| 1,037 | 1,364 | 1,500 | 1,699 | 1,946 |

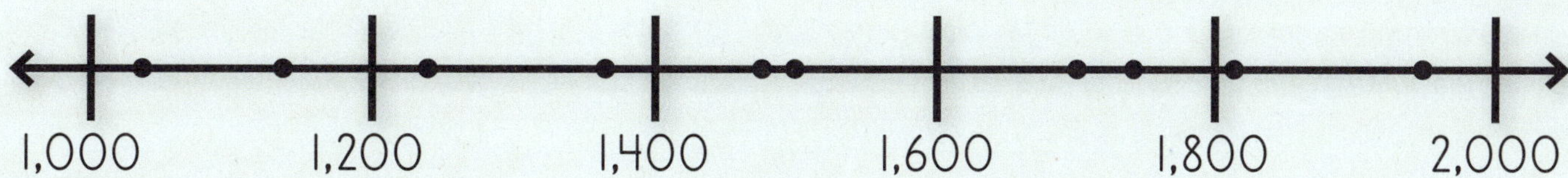

1,000   1,200   1,400   1,600   1,800   2,000

| 1,137 | 1,239 | 1,475 | 1,740 | 1,812 |

Write the number that comes before and after each number.

| 79 | 80 | 81 | | | 99 | |

| | 347 | | | | 2,694 | |

| | 999 | | | | 5,000 | |

Complete with <, >, or =.

40 + 7 ◯ 40 + 8

40 − 7 ◯ 40 − 8

30 + 6 ◯ 6 + 30

200 + 5 ◯ 500 + 2

Match pairs that equal 500.

400		250
300		100
250		350
150		200

Lesson Activities

A

Multiples of 6	6	12	18	24	30	36	42	48	54	60
Multiples of 7	7	14	21		35	42		56	63	70
Multiples of 8	8		24		40		56		72	
Multiples of 9	9				45					90

B

$7 \times 9 = \boxed{}$ $8 \times 8 = \boxed{}$ $6 \times 9 = \boxed{}$

C

Multiples Four in a Row

64	49	42	72	36
63	36	48	81	56
48	42	54	56	48
56	81	63	42	64
54	36	72	49	54

Practice

Complete the missing numbers in the mixed-up multiplication charts. Then, use the charts to answer the questions.

×	3	6	2	10	8	1	9			
2	6	12				2	18	10	14	8

×	2	10	1			7		9	6	
3	6	30	3	24	15		12			9

×	5	6		1		2		10		9
4	20		12		32		16		28	

×	8		3		4		1		5	
5		35		50		30		45		10

Is 10 a multiple of 2?	Is 10 a multiple of 3?
Is 15 a multiple of 3?	Is 15 a multiple of 5?
Is 16 a multiple of 4?	Is 16 a multiple of 2?
Is 20 a multiple of 2?	Is 20 a multiple of 3?
Is 20 a multiple of 4?	Is 20 a multiple of 5?

1.2

Color the multiples in order from Start to End.

Multiples of 6

8	10	14	56	60
6	12	15	48	54
21	18	25	42	45
20	24	30	36	40
25	27	32	52	39

Start (→ row 2), **END**

Multiples of 7

14	21	28	35	48
7	25	32	42	49
12	15	40	54	56
16	18	30	60	63
24	20	81	72	70

Start (→ row 2), **END**

Circle the odd numbers. X the even numbers.

73	978	1,000
456	45	9,732
1,374	8,643	2,001

Complete.

$ ____

$ ____

Complete each blank with the greatest possible number.

$3 \times \boxed{2} < 8$ $\qquad$ $4 \times \boxed{} < 10$ $\qquad$ $5 \times \boxed{} < 11$

$4 \times \boxed{} < 13$ $\qquad$ $7 \times \boxed{} < 15$ $\qquad$ $6 \times \boxed{} < 16$

$6 \times \boxed{} < 20$ $\qquad$ $4 \times \boxed{} < 21$ $\qquad$ $3 \times \boxed{} < 25$

Lesson Activities 👥

A

12 children split into groups of 4.
How many groups do they make?

$12 \div 4 =$ ☐

total — size of each group — number of groups

12 children split into 4 equal groups.
How many children are in each group?

$12 \div 4 =$ ☐

total — number of groups — size of each group

B

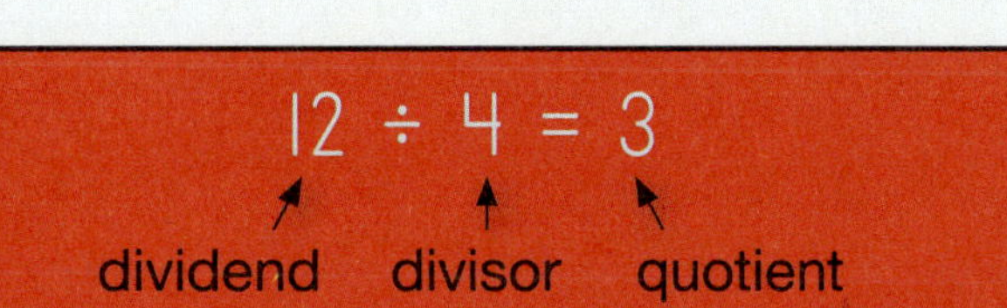

C

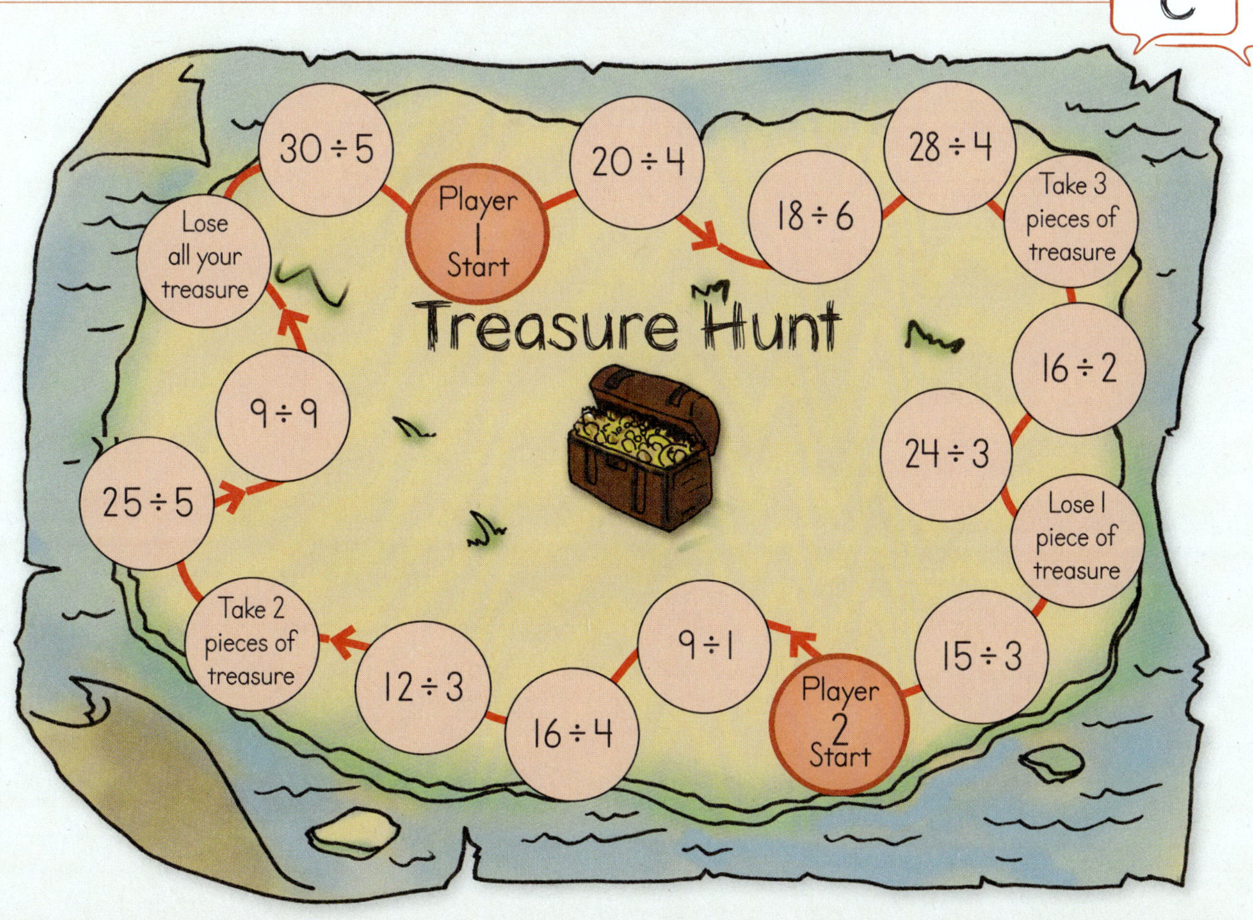

Practice

Complete.

$20 \div 5 =$ ☐ $90 \div 10 =$ ☐ $16 \div 2 =$ ☐

$30 \div 10 =$ ☐ $25 \div 5 =$ ☐ $15 \div 5 =$ ☐

$10 \div 1 =$ ☐ $20 \div 2 =$ ☐ $50 \div 5 =$ ☐

$45 \div 5 =$ ☐ $40 \div 10 =$ ☐ $14 \div 2 =$ ☐

$18 \div 2 =$ ☐ $35 \div 5 =$ ☐ $70 \div 10 =$ ☐

Color the problems that match the number in the star.

| $15 \div 3$ |
| $24 \div 4$ |
| $30 \div 6$ |

| $24 \div 3$ |
| $32 \div 4$ |
| $36 \div 6$ |

| $18 \div 3$ |
| $16 \div 4$ |
| $24 \div 6$ |

| $27 \div 3$ |
| $24 \div 4$ |
| $30 \div 5$ |

| $30 \div 3$ |
| $36 \div 4$ |
| $27 \div 3$ |

| $21 \div 3$ |
| $32 \div 4$ |
| $35 \div 5$ |

Review

Color the multiples in order from Start to End.

Multiples of 8

Start →

8	16	24	32	40
14	12	36	56	48
27	44	54	64	72
15	25	45	70	80
20	21	50	49	100

END

Multiples of 9

24	30	32	35	80
18	27	36	40	90
9	12	45	48	81
15	20	54	63	72
21	25	56	70	64

Start →

END

Complete.

1 year = ____ months

1 week = ____ days

1 day = ____ hours

1 hour = ____ minutes

1 minute = ____ seconds

Match pairs that equal 100.

79		33
67		42
58		55
45		21

Write the time.

Lesson Activities

A

$$\square \times \square = \square$$
$$\square \times \square = \square$$
$$\square \div \square = \square$$
$$\square \div \square = \square$$

B

$$35 \div 5 = \square \qquad 48 \div 6 = \square$$

$$5 \times \square = 35 \qquad 6 \times \square = 48$$

C

How to Read Word Problems

1. Read the problem.
2. Identify the goal.
3. Read the problem again.
   - Read slowly and carefully.
   - Imagine what's happening.
   - Stop after each sentence to make sure you understand it.
4. Solve.

Sammy is making bows from ribbon.
She wants to make 5 bows.
She needs 8 in. of ribbon for each bow.
How much ribbon does she need?

Charlie is making bows from ribbon.
He has 36 cm of ribbon. He wants to cut the ribbon into 4 equal parts. How long should he make each piece of ribbon?

Practice

Complete.

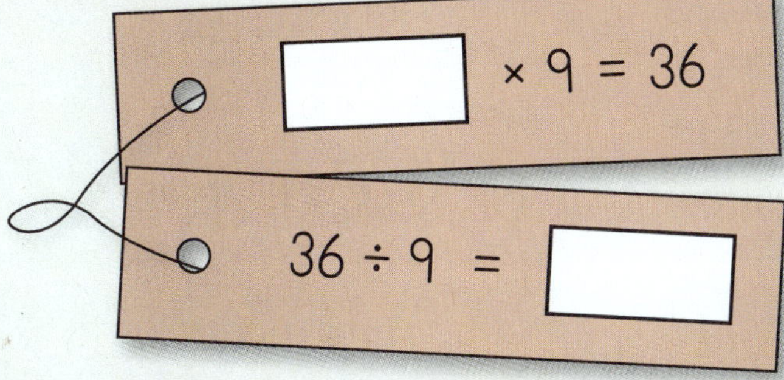

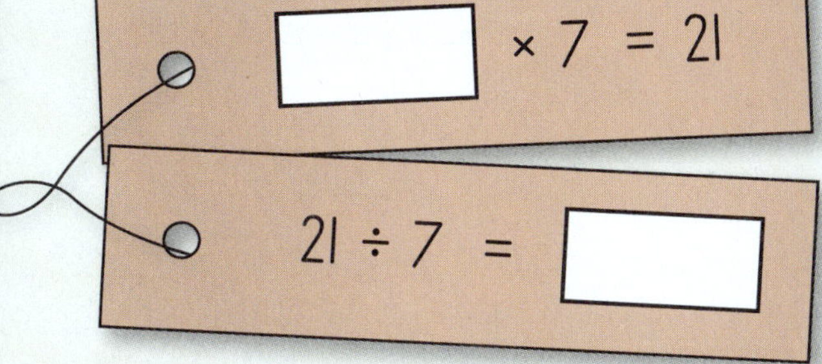
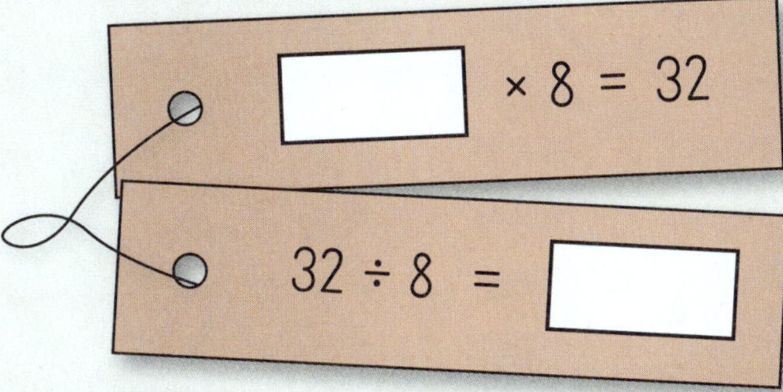

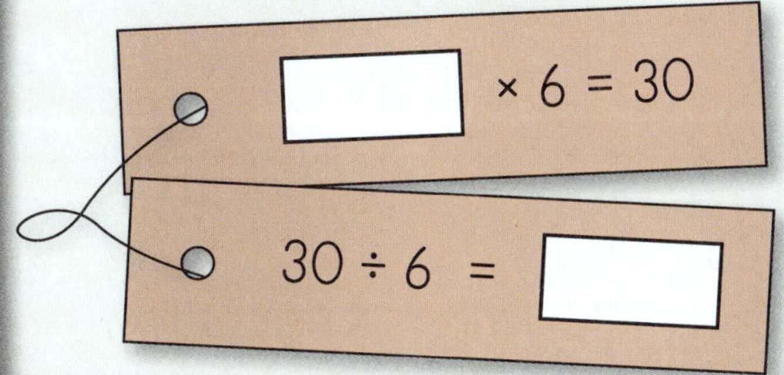
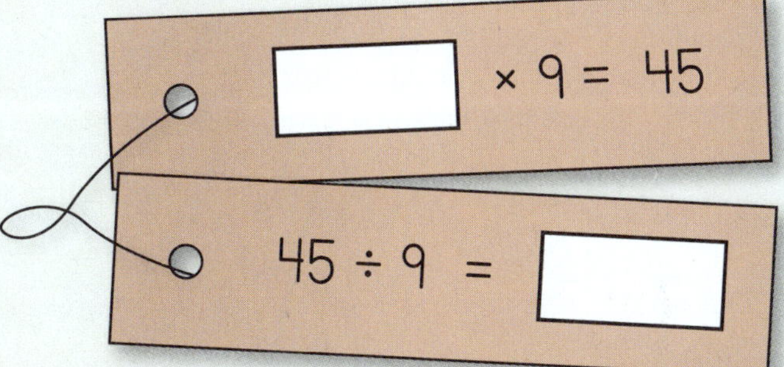

Solve. Write the equations you use.

The choir is setting up chairs for their concert. They have 36 chairs.
They put 9 chairs in each row.
How many rows can they make?

The actors are setting up chairs for their performance. They put 5 chairs in each row.
They make 6 rows.
How many chairs do they use?

Review

Complete.

Start

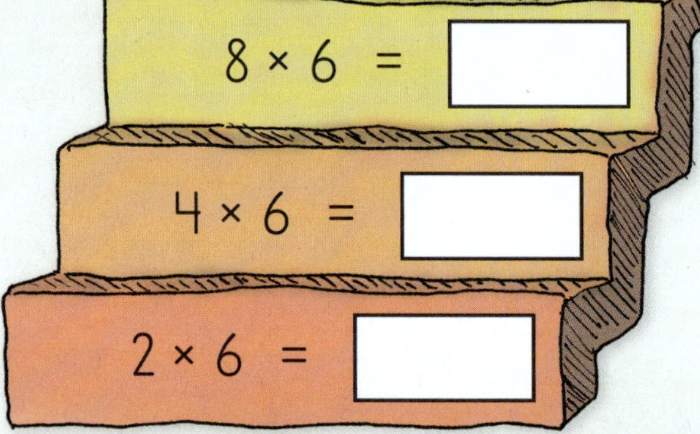

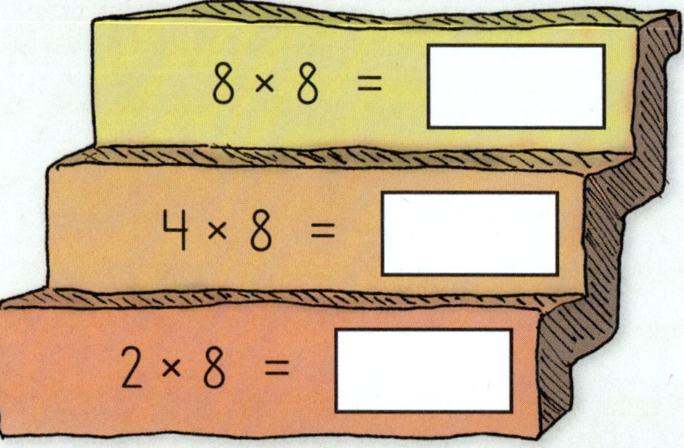

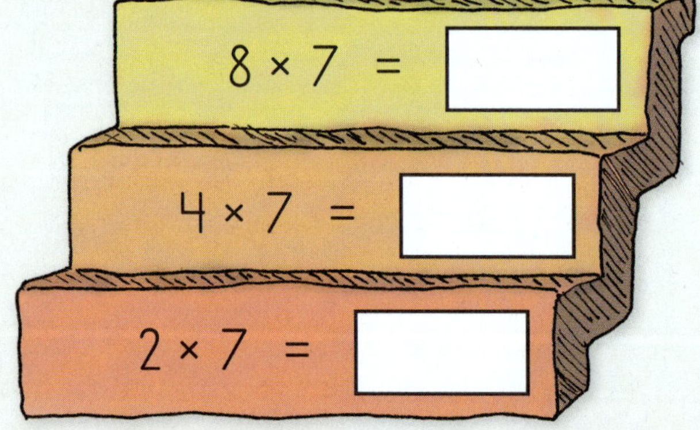

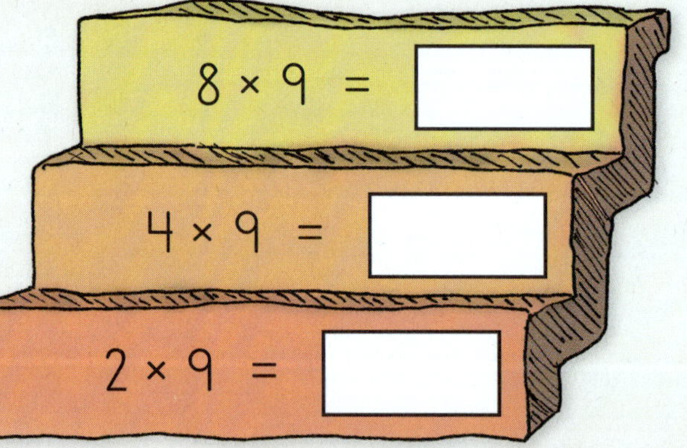

Choose the more sensible measurement for each item.

Height of a chair

| 1 centimeter | 1 meter |

Length of a ladybug

| 1 centimeter | 1 meter |

Length of a hike

| 1 meter | 1 kilometer |

Lesson Activities

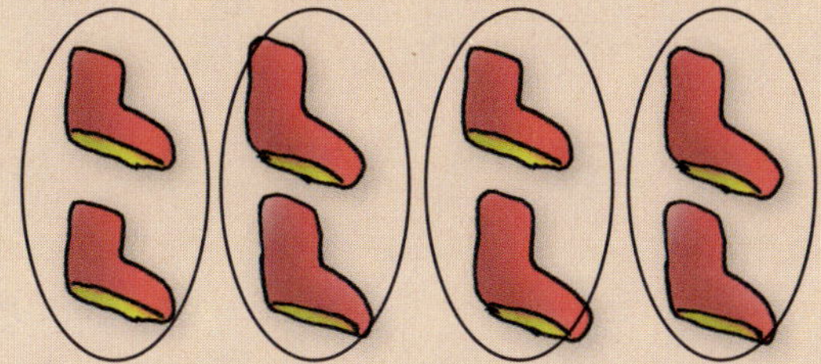

8 can be evenly divided by 2.
8 is divisible by 2.

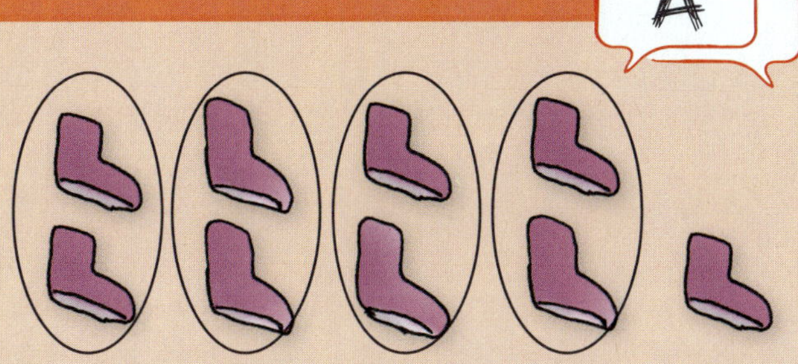

9 cannot be evenly divided by 2.
9 is not divisible by 2.

$12 \div 3 =$ ____	$15 \div 3 =$ ____	$16 \div 3 =$ ____
$12 \div 4 =$ ____	$15 \div 4 =$ ____	$16 \div 4 =$ ____
$12 \div 5 =$ ____	$15 \div 5 =$ ____	$16 \div 5 =$ ____

Multiples of 2

2	4	6	8	10
12	14	16	18	20

Numbers divisible by 2 have ____ in the ones-place.

Multiples of 5

5	10	15	20	25
30	35	40	45	50

Numbers divisible by 5 have ____ in the ones-place.

Multiples of 10

10	20	30	40	50
60	70	80	90	100

Numbers divisible by 10 have ____ in the ones-place.

Practice

Circle the numbers that match the description.
X the numbers that do not match the description.

Divisible by 2	Divisible by 10	Divisible by 5

Divisible by 2: 38 41 96 790 205 324

Divisible by 10: 70 68 90 500 130 704

Divisible by 5: 37 80 35 100 95 453

Complete. Then, use the problems to answer the questions.

$8 \div 3 =$ ☐

$9 \div 3 =$ ☐

$10 \div 3 =$ ☐

$16 \div 4 =$ ☐

$17 \div 4 =$ ☐

$18 \div 4 =$ ☐

$22 \div 6 =$ ☐

$23 \div 6 =$ ☐

$24 \div 6 =$ ☐

Is 8 divisible by 3?

Is 9 divisible by 3?

Is 16 divisible by 4?

Is 17 divisible by 4?

Is 18 divisible by 4?

Is 22 divisible by 6?

Is 23 divisible by 6?

Is 24 divisible by 6?

Review   Complete.

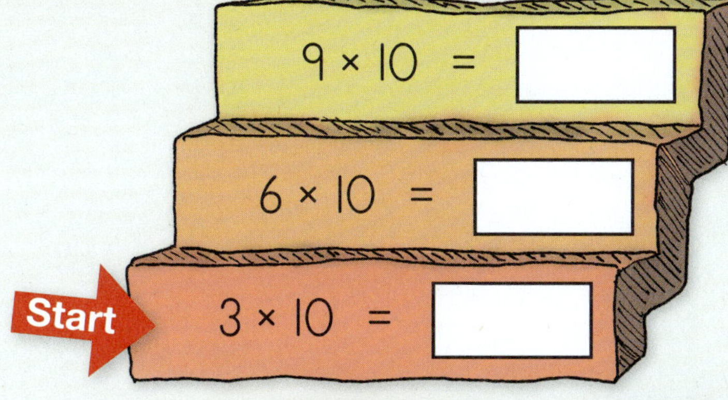

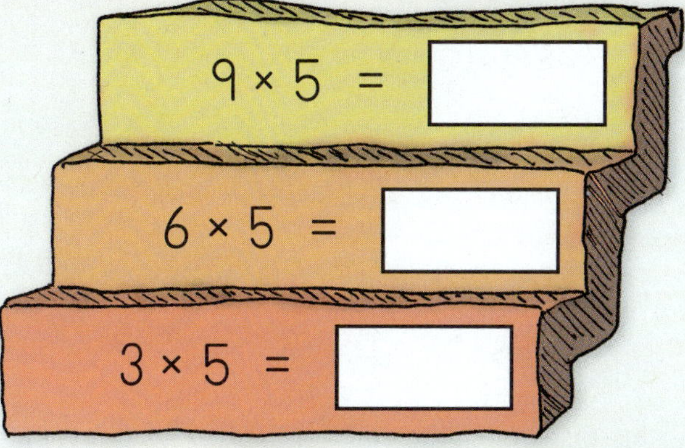

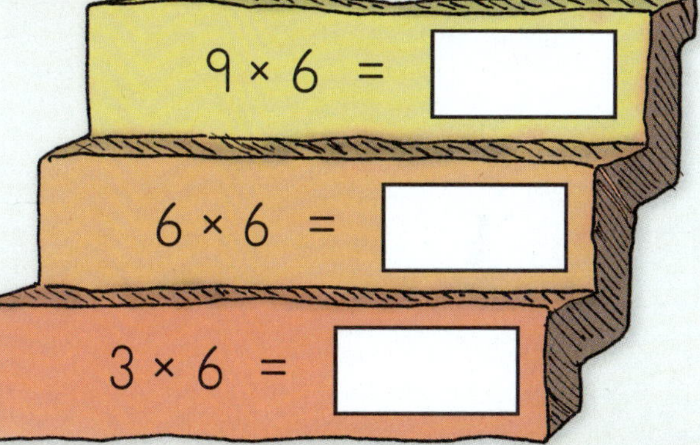

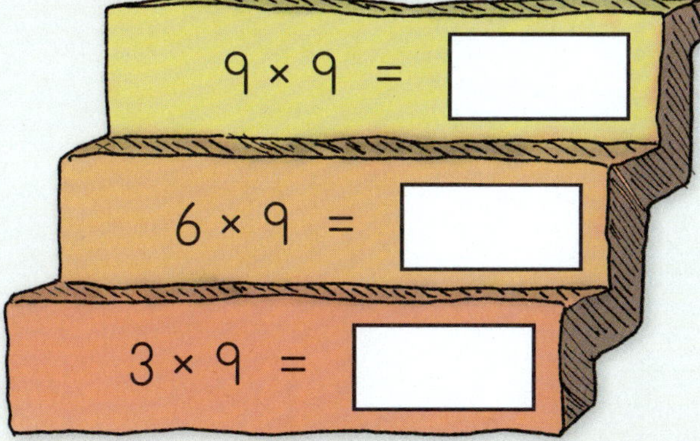

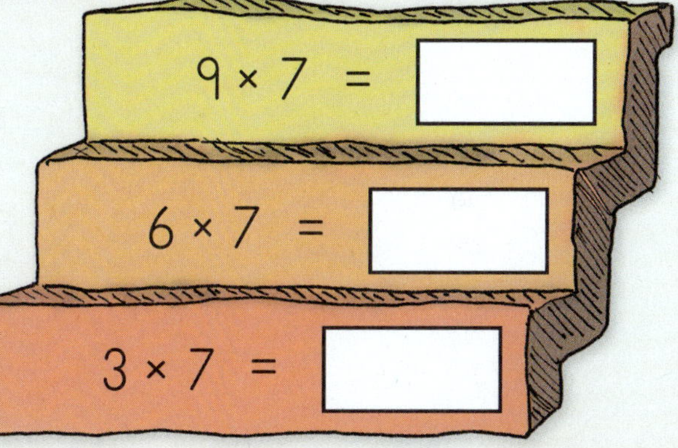

Choose the more sensible measurement for each item.

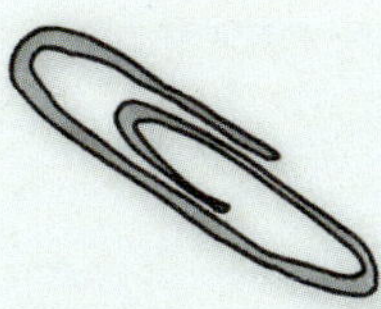

Length of a paper clip

| inch | foot |

Length of a baseball bat

| foot | yard |

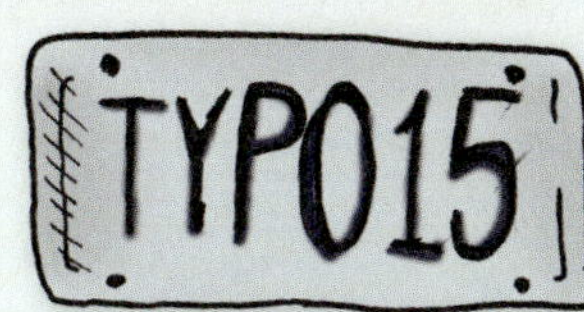

Width of a license plate

| foot | yard |

Lesson Activities

A

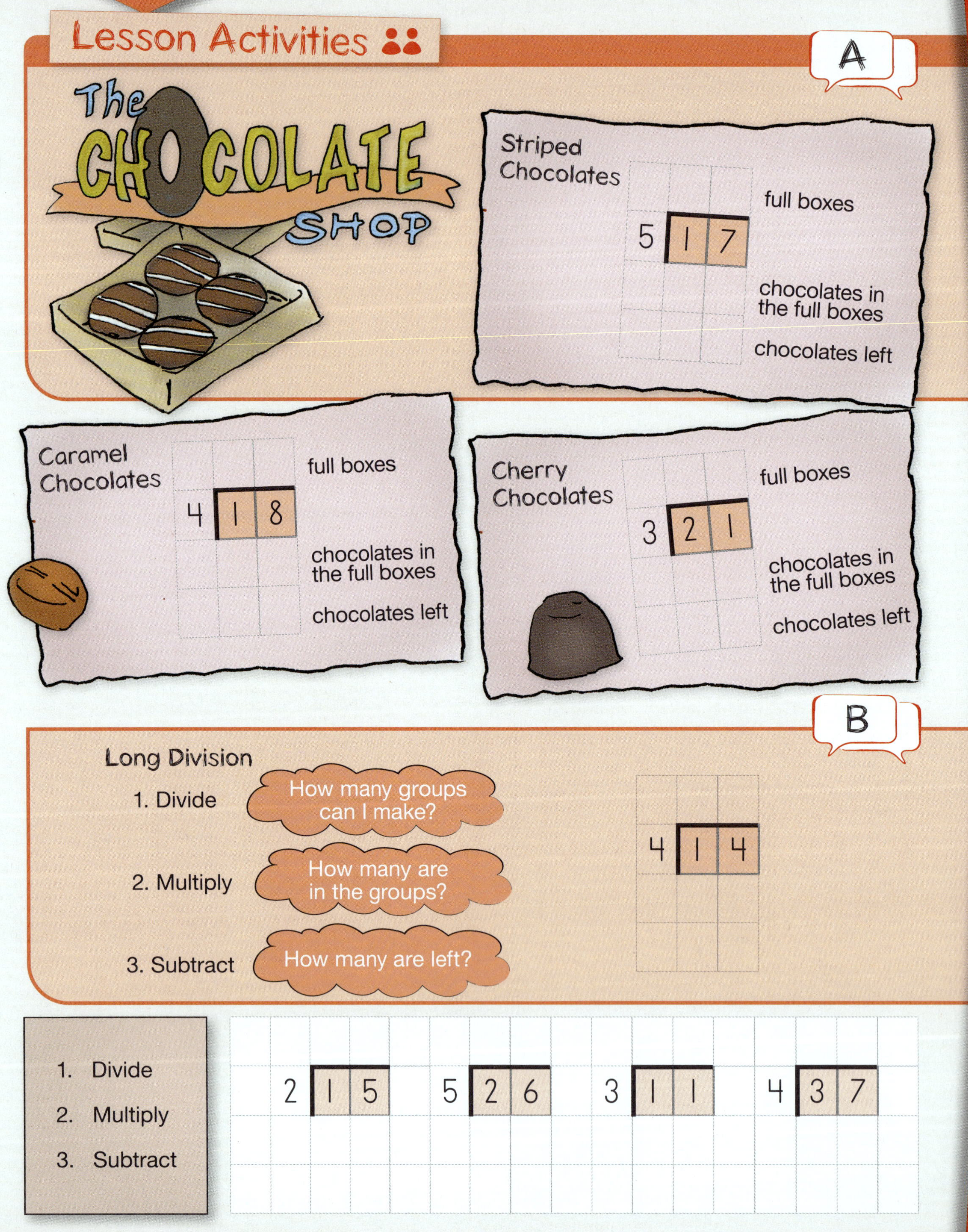

Roll and Divide

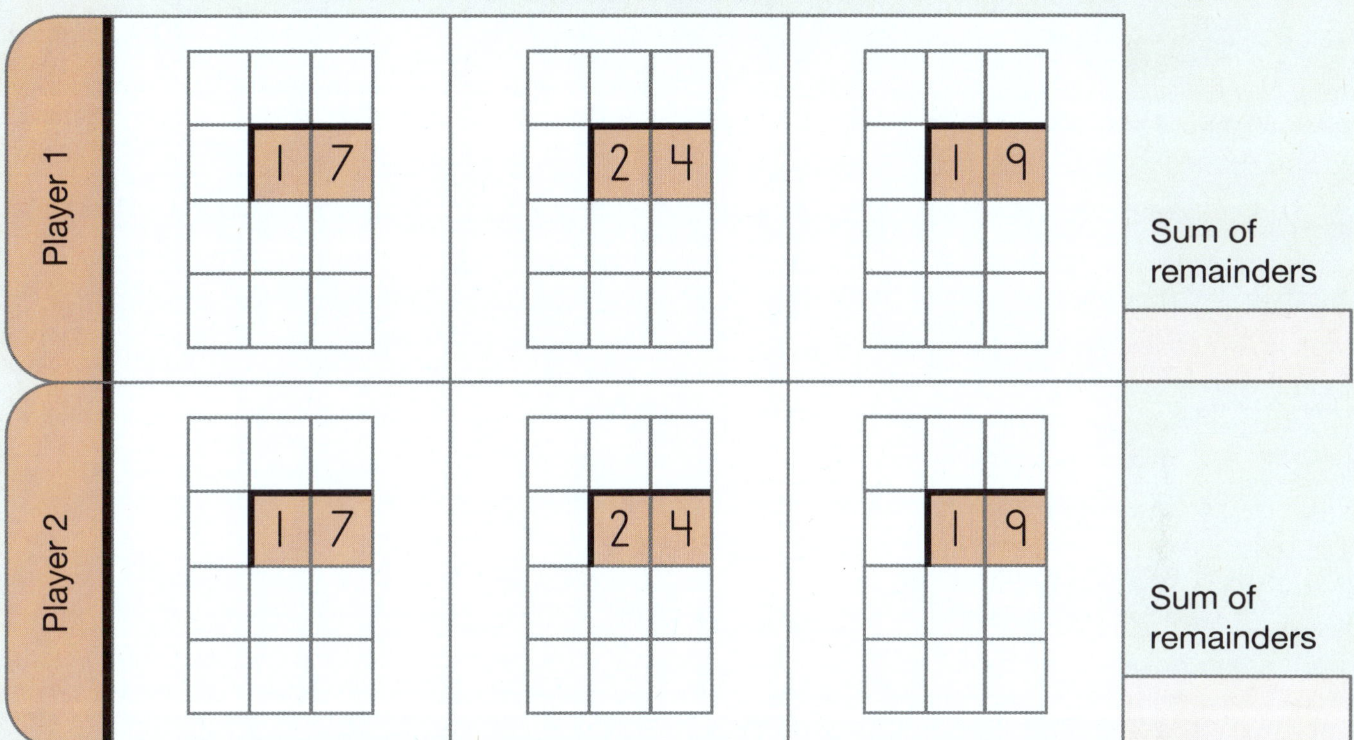

				Sum of remainders
Player 1	1 7	2 4	1 9	
Player 2	1 7	2 4	1 9	Sum of remainders

Practice

Complete. Follow the steps.

1. Divide
2. Multiply
3. Subtract

5 | 1 | 8   5 | 2 | 3   9 | 3 | 2   4 | 2 | 6

Solve. Write the equations you use.

Oscar's mom runs 5 km every day. How many days does it take her to run 30 km?

Sophie's dad bikes 9 miles each day. How many days does it take for him to bike 45 miles?

Review

Choose the more sensible measurement for each item.

Slice of bread

| ounce | pound |

Loaf of bread

| ounce | pound |

Can of tomatoes

| ounce | pound |

Complete.

8:00 — 1 hr. → ☐

8:00 — 1 hr. 15 min. → ☐

8:00 — 1 hr. 30 min. → ☐

8:00 — 2 hr. → ☐

Complete.

	Double
30	60
40	
50	
12	
15	
17	

Circle the greatest number in each row.

7,014	7,040	7,004
8,296	8,298	8,030
6,405	6,350	6,399

Complete.

```
   3 8        9 6
 + 2 7      + 4 5
 -----      -----

   8 7        9 1
 - 2 3      - 4 8
 -----      -----
```

Lesson Activities

Factor Pairs of 10		Factors of 10			
1 × 10	2 × 5	1	2	5	10

Factor pairs of 20

1 × ☐

2 × ☐

☐ × 5

Factor pairs of 16

1 × ☐

2 × ☐

☐ × 4

Factor pairs of 11

1 × ☐

Factors Four in a Row

10	8	28	8	20
27	25	9	35	6
18	2	40	16	30
11	36	15	4	32
12	5	21	24	13

Practice

Complete the missing factors in the factor pairs.

Factor pairs of 6	Factor pairs of 7	Factor pairs of 9
1 × ☐	☐ × 7	1 × ☐
2 × ☐		☐ × ☐

Factor pairs of 40	Factor pairs of 12	Factor pairs of 29
☐ × 40	1 × ☐	☐ × ☐
2 × 20	2 × ☐	
4 × ☐	3 × ☐	
5 × ☐		

Complete the factor triangles so each number in a box is the product of the factors in the adjoining circles.

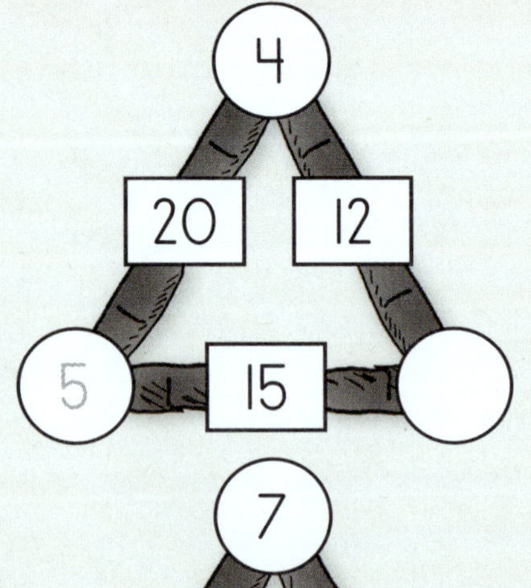

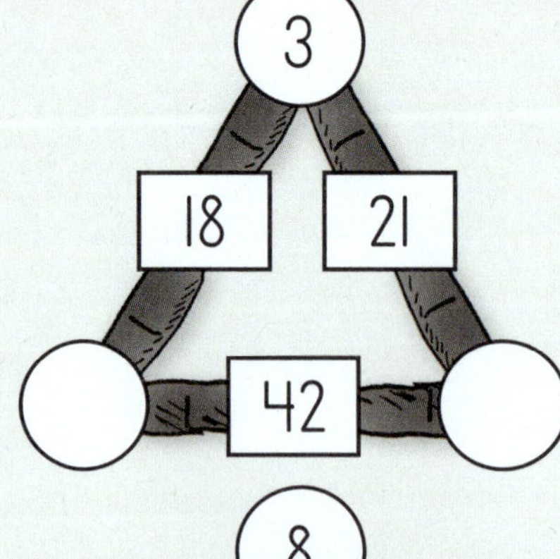

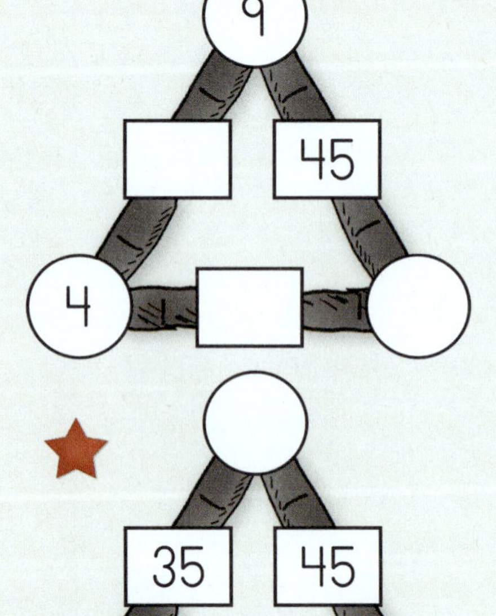

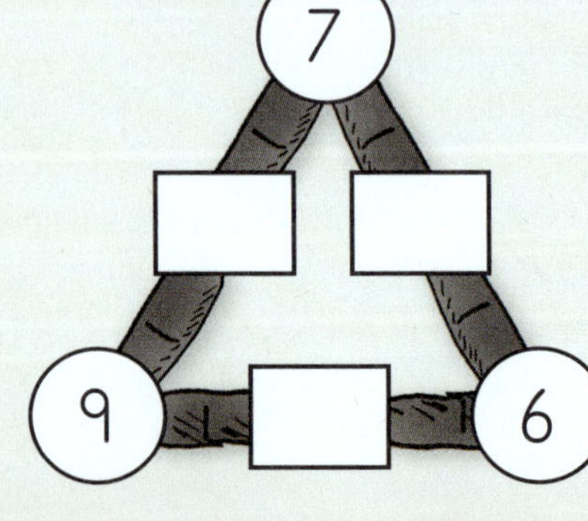

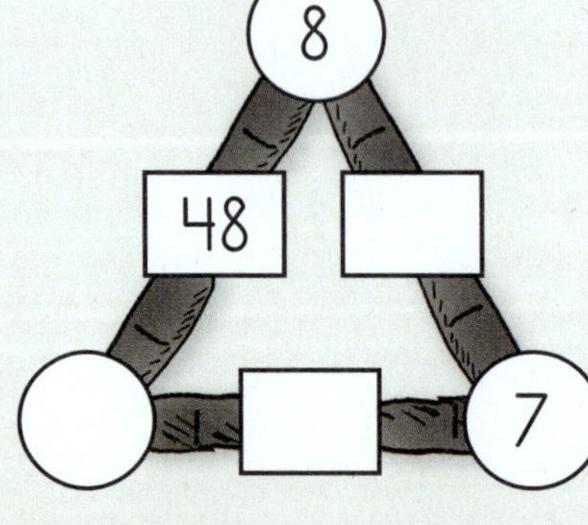

Review

Complete. Follow the steps.

1. Divide
2. Multiply
3. Subtract

7 | 3 0   4 | 2 1   8 | 3 6   5 | 4 7

Match.

6 × 7		54
6 × 10		42
6 × 9		36
6 × 6		60
6 × 8		48

7 × 10		70
7 × 8		63
7 × 9		42
7 × 7		56
7 × 6		49

Color the shapes to match the fractions. Then, complete with <, >, or =.

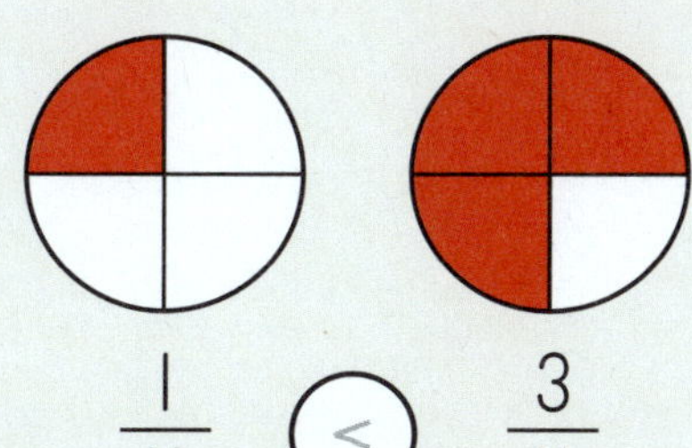

$\frac{1}{4}$ < $\frac{3}{4}$

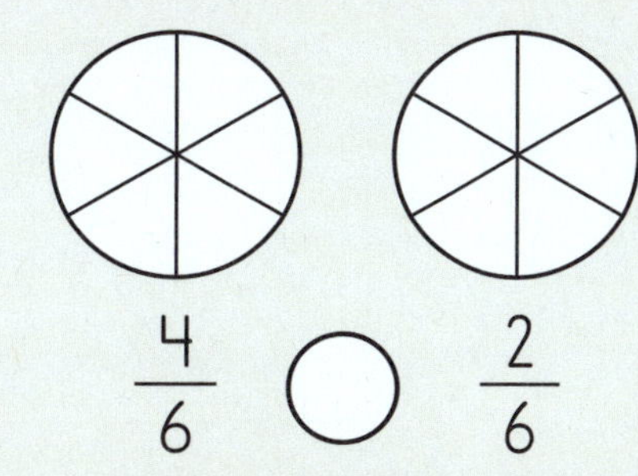

$\frac{4}{6}$ ◯ $\frac{2}{6}$

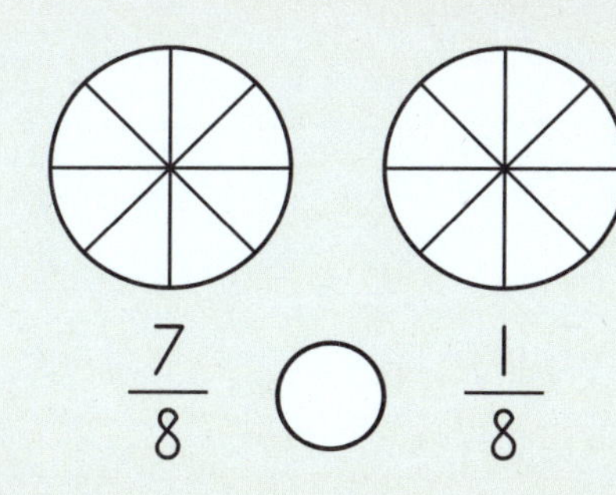

$\frac{7}{8}$ ◯ $\frac{1}{8}$

Lesson Activities

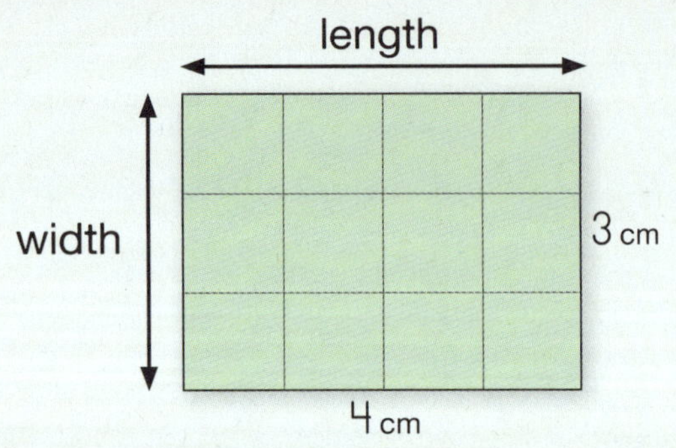

Perimeter of a Rectangle

length + width + length + width

Area of a Rectangle

length × width

B

Factor pairs of 12	Factor pairs of 16	Factor pairs of 9
Factor pairs of 6	Factor pairs of 8	Factor pairs of 10

C

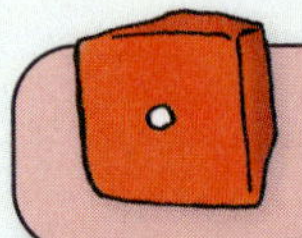

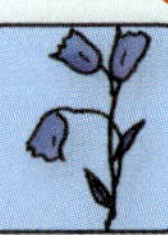

Player 1

Player 2

Practice

Draw a rectangle with the given dimensions. Then, find the area and perimeter of the rectangle.

Length: 6 cm

Width: 4 cm

Perimeter: ____________ cm

Area: ____________ sq. cm

Length: 5 cm

Width: 5 cm

Perimeter: ____________ cm

Area: ____________ sq. cm

Find all factor pairs for each number. Then, draw a rectangle to match each factor pair.

Factor pairs of
18

Factor pairs of
20

Review

Choose the more sensible unit for each item.

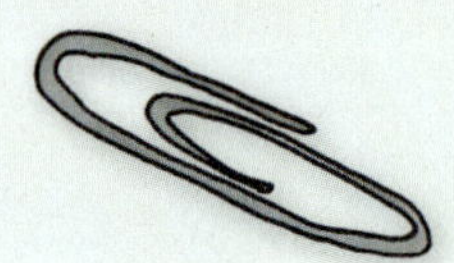

Paper clip

| 1 gram | 1 kilogram |

Pineapple

| 1 gram | 1 kilogram |

Tack

| 1 gram | 1 kilogram |

Match.

8 × 8		72
8 × 9		48
8 × 7		64
8 × 6		80
8 × 10		56

9 × 9		54
9 × 6		90
9 × 10		63
9 × 7		72
9 × 8		81

Complete.

3 weeks = ☐ days

3 weeks, 5 days = ☐ days

28 days = ☐ weeks

30 days = ☐ weeks, ☐ days

Lesson Activities

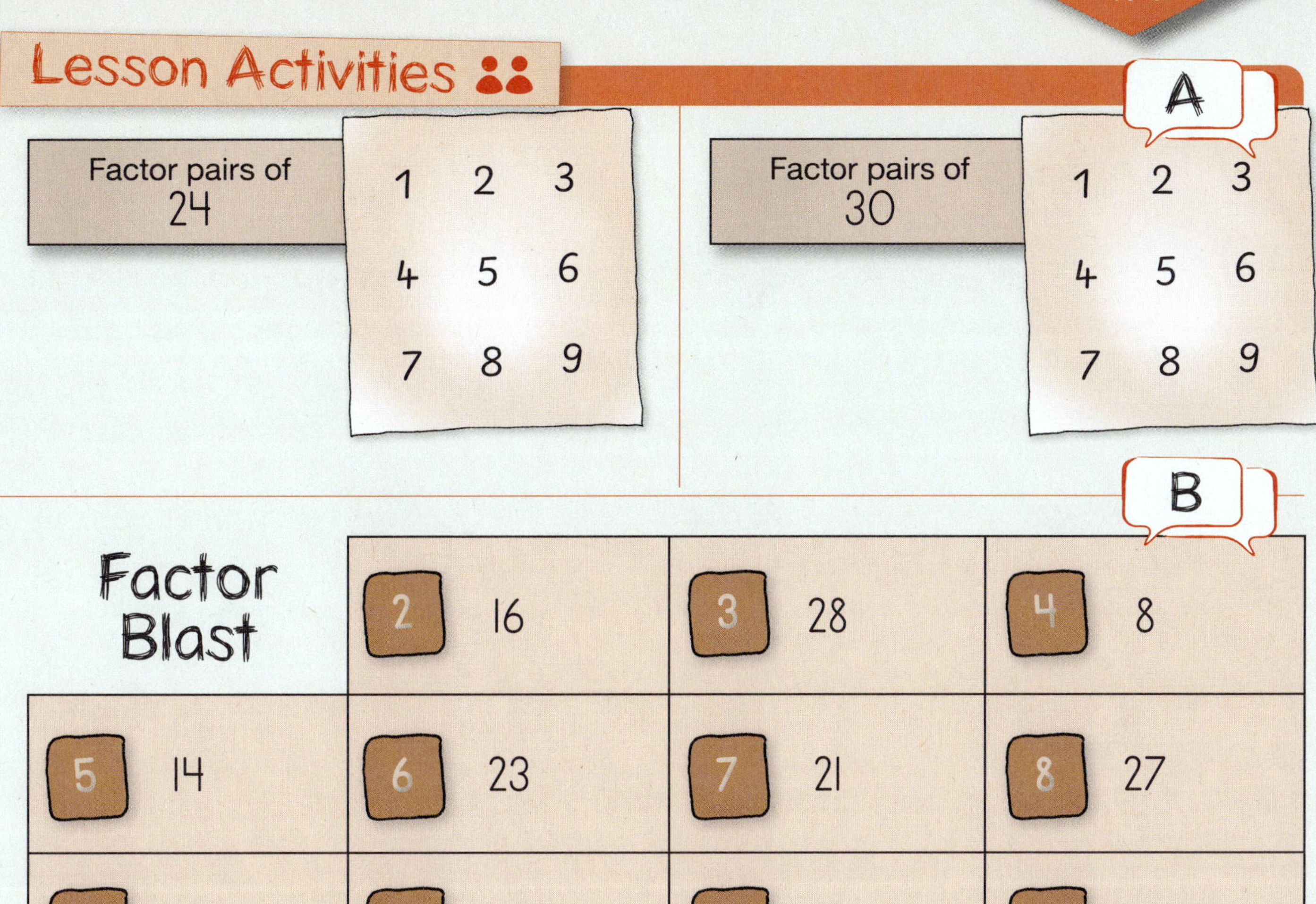

Number	Factor Pairs	Sum of Factors	Number	Factor Pairs	Sum of Factors
	Player 1 Total			Player 2 Total	

Practice

Find all factor pairs for each number.

Factor pairs of **14**

1	2	3
4	5	6
7	8	9

Factor pairs of **28**

1	2	3
4	5	6
7	8	9

Factor pairs of **15**

1	2	3
4	5	6
7	8	9

Factor pairs of **35**

1	2	3
4	5	6
7	8	9

Factor pairs of **23**

1	2	3
4	5	6
7	8	9

Factor pairs of **27**

1	2	3
4	5	6
7	8	9

Factor pairs of **32**

1	2	3
4	5	6
7	8	9

★ Factor pairs of **36**

1	2	3
4	5	6
7	8	9

Review

Find the perimeter and area of each shape.

7 cm

2 cm

Perimeter: ____ cm

Area: ____ sq. cm

6 cm

3 cm

Perimeter: ____ cm

Area: ____ sq. cm

Complete.

×	6	7	8	9	10
5					
6					
7					
8					
9					

Complete.

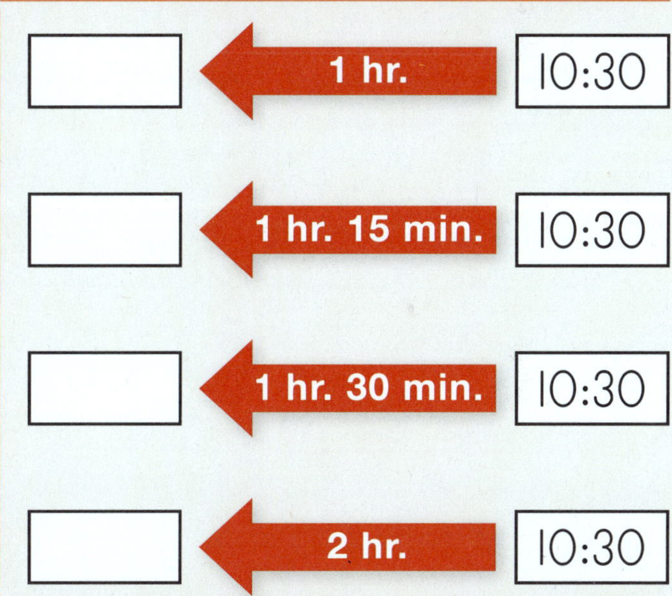

____ ← 1 hr. — 10:30

____ ← 1 hr. 15 min. — 10:30

____ ← 1 hr. 30 min. — 10:30

____ ← 2 hr. — 10:30

Solve. Write the equations you use.

There are 6 groups of children at day camp. There are 8 children in each group. How many children are at day camp?

There are 45 children at gymnastics lessons. The teachers divide the children into 5 equal groups. How many children are in each group?

Lesson Activities 👥

Prime numbers have exactly 2 factors: 1 and the number itself.

2	5	19
1×2	1×5	1×19

Composite numbers have more than 2 factors.

4	12	21
1×4	1×12	1×21
2×2	2×6	3×7
	3×4	

1	2	3	4	5	6	7	8	9	10
11	12	13	14	15	16	17	18	19	20

Number Knock-Out

Player 1

40 47 44 43
37 30 23 25
21 49 27 42
38 29 35 31

Player 2

40 47 44 43
37 30 23 25
21 49 27 42
38 29 35 31

Practice

Find all factor pairs for each number.

Factor pairs of 18		
1	2	3
4	5	6
7	8	9

Factor pairs of 31		
1	2	3
4	5	6
7	8	9

Factor pairs of 12		
1	2	3
4	5	6
7	8	9

Factor pairs of 50		
1	2	3
4	5	6
7	8	9

Is 18 prime or composite?

Is 31 prime or composite?

Is 12 prime or composite?

Is 50 prime or composite?

List the factors of 18 in order from least to greatest.

List the factors of 50 in order from least to greatest.

Is 4 a factor of 12?

Is 4 a factor of 50?

Review

Circle the description that matches the angle.

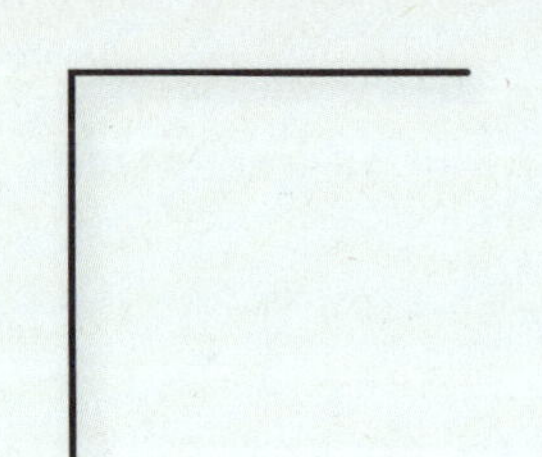

Right angle
Smaller than a right angle
Larger than a right angle

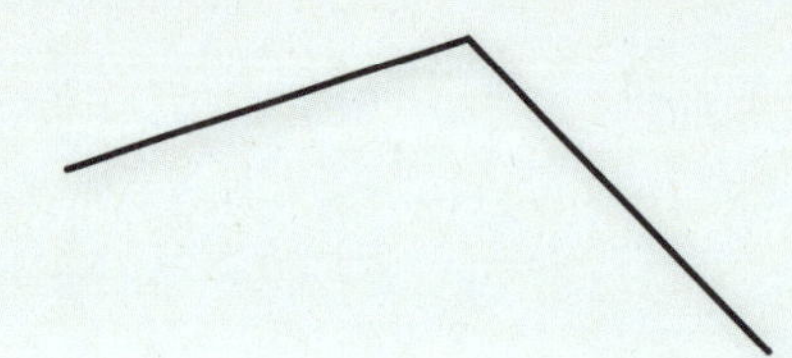

Right angle
Smaller than a right angle
Larger than a right angle

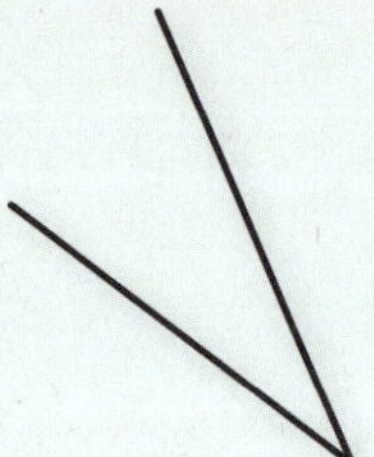

Right angle
Smaller than a right angle
Larger than a right angle

Complete.

1. Divide
2. Multiply
3. Subtract

8 ⟌ 2 5   2 ⟌ 1 7   6 ⟌ 4 0   7 ⟌ 6 8

Complete.

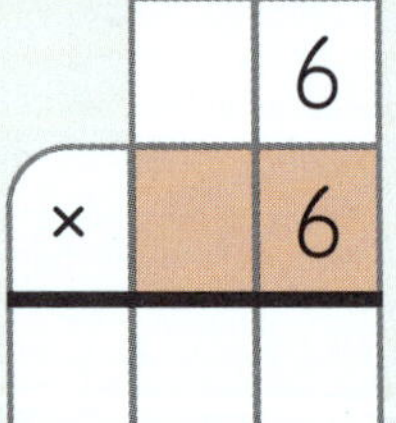

		6
×		6

		8
×		9

		9
×		6

		8
×		8

		3
×		7

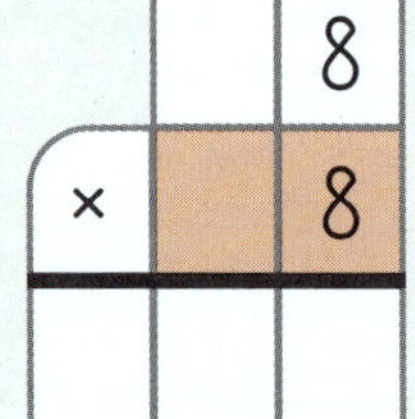

		8
×		6

		7
×		7

		7
×		8

		5
×		7

		9
×		9

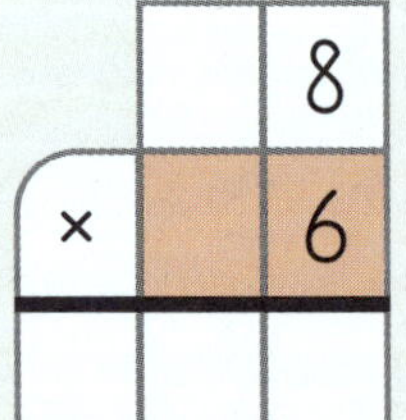

		9
×		5

		8
×		9

		7
×		4

		9
×		7

		6
×		7

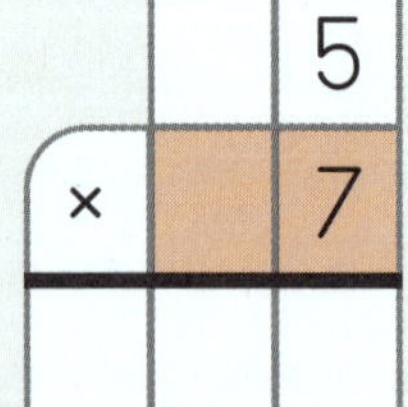
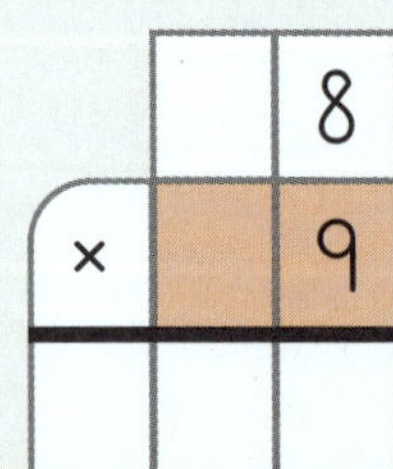

Unit Wrap-Up

**Circle the numbers that match the description.
X the numbers that do not match the description.**

Multiples of 4		
12	1	8
2	4	20

Multiples of 7		
27	7	17
14	70	35

Multiples of 5		
15	12	20
49	35	25

Factors of 16		
16	4	1
14	2	8

Factors of 7		
2	7	3
1	17	14

Factors of 9		
6	18	1
9	3	15

Divisible by 2		
8	54	81
49	36	27

Divisible by 10		
80	20	45
406	400	650

Divisible by 5		
25	35	100
215	50	95

Find all factor pairs for each number.

Factor pairs of 12

1	2	3
4	5	6
7	8	9

Factor pairs of 40

1	2	3
4	5	6
7	8	9

Unit Wrap-Up

**Circle the prime numbers.
X the composite numbers.**

| 7 | 13 | 9 | 11 | 25 |

| 18 | 2 | 5 | 14 | 23 |

Use these numbers to answer the riddles. You will not use every number.

| 10 | 15 | 17 | 20 | 25 | 27 | 29 | 36 | 42 |

This number is greater than 17.
It is a multiple of 5.
It is divisible by 2.

This number is greater than 17.
It is a multiple of 5.
It is not divisible by 2.

This number is less than 20.
It is a multiple of 3.

This number is less than 20.
It is prime.

This number has 1, 3, 9, and 27 as its factors.

This number is greater than 20.
It is prime.

This number is a multiple of 6.
It is also a multiple of 7.

This number is a multiple of 9.
It has 4 as one of its factors.

Lesson Activities

Standard Form	Expanded Form
3,217	3,000 + 200 + 10 + 7
4,605	
6,991	

B

600 + 800 = ☐

6 + 8 = ☐

1,200 – 300 = ☐

12 – 3 = ☐

C

Close to 3,000

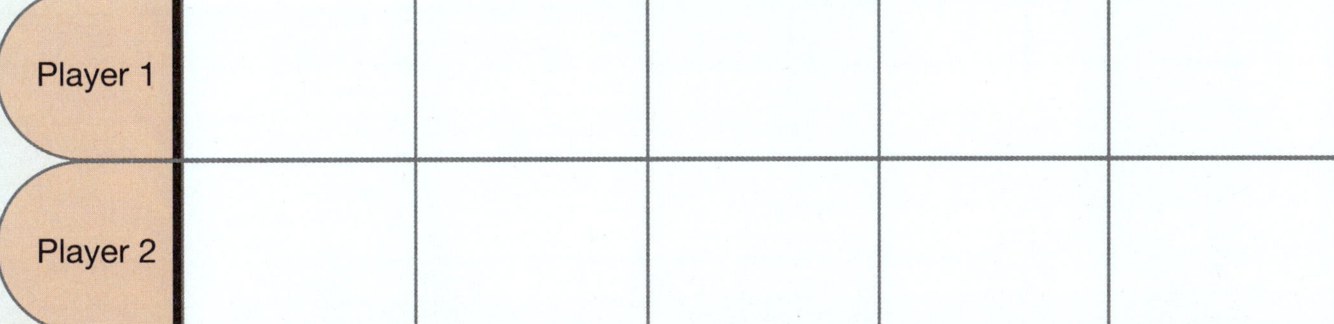

Player 1					
Player 2					

Practice 👤 Complete the missing numbers.

$$8{,}974 = 8{,}000 + 900 + 70 + \boxed{}$$

$$1{,}293 = 1{,}000 + \boxed{} + 90 + 3$$

$$3{,}040 = 3{,}000 + \boxed{}$$

$$\boxed{} = 5{,}000 + 7$$

Match.

1,300 + 600	1,700	2,200 - 300
1,700 + 300	1,900	2,400 - 400
1,900 + 600	2,000	2,000 - 300
800 + 900	2,200	3,100 - 600
1,400 + 800	2,500	3,000 - 800

Connect each number to its dot on the number line.

2,350	235	4,700	5,625	8,777

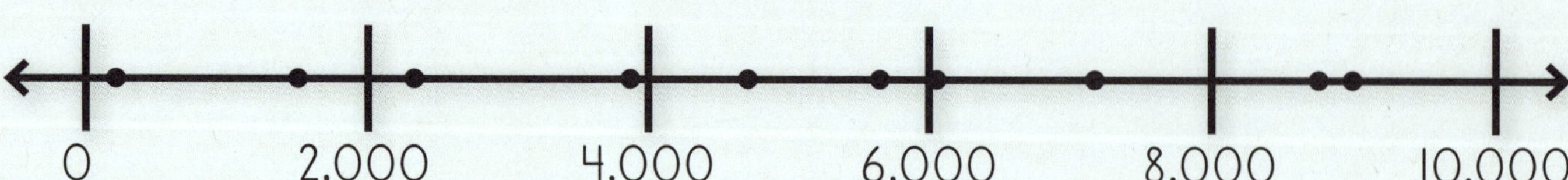

3,879	1,500	6,025	9,000	7,116

Review

Color the problems that match the number in the star.

5	4	2	3
35 ÷ 7	45 ÷ 9	16 ÷ 8	24 ÷ 8
32 ÷ 8	28 ÷ 7	27 ÷ 9	28 ÷ 7
45 ÷ 9	32 ÷ 8	14 ÷ 7	27 ÷ 9

Complete with <, >, or =.

4,302 ◯ 4,032

6,710 ◯ 6,701

8,056 ◯ 8,560

9,790 ◯ 979

1,099 ◯ 1,990

Complete.

2:40	15 min. →	
2:45	15 min. →	
2:50	15 min. →	
2:55	15 min. →	
3:00	15 min. →	

Use the clues to complete the chart.

- Sadie is 20 cm shorter than Cayden.
- Sadie is 6 cm taller than Ben.
- Sadie is 8 cm shorter than Leena.

Name	Height (cm)
Cayden	145
Sadie	
Ben	
Leena	

Lesson Activities 👥

A

Nearest Hundred

200   300

2̲74 ≈ ⬜

Nearest Ten

270   280

27̲4 ≈ ⬜

⬜   ⬜

4̲45 ≈ ⬜

⬜   ⬜

4̲45 ≈ ⬜

⬜   ⬜

8̲96 ≈ ⬜

⬜   ⬜

89̲6 ≈ ⬜

B

Rounding Four in a Row

570	8̲49	210	57̲1	300	4̲25
2̲96	400	9̲32	900	39̲8	800
300	21̲4	570	7̲50	400	2̲61
2̲07	800	8̲83	210	56̲5	900

Practice

Round each number to the nearest ten.
Use the number line to help.

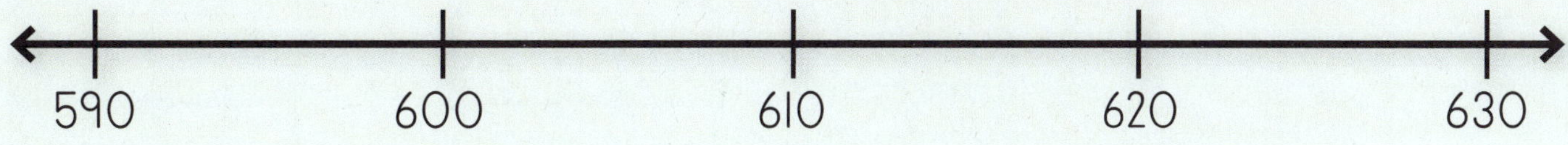

590   600   610   620   630

612 ≈ ________   604 ≈ ________

625 ≈ ________   591 ≈ ________

596 ≈ ________   619 ≈ ________

Round each number to the underlined place.

874 ≈ ________   919 ≈ ________

309 ≈ ________   735 ≈ ________

562 ≈ ________   404 ≈ ________

650 ≈ ________   698 ≈ ________

Round each price to the underlined place.

$797

438 ≈ ________   797 ≈ ________   964 ≈ ________

438 ≈ ________   797 ≈ ________   964 ≈ ________

Review

Complete.

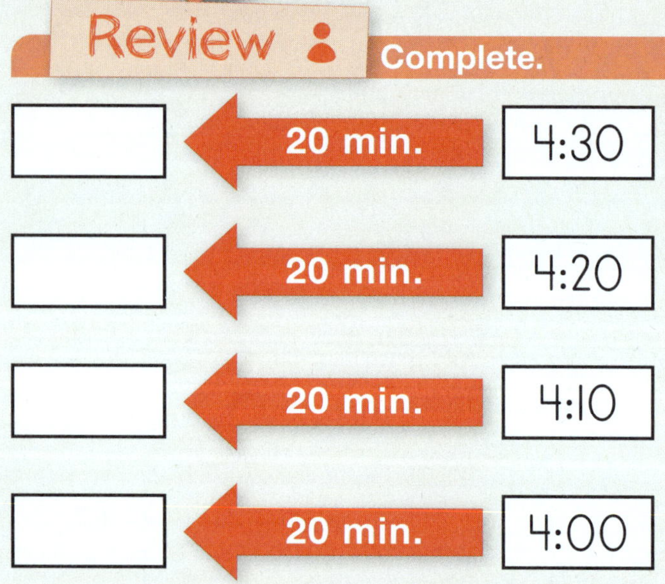

□	← 20 min.	4:30
□	← 20 min.	4:20
□	← 20 min.	4:10
□	← 20 min.	4:00

Complete.

$$\begin{array}{ccc} 3 & 9 & 7 \\ +\ 2 & 0 & 6 \\ \hline \end{array} \qquad \begin{array}{ccc} 4 & 2 & 8 \\ +\ 7 & 9 & 0 \\ \hline \end{array}$$

$$\begin{array}{ccc} 6 & 4 & 8 \\ -\ 1 & 7 & 3 \\ \hline \end{array} \qquad \begin{array}{ccc} 7 & 0 & 7 \\ -\ 2 & 4 & 5 \\ \hline \end{array}$$

Use the chart to answer the questions. Write the equations you use.

How much does skating cost for 4 guests?

How much does skating cost for 8 guests?

How much does skating and skate rental cost for 5 guests?

How much does skating and skate rental cost for 10 guests?

How much does skating, skate rental, and party favors cost for 10 guests?

 How much does skating, skate rental, and party favors cost for 11 guests?

Lesson Activities

Nearest Thousand

5,371 ≈ ☐

Nearest Hundred

5,371 ≈ ☐

Nearest Ten

5,371 ≈ ☐

4,628 ≈ ☐	8,409 ≈ ☐	6,965 ≈ ☐
4,628 ≈ ☐	8,409 ≈ ☐	6,965 ≈ ☐
4,628 ≈ ☐	8,409 ≈ ☐	6,965 ≈ ☐

Dice Tic-Tac Toe

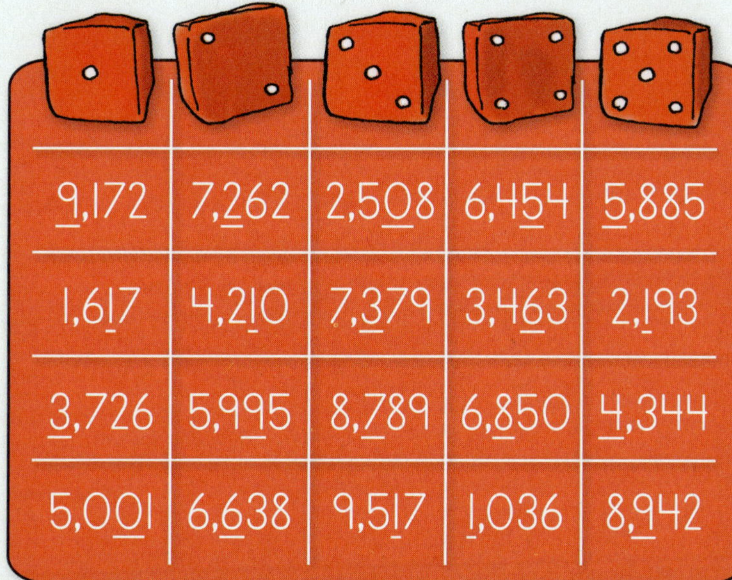

Practice 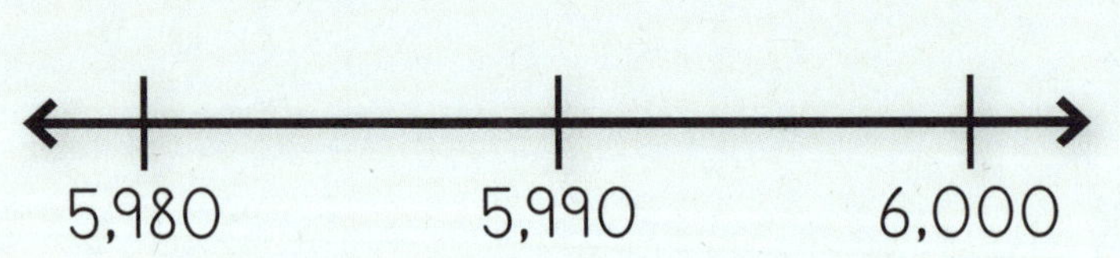

**Round each number to the nearest ten.
Use the number line to help.**

5,9<u>9</u>2 ≈ ☐

5,9<u>9</u>7 ≈ ☐

5,9<u>8</u>5 ≈ ☐

5,980   5,990   6,000

Round each number to the underlined place.

<u>5</u>,062 ≈ ☐   3,9<u>9</u>9 ≈ ☐

6,<u>0</u>49 ≈ ☐   2,<u>9</u>95 ≈ ☐

1,0<u>0</u>7 ≈ ☐   4,9<u>9</u>1 ≈ ☐

8,0<u>0</u>3 ≈ ☐   7,<u>9</u>93 ≈ ☐

Round each number to the underlined place.

Weight of a hippopotamus:

2,864 kilograms

<u>2</u>,864 ≈ ☐

2,<u>8</u>64 ≈ ☐

2,8<u>6</u>4 ≈ ☐

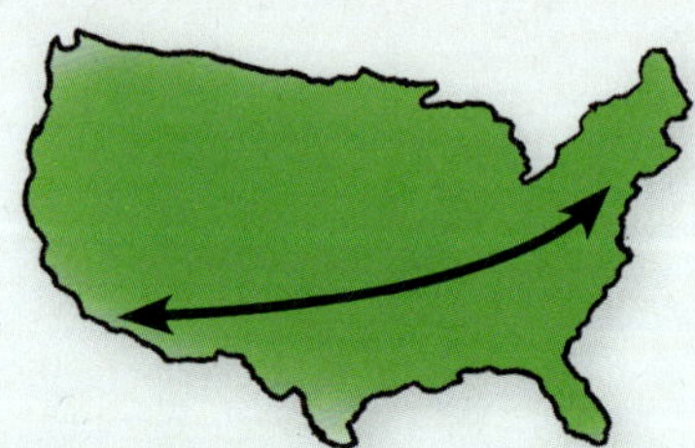

Distance from Los Angeles
to New York City:

4,473 kilometers

<u>4</u>,473 ≈ ☐

4,<u>4</u>73 ≈ ☐

4,4<u>7</u>3 ≈ ☐

Review — Match.

70 ÷ 7	6	48 ÷ 6
42 ÷ 7	7	36 ÷ 6
63 ÷ 7	8	60 ÷ 6
49 ÷ 7	9	42 ÷ 6
56 ÷ 7	10	54 ÷ 6

Find the perimeter and area.

3 ft.

2 ft.

Perimeter: ____ ft.

Area: ____ sq. ft.

2 km

1 km

Perimeter: ____ km

Area: ____ sq. km

5 in.

8 in.

Perimeter: ____ in.

Area: ____ sq. in.

Circle the prime numbers.

(2)	(3)	4
5	6	7
8	9	10
11	12	13
14	15	16
17	18	19

Complete.

$100 = 90 + \boxed{}$

$\boxed{} = 250 + 250$

$400 = \boxed{} + 300$

$\boxed{} = 300 - 50$

$150 = 250 - \boxed{}$

$100 = \boxed{} - 50$

Lesson Activities

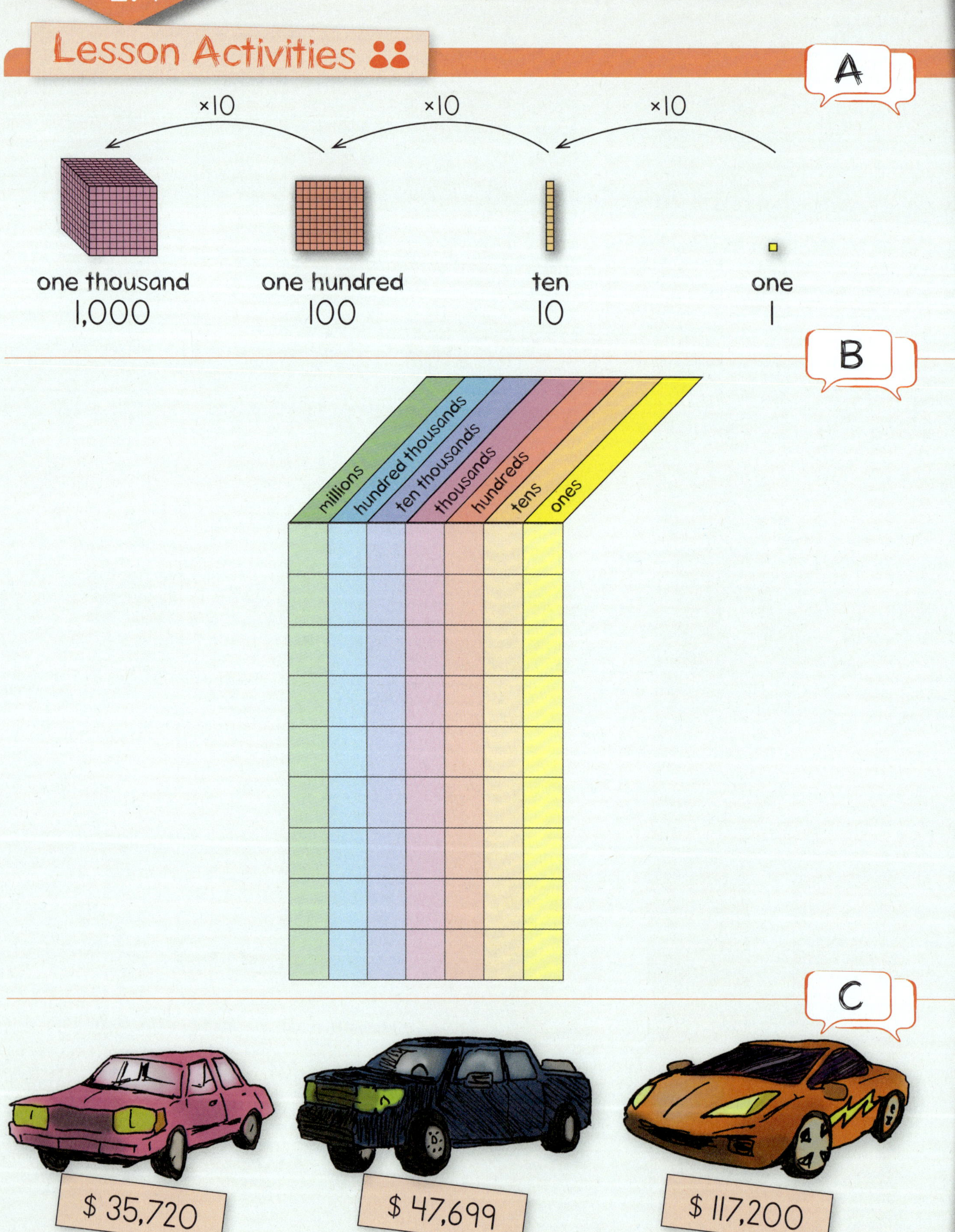

Practice 

Write each number in the place-value chart.

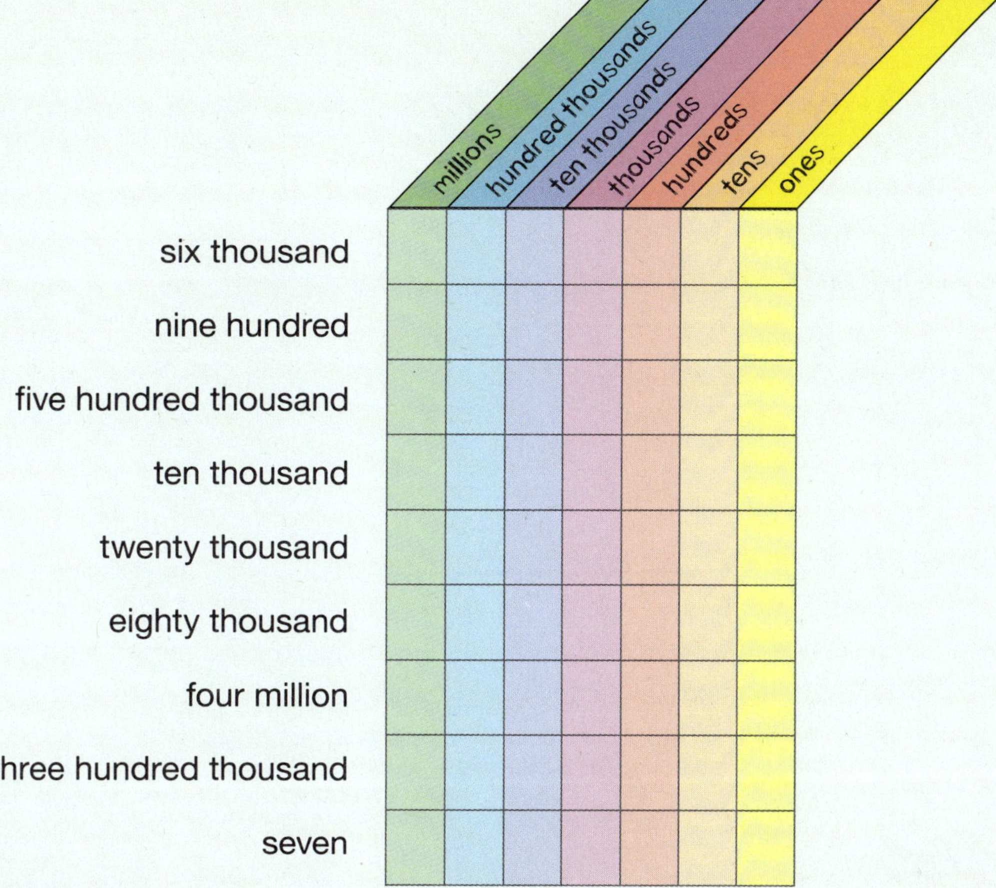

	millions	hundred thousands	ten thousands	thousands	hundreds	tens	ones
six thousand							
nine hundred							
five hundred thousand							
ten thousand							
twenty thousand							
eighty thousand							
four million							
three hundred thousand							
seven							

Match.

200,907   twenty-nine thousand seven hundred

29,700   twenty thousand nine hundred seven

209,070   two hundred thousand nine hundred seven

20,907   two hundred nine thousand seventy

Review

Complete the mixed-up multiplication chart.

×	2	4	10	9	1	3	5	6	8	7
5	10	20	50	45	5	15	25	30	40	35
6			60		6		30			
7	14		70		7					

Complete.

	3,	9	4	2
+	4,	3	0	8

	6,	9	8	1
−	4,	6	3	5

	3,	2	2	4
−	1,	3	8	6

Choose the more sensible unit for each item.

Capacity of a tea cup

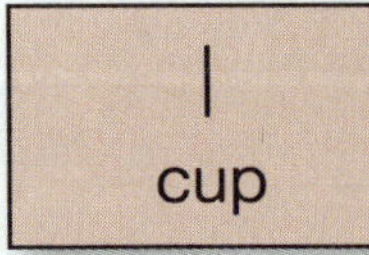
1 cup

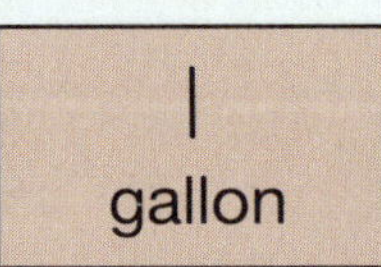
1 gallon

Capacity of a watering can

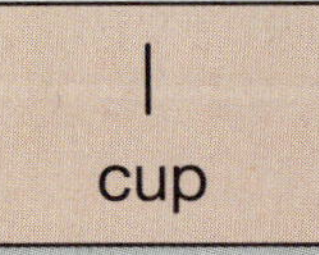
1 cup

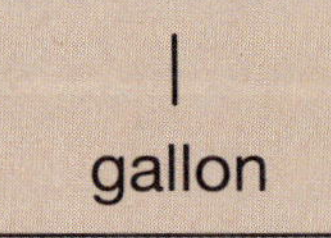
1 gallon

Capacity of a pitcher

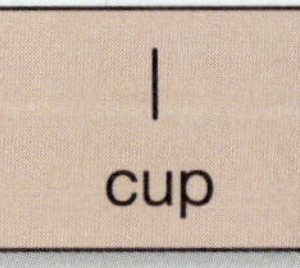
1 cup

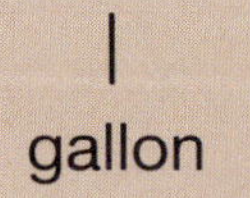
1 gallon

Answer the questions.

Is 45 a multiple of 5?

Is 32 a multiple of 6?

Is 27 divisible by 2?

Is 40 divisible by 10?

Is 4 a factor of 18?

Is 6 a factor of 24?

Lesson Activities

A

millions	hundred thousands	ten thousands	thousands	hundreds	tens	ones
		4	6, 2	0	5	
		2	0, 3	8	6	
	4	0	7, 0	3	1	
1,	0	6	0, 4	2	7	

B

sailboat

$

airboat

$

speed boat

$

yacht

$

pontoon boat

$

cabin cruiser

$

Practice 👤 Complete.

Standard Form	Expanded Form
24,923	
35,607	
	50,000 + 4,000 + 900 + 80 + 5
120,082	
	500,000 + 40,000 + 10 + 9

Complete with <, >, or =.

96,000 ◯ 97,000	36,845 ◯ 51,936	401,560 ◯ 401,506
85,422 ◯ 85,088	77,201 ◯ 77,201	635,785 ◯ 695,014
19,874 ◯ 20,000	46,500 ◯ 45,600	999,999 ◯ 999,998

Circle the greatest number in each group.

37,405	543,000	197,452
36,943	529,999	197,099
38,000	500,682	197,800

Review 👤 — Complete. Follow the steps.

1. Divide
2. Multiply
3. Subtract

5  | 9   5  9   5   9   5  9

Match pairs that equal 10,000.

9,000	2,000
8,500	3,000
8,000	1,000
7,500	2,500
7,000	1,500

Complete.

8:00	20	min. →	8:20
8:20		min. →	8:40
8:40		min. →	8:55
8:55		min. →	9:00
9:00		min. →	9:25

Solve. Write the equations you use.

The remote-controlled car costs $59.
The remote-controlled helicopter costs
$33 more than the car.
How much does it cost to buy both?

Jonah has $35.
He wants to buy a video game
controller that costs $54.
How much more money
does he need?

Lesson Activities 

53,900 ≈ [ ]

19,823 ≈ [ ]

26,125 ≈ [ ]

165,498 ≈ [ ]

Practice

Round each number to the nearest thousand. Use the number line to help.

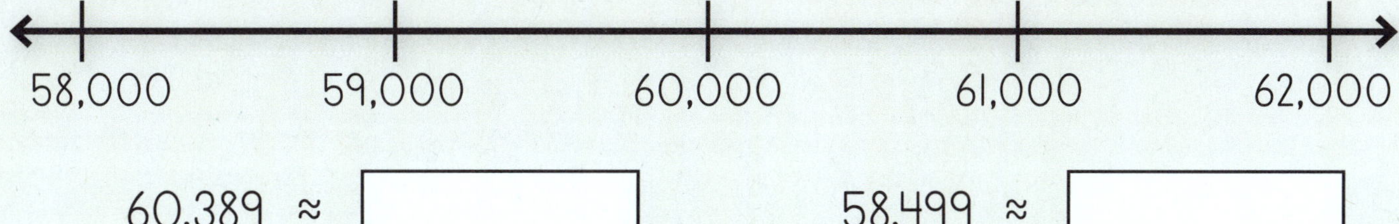

58,000   59,000   60,000   61,000   62,000

60,389 ≈ ____   58,499 ≈ ____

61,700 ≈ ____   59,825 ≈ ____

59,074 ≈ ____   61,009 ≈ ____

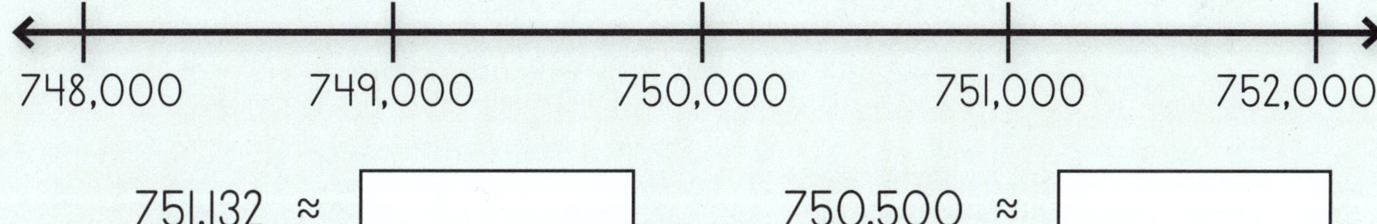

748,000   749,000   750,000   751,000   752,000

751,132 ≈ ____   750,500 ≈ ____

748,510 ≈ ____   749,999 ≈ ____

751,647 ≈ ____   751,008 ≈ ____

Round each number to the nearest thousand to complete the chart.

Zoo Attendance

Month	Attendance	Rounded to Nearest Thousand
May	225,882	
June	358,947	
July	429,694	
August	344,006	

Review

Find all factor pairs.

Factor pairs of 18

1 2 3
4 5 6
7 8 9

Factor pairs of 24

1 2 3
4 5 6
7 8 9

Complete.

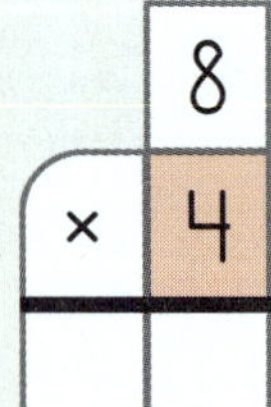
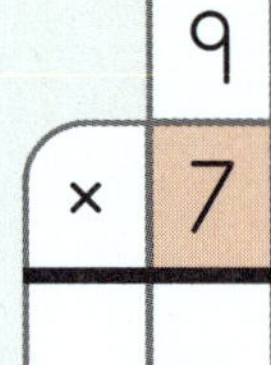
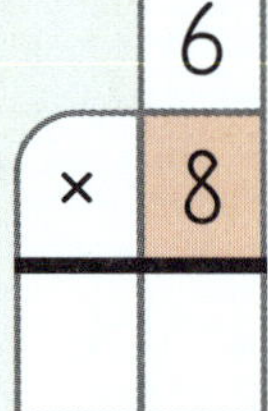

Circle the shapes that have 4 right angles.
X the shapes that do not have 4 right angles.

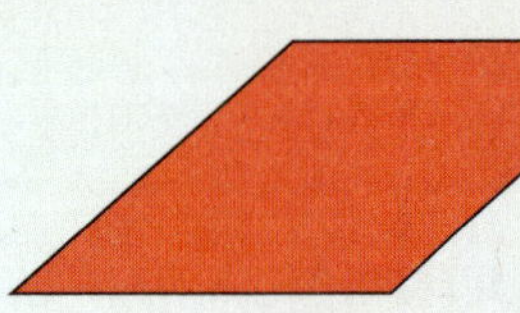
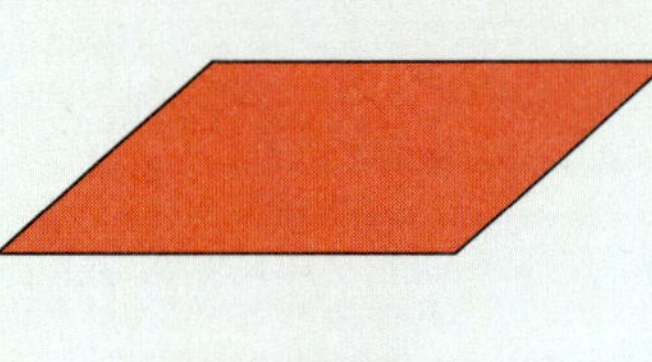
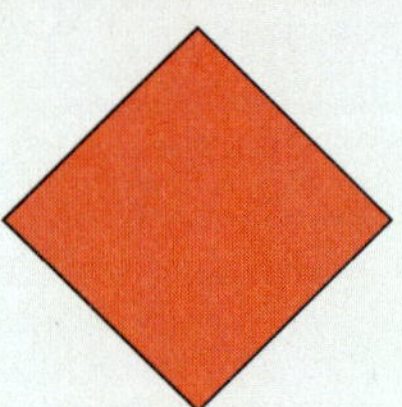

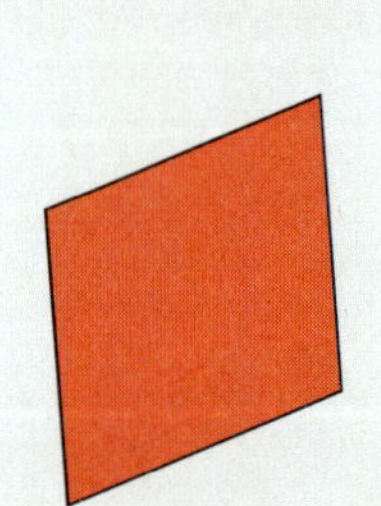
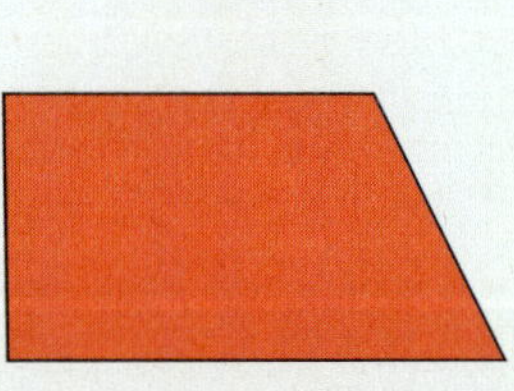

Complete.

6 weeks = [ ] days

6 weeks, 1 day = [ ] days

9 weeks = [ ] days

9 weeks, 5 days = [ ] days

28 days = [ ] weeks

29 days = [ ] weeks, [ ] day(s)

49 days = [ ] weeks

50 days = [ ] weeks, [ ] day(s)

Lesson Activities

$35{,}000 + 5{,}000 =$ ___________

$35 + 5 =$ ___________

$142{,}000 + 100{,}000 =$ ___________

$142 + 100 =$ ___________

$90{,}000 - 30{,}000 =$ ___________

$90 - 30 =$ ___________

$200{,}000 - 50{,}000 =$ ___________

$200 - 50 =$ ___________

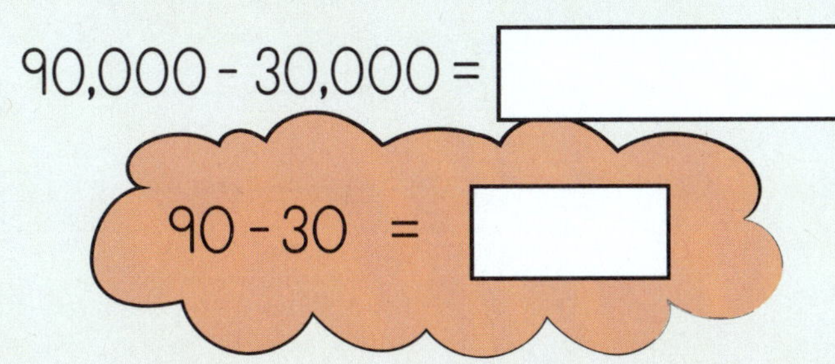

Race to 500,000

Player 1	Player 2

Practice

Match pairs that equal 100,000.

50,000	25,000
99,000	10,000
75,000	50,000
90,000	15,000
85,000	1,000

Complete.

$60{,}000 + 50{,}000 =$ ☐ $100{,}000 + 200{,}000 =$ ☐

$80{,}000 - 10{,}000 =$ ☐ $300{,}000 + 50{,}000 =$ ☐

$45{,}000 + 5{,}000 =$ ☐ $300{,}000 - 50{,}000 =$ ☐

$50{,}000 - 25{,}000 =$ ☐ $400{,}000 - 100{,}000 =$ ☐

Solve. Write the equations you use.

Peter bikes 20,000 meters on Monday and 13,000 meters on Tuesday.
How much further does he bike on Monday than Tuesday?

Vanshika's mom runs 6,000 meters on Saturday and 8,000 meters on Sunday.
How far does she run in all?

Review 👤 Match.

90 ÷ 9		6		72 ÷ 8
72 ÷ 9		7		56 ÷ 8
54 ÷ 9		8		48 ÷ 8
81 ÷ 9		9		80 ÷ 8
63 ÷ 9		10		64 ÷ 8

Match.

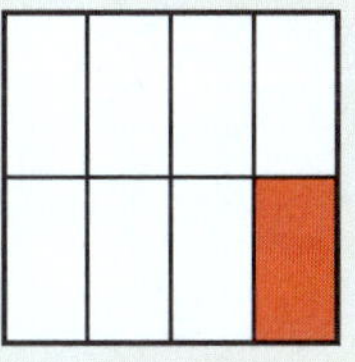

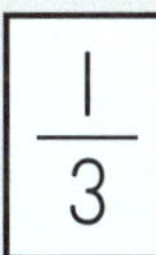

$\frac{1}{3}$

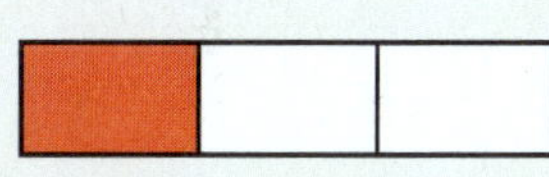

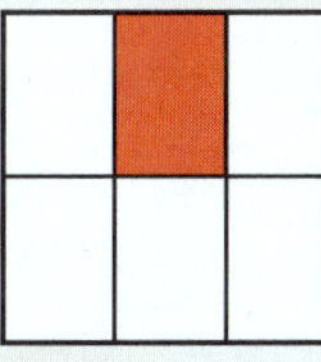

$\frac{1}{6}$

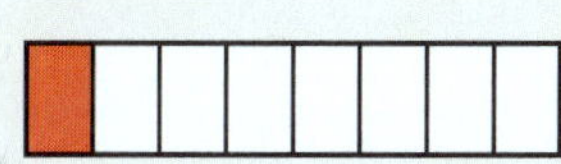

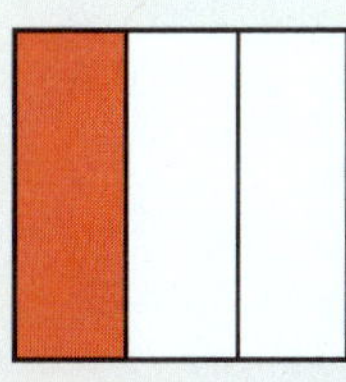

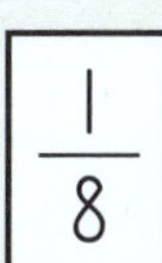

$\frac{1}{8}$

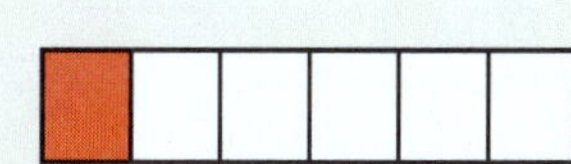

Solve. Write the equations you use.

On Saturday, the ice cream shop sold 125 ice cream cones. 50 were chocolate. 35 were vanilla. The rest were strawberry. How many were strawberry?

Bobby's family bought 4 chocolate cones and 3 strawberry cones. Each cone cost $6. How much did they pay for all the ice cream cones?

Lesson Activities 👥

A

	2	4	9 ,	3	1	2
+	1	0	6 ,	8	4	8

	6	5	7 ,	9	0	8
−	2	6	1 ,	3	5	4

B

Leaf Fight

Player 1	Player 2
+	+
+	+
−	−
−	−

Practice 

Complete.

	5	3	9	,	0	8	7
+	2	4	6	,	3	5	3

	5	3	9	,	0	8	7
−	2	4	6	,	3	5	3

Review 

Choose the more sensible unit for each item.

Capacity of an eyedropper

mL	L

Capacity of a water bottle

mL	L

Capacity of a pitcher

mL	L

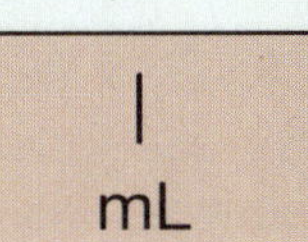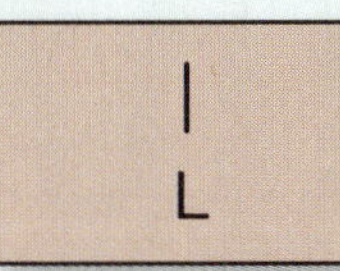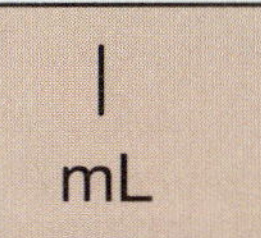

Round to the underlined place.

7<u>3</u>8 ≈

4,3<u>6</u>2 ≈

8,<u>9</u>74 ≈

3<u>6</u>,527 ≈

84,<u>0</u>14 ≈

Complete.

3 × 8 =   9 × 7 =

7 × 7 =   4 × 9 =

8 × 9 =   8 × 7 =

9 × 3 =   4 × 7 =

7 × 6 =   9 × 9 =

Lesson Activities 👥

37,406 people came to the baseball game on Thursday.
48,694 people came to the baseball game on Friday.
What was the total attendance for both games?

➡️ How many more people came to the baseball game on Friday than the game on Thursday?

The aquarium sold 137,892 child tickets in October.
It sold 45,624 fewer adult tickets than child tickets.
How many adult tickets did the aquarium sell?

➡️ How many child and adult tickets did the aquarium sell in all?

Practice

Use the chart to answer the questions.
Write the equations you use.

State	Population in 1900	Population in 2000
North Dakota	319,146	642,200
South Dakota	401,570	754,844

How many people lived in North Dakota and South Dakota in 1900?

How many more people lived in South Dakota than North Dakota in 2000?

How much did North Dakota's population grow from 1900 to 2000?

How much did South Dakota's population grow from 1900 to 2000?

Review

Color the problems that match the number in the star.

7	6	9	8
49 ÷ 7	54 ÷ 9	72 ÷ 8	72 ÷ 8
56 ÷ 8	56 ÷ 7	81 ÷ 9	56 ÷ 7
90 ÷ 9	48 ÷ 8	56 ÷ 7	72 ÷ 9
28 ÷ 4	30 ÷ 5	36 ÷ 4	24 ÷ 3

Tell how many right angles each shape has.

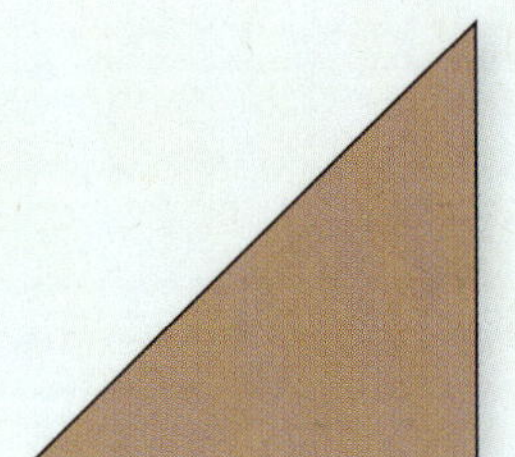

___ right angle(s)   ___ right angle(s)   ___ right angle(s)

Match.

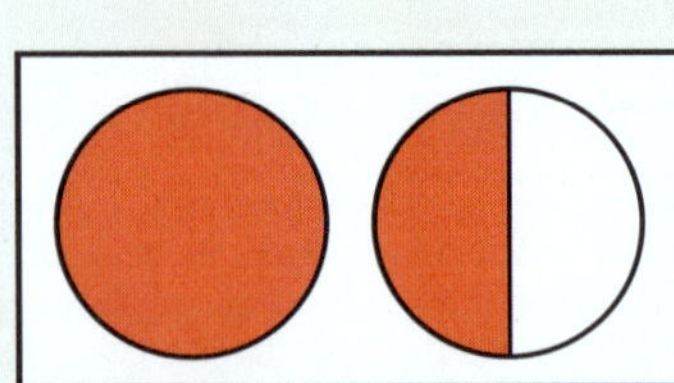
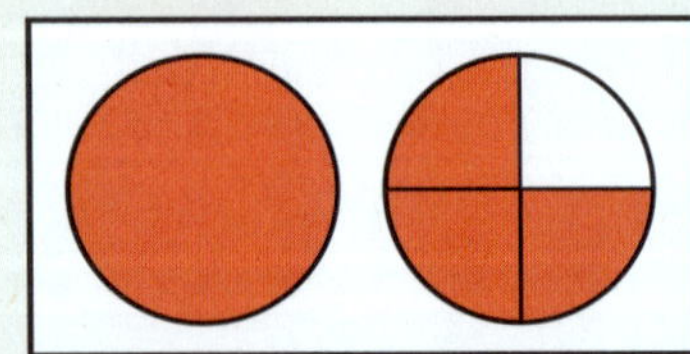

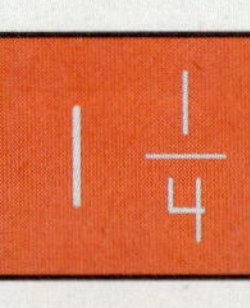
$1\frac{1}{4}$

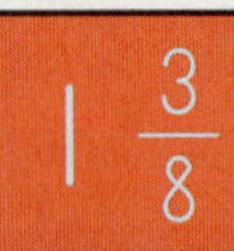
$1\frac{3}{8}$

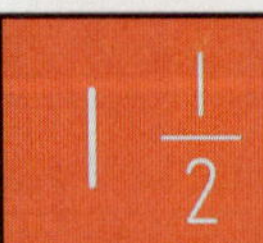
$1\frac{1}{2}$

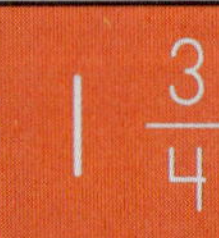
$1\frac{3}{4}$

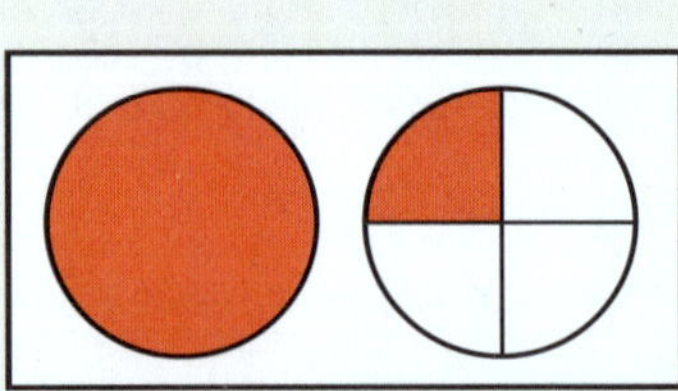
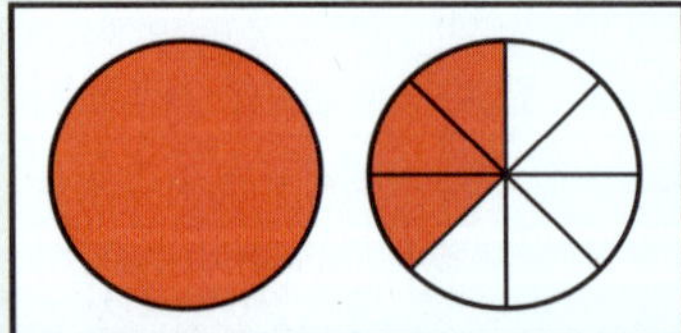

Lesson 2.9

Unit Wrap-Up

Write each number in standard form.

Words	Standard Form
five hundred thousand six hundred twenty	
five hundred six thousand twenty	
fifty-six thousand two hundred	
fifty-six thousand two	
five hundred sixty-two thousand	

Write each number in expanded form.

75,978 =

395,100 =

130,891 =

Round to the underlined place.

3,7<u>8</u>2 ≈

4,9<u>6</u>1 ≈

5,9<u>8</u>5 ≈

36,<u>8</u>47 ≈

65<u>9</u>,285 ≈

Use the clues to solve the number riddle.

- I am greater than 80,000 and less than 81,000.

- The digit in my tens-place is 3.

- The digit in my hundreds-place is 2 more than the digit in my tens-place.

- I am divisible by 10.

Unit Wrap-Up

Complete.

300,000 + 100,000 = ______

300,000 + 37,000 = ______

99,000 + 3,000 = ______

100,000 - 35,000 = ______

100,000 - 1,000 = ______

150,000 - 25,000 = ______

Complete with <, >, or =.

99,999 ◯ 100,000

74,017 ◯ 74,701

513,284 ◯ 531,284

680,562 ◯ 680,000

739,865 ◯ 739,864

297,842 ◯ 297,842

Complete.

	5	9	7,	3	4	6
+	1	0	2,	6	5	4

	6	7	4,	0	3	9
−	2	9	1,	5	2	8

	2	9	9,	9	9	9
+	3	7	5,	8	6	4

	5	7	5,	1	7	5
−	1	6	2,	3	8	5

Solve. Write the equations you use.

The bookstore had $474,968 in sales this year. It had $439,470 in sales last year. What were its total sales for both years?

➡ How much greater were the bookstore's sales this year than last year?

Lesson Activities

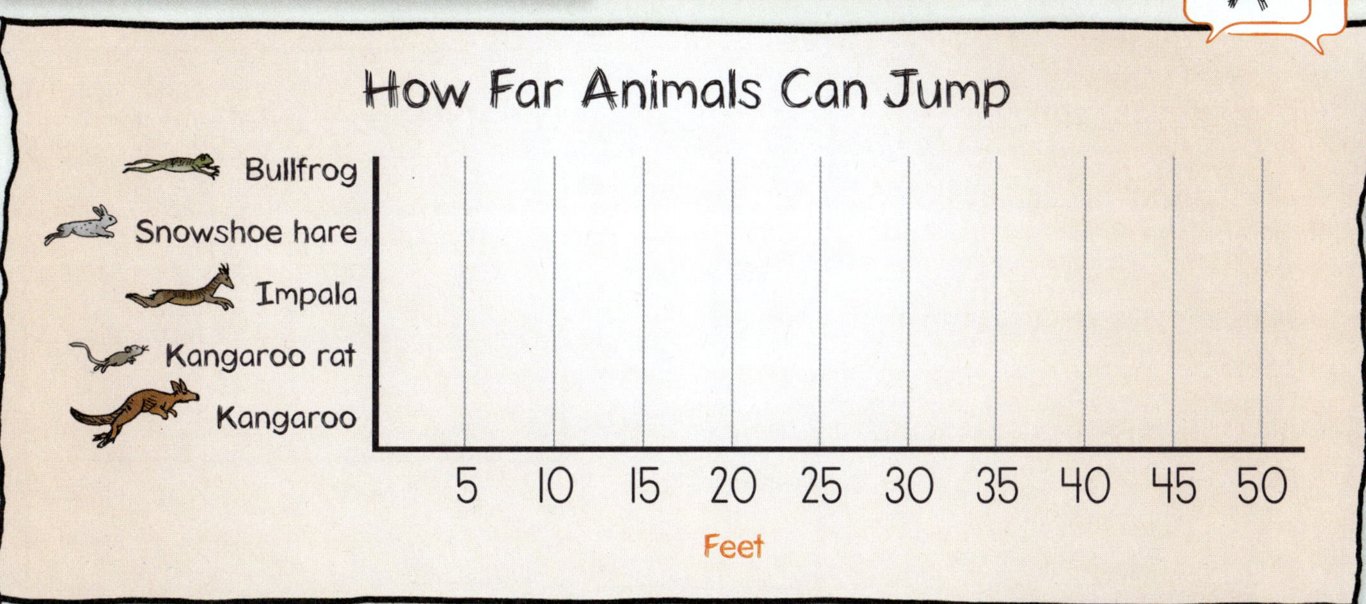

A bullfrog can jump 6 ft. A snowshoe hare can jump 2 times as far as a bullfrog. How far can a showshoe hare jump?

➜ How many feet farther can a snowshoe hare jump than a bullfrog?

An impala can jump 5 times as far as a bullfrog. How far can an impala jump?

➜ How many feet less can a bullfrog jump than an impala?

A kangaroo can jump 45 ft. That's 5 times as far as a kangaroo rat can jump. How far can a kangaroo rat jump?

➜ How many feet farther can a kangaroo jump than a kangaroo rat?

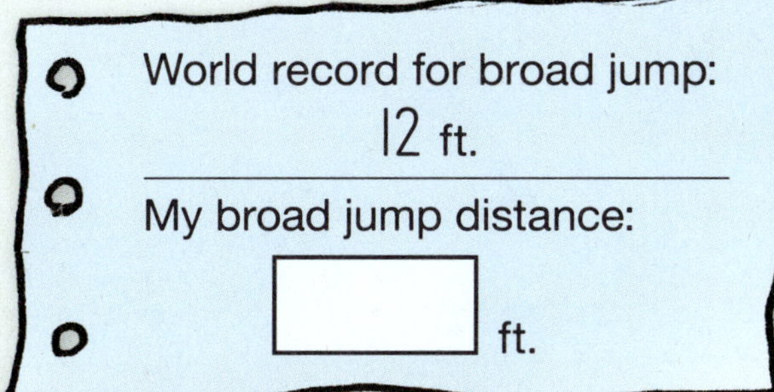

The world record is ______________ feet longer than my jump.

The world record is ______________ times as long as my jump.

Practice

Betsy asked people what their favorite season is. Use the clues to complete her bar graph.

- 6 people chose spring.

- 2 fewer people chose summer than spring.

- Twice as many people chose fall as summer.

- 4 times as many people chose fall as winter.

Use the clues to complete the chart.

- Peter is 2 years older than Nora.

- Hannah is twice as old as Nora.

- Mom is 6 times as old as Peter.

- Dad is 5 times as old as Hannah.

Name	Age
Nora	4
Peter	
Hannah	
Mom	
Dad	

Use the clues to complete the prices.

- The pogo stick costs 6 times as much as the jump rope.

- The skateboard costs $2 less than the pogo stick.

- The mini trampoline costs twice as much as the skateboard.

Review

Complete. Follow the steps.

1. Divide
2. Multiply
3. Subtract

| 4 | 3 6 | | 5 | 3 6 | | 6 | 3 6 | | 7 | 3 6 |

Write the quantities in the place-value chart.

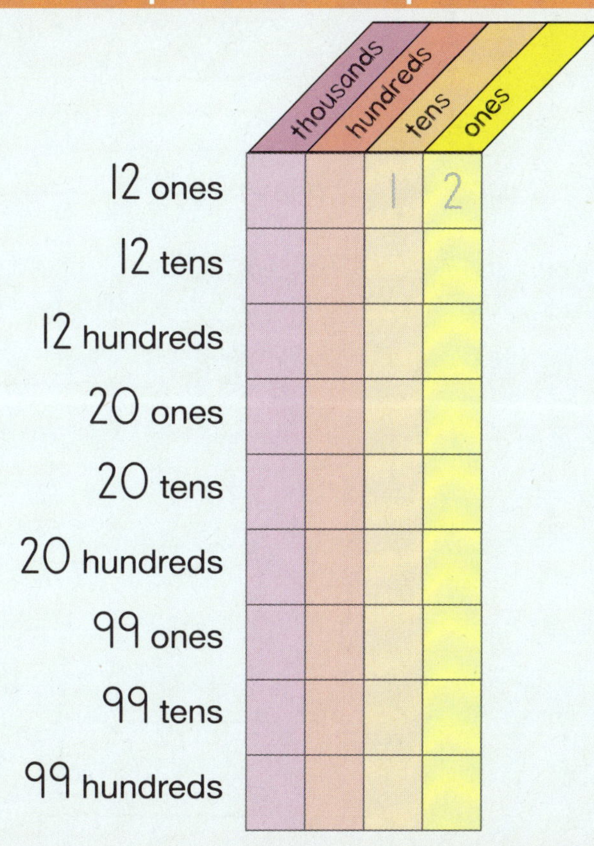

12 ones

12 tens

12 hundreds

20 ones

20 tens

20 hundreds

99 ones

99 tens

99 hundreds

Complete.

	5	4,	3	9	2
+	8	7,	1	0	6

	9	7,	3	0	4
−	4	5,	6	1	7

Solve the number riddles.

The product of two numbers is 12.
The sum of the numbers is 7.
What are the two numbers?

The product of two numbers is 40.
The difference between the numbers is 3.
What are the two numbers?

The product of two numbers is 19.
The sum of the numbers is 20.
What are the two numbers?

 The product of two numbers is 100.
The sum of the numbers is 25.
What are the two numbers?

Lesson Activities

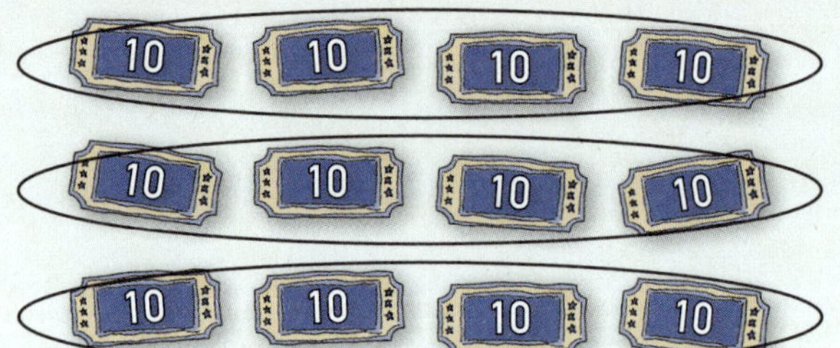

3 × 40 = [ ]

4 × 500 = [ ]

3 × 4 tens = [ ] tens

4 × 5 hundreds = [ ] hundreds

2 × 8,000 = [ ]

2 × 8 thousands = [ ] thousands

1. Underline the place-holder zeros.

2. Multiply the non-zero digits.

3. Tack on the place-holder zeros.

4 × 60 = [ ]

3 × 700 = [ ]

5 × 2,000 = [ ]

2 × 90 = [ ]

8 × 4,000 = [ ]

5 × 3,000 = [ ]

4 × 400 = [ ]

8 × 500 = [ ]

5 × 60 = [ ]

MENTAL MATH ARCADE

PRIZES

	×							
	×	80						
	×	500						
	×	700						
	×	2,000						
	×	3,000						
Total Points								

6,000

8,000

15,000

20,000

Practice Complete.

2 × 7,000 = ☐   5 × 600 = ☐

9 × 40 = ☐   3 × 8,000 = ☐

6 × 800 = ☐   4 × 70 = ☐

7 × 500 = ☐   9 × 9,000 = ☐

★ ☐ × 6,000 = 36,000   ★ 8 × ☐ = 40,000

Review

Circle the numbers that match the description.
X the numbers that do not match the description.

Divisible by 2	Divisible by 5	Divisible by 10
3,295 7,438	3,295 7,438	3,295 7,438
2,100 5,335	2,100 5,335	2,100 5,335
1,926 8,750	1,926 8,750	1,926 8,750

Complete with <, >, or =.

694,228 ◯ 64,228

135,017 ◯ 301,000

42,986 ◯ 429,861

543,908 ◯ 543,908

76,209 ◯ 76,290

Match.

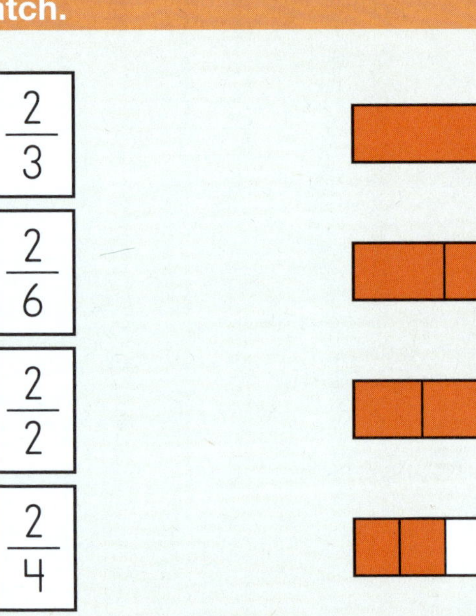

$\frac{2}{3}$

$\frac{2}{6}$

$\frac{2}{2}$

$\frac{2}{4}$

Solve. Write the equations you use.

Sean's parents pay $2,694 for new carpet.
They pay $3,047 for new furniture.
How much do they spend in all?

 How much more does the furniture cost than the carpet?

Lesson Activities 👥

$3 \times 900 =$ ☐ $4 \times 4{,}000 =$ ☐

$20 \times 30 =$ ☐

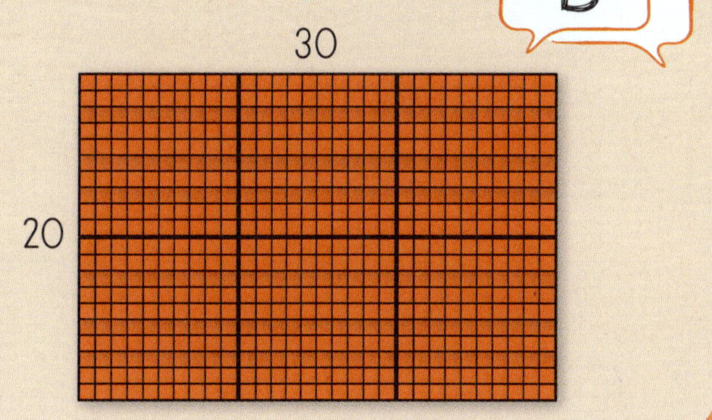

$40 \times 40 =$ ☐ $60 \times 30 =$ ☐ $80 \times 50 =$ ☐

SPIN TO **WIN!**

			Product
	×		
	×		
	×		
	×		

Player 1 Total ☐

			Product
	×		
	×		
	×		
	×		

Player 2 Total ☐

Practice

Complete.

30 × 30 = [ ]   20 × 90 = [ ]

10 × 70 = [ ]   60 × 50 = [ ]

7 × 70 = [ ]   90 × 90 = [ ]

60 × 60 = [ ]   6 × 800 = [ ]

80 × 70 = [ ]   70 × 60 = [ ]

8 × 9,000 = [ ]   40 × 90 = [ ]

Solve. Write the equations you use.

There are 50 paper clips in each box.
How many paper clips are in 20 boxes?

Logan earns $30 per hour.
He works 40 hours per week.
How much does he earn in one week?

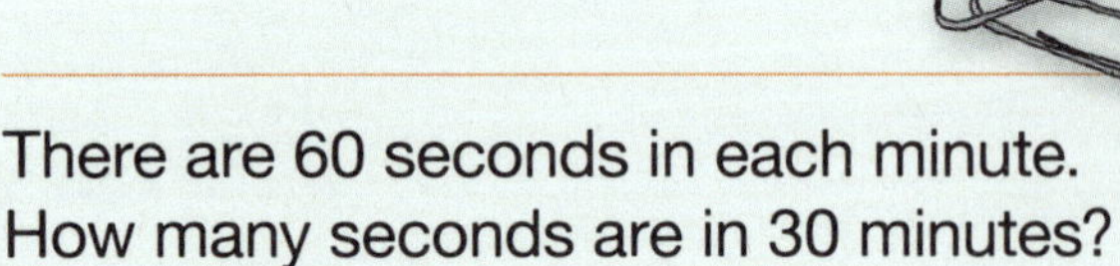

There are 60 seconds in each minute.
How many seconds are in 30 minutes?

There are 60 seconds in each minute.
How many seconds are in 60 minutes?

Review

Find all factors of each number. Then, answer the questions.

Factor pairs of 19	Factor pairs of 20
1 2 3 4 5 6 7 8 9	1 2 3 4 5 6 7 8 9

Is 19 prime or composite?

Is 19 a multiple of 4?

Is 5 a factor of 19?

Is 20 prime or composite?

Is 20 a multiple of 4?

Is 5 a factor of 20?

Round to the underlined place.

4,3<u>8</u>5 ≈ ☐

6,2<u>4</u>1 ≈ ☐

8,2<u>9</u>9 ≈ ☐

<u>1</u>,875 ≈ ☐

5,9<u>9</u>6 ≈ ☐

Match pairs that equal 10,000.

7,800	200
9,800	1,200
8,800	2,200
6,800	3,200
5,800	4,200

Lesson Activities

Parentheses mean "do this first!"

$(3 + 2) \times 4 =$ ☐ $\qquad$ $3 + (2 \times 4) =$ ☐

$(16 \div 4) - 2 =$ ☐ $\qquad$ $16 \div (4 - 2) =$ ☐

$(6 \times 7) + 1 =$ ☐ $\qquad$ $6 \times (7 + 1) =$ ☐

4 chicken sandwiches
5 chips

$(4 \times 8) + (5 \times 3) =$ ☐

Concession Stand Menu

Chicken Sandwich $8
Veggie Wrap $8
Pizza Slice $4
Hot Dog $3
Chips.. $3
Bottled Water $2
Candy $2

4 pizza slices
3 chips

5 pizza slices
1 chicken sandwich

1 veggie wrap
7 candies

2 chicken sandwiches
3 pizza slices
5 bottled waters

Practice 👤 Complete.

$(7 \times 4) + 2 =$ ______
28

$5 \times (6 + 1) =$ ______
______

$(9 - 5) \times 4 =$ ______

$(2 \times 10) + (3 \times 10) =$ ______

$20 - (4 \times 3) =$ ______

$14 \div (5 + 2) =$ ______

$9 \times (2 \times 4) =$ ______

$(48 \div 6) \times 6 =$ ______

Use the numbers to complete the equations.

| 5 | 4 |
| 3 | 10 |

$(6 \times \boxed{}) + \boxed{} = 34$

$(\boxed{} \times 9) - \boxed{} = 87$

| 7 | 2 |
| 8 | 6 | 9 |

$(5 \times \boxed{}) + (3 \times \boxed{}) = 31$

⭐ $\boxed{} + (\boxed{} \times \boxed{}) = 78$

Review Complete.

89 + 1 = ⬚	89 + 10 = ⬚
899 + 1 = ⬚	899 + 10 = ⬚
8,999 + 1 = ⬚	8,999 + 10 = ⬚
80 - 1 = ⬚	80 - 10 = ⬚
800 - 1 = ⬚	800 - 10 = ⬚
8,000 - 1 = ⬚	8,000 - 10 = ⬚

Complete. Follow the steps.

1. Divide
2. Multiply
3. Subtract

5 **2** 2   5 **3** 2   5 **4** 2   5 **5** 2

Use the clues to complete the chart.

- Jake biked 3 times as far as Kendall.

- Jake biked 6 times as far as Aiden.

- Luna biked 5 kilometers less than Jake.

- Brynn biked twice as far as Kendall.

Name	Distance Biked
Kendall	10 km
Jake	
Aiden	
Luna	
Brynn	

Lesson Activities

Concession Stand Menu

Chicken Sandwich $8
Veggie Wrap $8
Pizza Slice $4
Hot Dog $3
Chips $3
Bottled Water $2
Candy $2

A

4 bottled waters
3 candies

Multiply, then add.

$$(4 \times 2) + (3 \times 2) = \boxed{}$$

Add, then multiply.

$$(4 + 3) \times 2 = \boxed{}$$

B

3 chicken sandwiches
7 veggie wraps

5 hot dogs
4 chips

3 chicken sandwiches
3 bottled waters

5 pizza slices
5 chips

Practice

Complete. Then, match the equations with the same answer.

$(5 \times 8) + (1 \times 8) = \boxed{}$

$(4 + 5) \times 9 = \boxed{}$

$(6 \times 7) + (4 \times 7) = \boxed{}$

$(5 + 1) \times 8 = \boxed{}$

$(4 \times 8) + (4 \times 8) = \boxed{}$

$(6 + 4) \times 7 = \boxed{}$

$(4 \times 9) + (5 \times 9) = \boxed{}$

$(4 + 4) \times 8 = \boxed{}$

Complete the blanks to match the word problem. Then, solve.

Annika bought 8 boxes of chocolate chip granola bars and 2 boxes of peanut granola bars. Each box had 6 granola bars. How many granola bars did she buy?

Hakeem bought 7 paperback books and 7 hardcover books at the used book sale. The paperback books cost $4 each. The hardcover books cost $6 each. How much did he pay for the books?

$(\boxed{} + \boxed{}) \times \boxed{} = \boxed{}$

$(\boxed{} + \boxed{}) \times \boxed{} = \boxed{}$

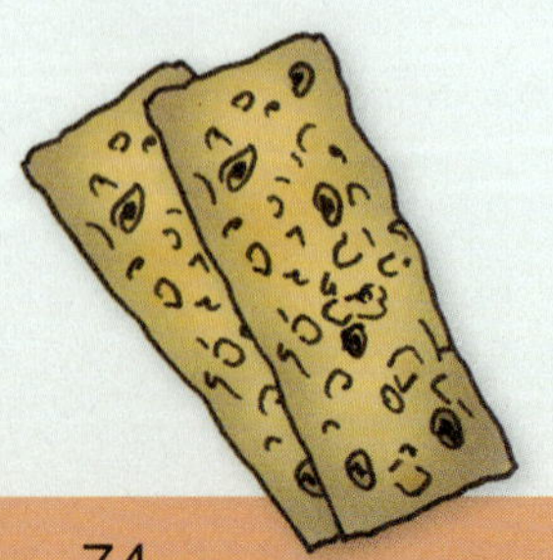

Review
Complete the sequences.

Use the diagram to answer the questions.

What is the area of the living room?

What is the area of the dining room?

What is the total area of both rooms?

Complete.

$(20 + 40) + 30 =$ ☐

$20 + (40 + 30) =$ ☐

$(50 - 30) + 20 =$ ☐

$50 - (30 + 20) =$ ☐

$(2 \times 3) \times 5 =$ ☐

$2 \times (3 \times 5) =$ ☐

Complete.

$7 \times 8 =$ ☐

$70 \times 8 =$ ☐

$7 \times 800 =$ ☐

$7 \times 8,000 =$ ☐

$8 \times 70 =$ ☐

$80 \times 70 =$ ☐

Lesson Activities

$3 \times 11 = (3 \times 10) + (3 \times 1) =$ ☐

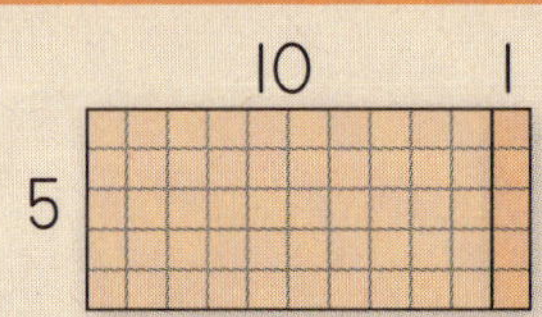

$5 \times 11 = (5 \times 10) + (5 \times 1) =$ ☐

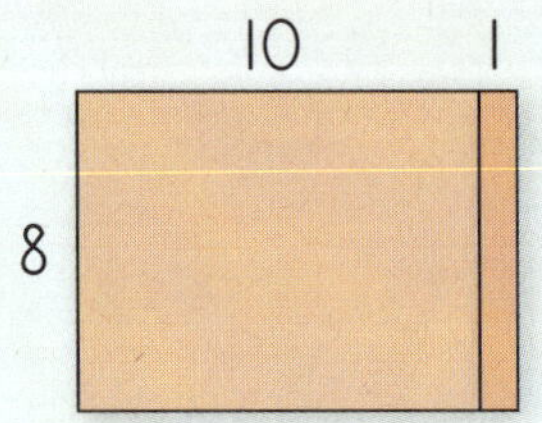

$8 \times 11 =$ ☐

$6 \times 11 =$ ☐

$4 \times 11 =$ ☐ $9 \times 11 =$ ☐ $2 \times 11 =$ ☐

$10 \times 11 =$ ☐ $11 \times 11 =$ ☐ $12 \times 11 =$ ☐

Four in a Row

11	3 × 11	10 × 11	33	5 × 11
8 × 11	12 × 11	121	2 × 11	77
44	6 × 11	110	88	9 × 11
132	99	4 × 11	11 × 11	66
1 × 11	55	7 × 11	22	11

Practice   Complete.

$2 \times 11 =$ ☐ $6 \times 11 =$ ☐ $4 \times 11 =$ ☐

$8 \times 11 =$ ☐ $1 \times 11 =$ ☐ $9 \times 11 =$ ☐

$3 \times 11 =$ ☐ $10 \times 11 =$ ☐ $5 \times 11 =$ ☐

$7 \times 11 =$ ☐   ★ $11 \times 11 =$ ☐   ★ $12 \times 11 =$ ☐

Use the clues to complete the chart.

- Mom is 3 times as old as Eduardo.

- Dad is 4 times as old as Eduardo.

- Grandpa is 6 times as old as Eduardo.

- Great-grandma is 8 times as old as Eduardo.

Name	Age
Eduardo	11
Mom	
Dad	
Grandpa	
Great-grandma	

Solve. Write the equations you use.

8 teams play in the soccer tournament.
Each team has 11 players.
How many players are in the tournament?

Tickets to the play cost $11.
How much does it cost to buy 6 tickets?

Review

Complete the missing numbers.

$38{,}215 = \boxed{} + 8{,}000 + 200 + 10 + 5$

$96{,}760 = 90{,}000 + 6{,}000 + 700 + \boxed{}$

$149{,}304 = 100{,}000 + \boxed{} + 9{,}000 + 300 + 4$

$\boxed{} = 700{,}000 + 3{,}000 + 700 + 3$

$\boxed{} = 70{,}000 + 3{,}000 + 70 + 3$

Complete.

$4 \times 20 = \boxed{}$

$4 \times 200 = \boxed{}$

$4 \times 2{,}000 = \boxed{}$

$40 \times 20 = \boxed{}$

Color the bar to match the fraction.

$\dfrac{1}{6}$

$\dfrac{3}{6}$

$\dfrac{6}{6}$

Solve. Write the equations you use.

1,148 people came to the play on Friday. 296 fewer people came on Saturday than Friday.
How many people came on Saturday?

How many people came to the play on Friday and Saturday in all?

Lesson Activities 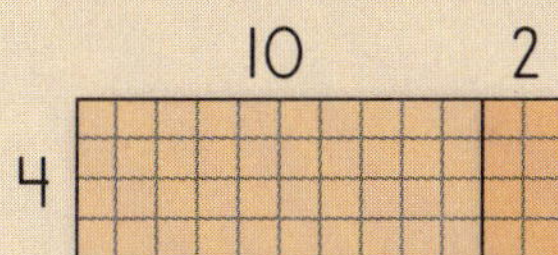

10   2

4

$4 \times 12 = (4 \times 10) + (4 \times 2) =$ ☐

10   2

6

$6 \times 12 = (6 \times 10) + (6 \times 2) =$ ☐

10   2

5

$5 \times 12 =$ ☐

10   2

7

$7 \times 12 =$ ☐

$3 \times 12 =$ ☐ $8 \times 12 =$ ☐ $9 \times 12 =$ ☐

$10 \times 12 =$ ☐ $11 \times 12 =$ ☐ $12 \times 12 =$ ☐

Egg Scramble

Dozens of Eggs	Number of Eggs	Dozens of Eggs	Number of Eggs
Player 1 Total		Player 2 Total	

Practice 👤 Complete.

3 × 12 = ⬜   7 × 12 = ⬜   4 × 12 = ⬜

6 × 12 = ⬜   10 × 12 = ⬜   1 × 12 = ⬜

2 × 12 = ⬜   5 × 12 = ⬜   9 × 12 = ⬜

8 × 12 = ⬜   ⭐ 11 × 12 = ⬜   ⭐ 12 × 12 = ⬜

Complete the charts.

1 dozen = 12 donuts

Dozens	1	3	5	8
Donuts	12			

1 foot = 12 inches

Feet	2	6	10	12
Inches				

1 year = 12 months

Years	4	7	9	11
Months				

Review

Complete.

$100 - (5 \times 5) =$ ☐

$(10 \times 9) + (2 \times 9) =$ ☐

$(10 + 2) \times 9 =$ ☐

Draw the missing halves for the symmetric shapes.

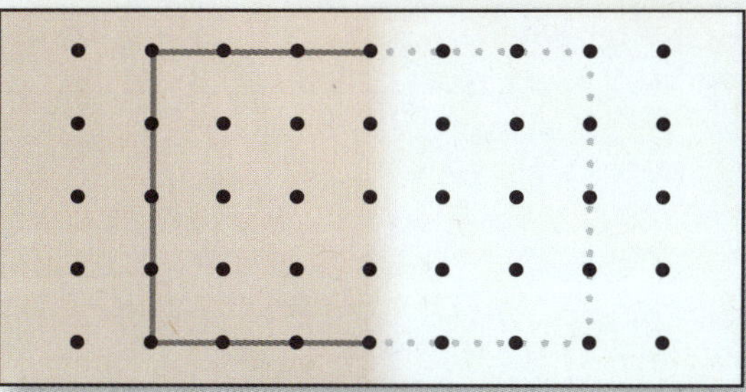

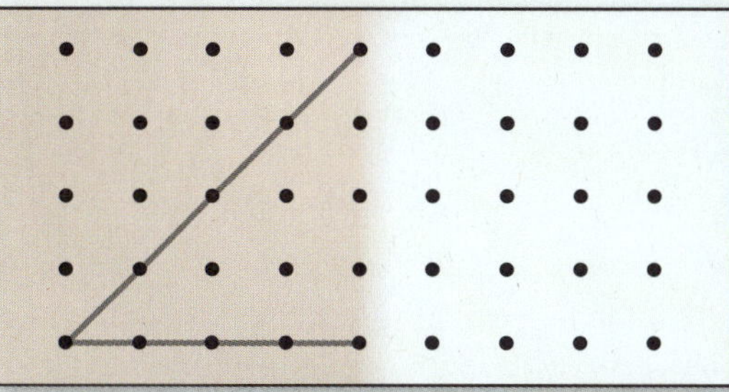

Round to the underlined place.

$450{,}128 \approx$ ☐

$450{,}728 \approx$ ☐

$79{,}841 \approx$ ☐

$79{,}341 \approx$ ☐

Complete. All times are p.m.

1:00	3 hr.	4:00
1:00	☐ hr.	6:00
1:30	☐ hr.	5:30
1:55	☐ hr.	5:55

Solve. Write the equations you use.

Niall bought 4 packs of cupcakes for a party.
Each pack cost $9.
He bought 3 tubs of ice cream.
Each tub cost $6.
How much did he spend in all?

Samantha mowed the lawn 6 times.
She earned $8 each time.
Then, she spent $15.
How much of her lawn-mowing money
did she have left?

Lesson Activities

Area Model

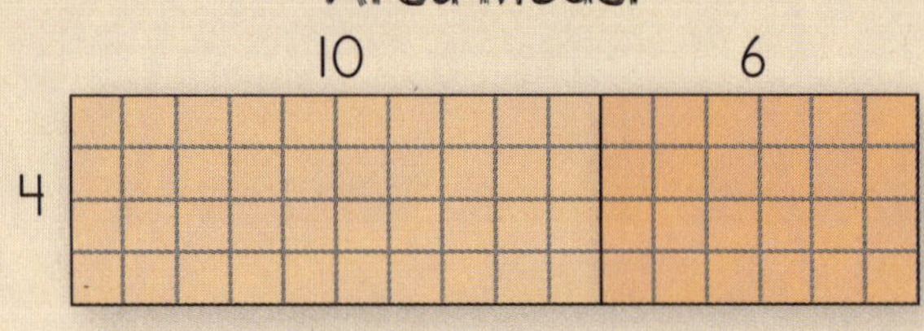

4 × 16 = [ ]

Box Method

10   6
4

4 × 16 = [ ]

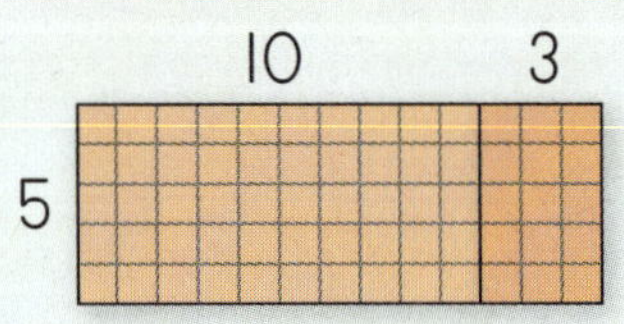

5 × 13 = [ ]

5 × 13 = [ ]

7 × 21 = [ ]

4 × 35 = [ ]

Roll and Multiply

Player 1	Player 2
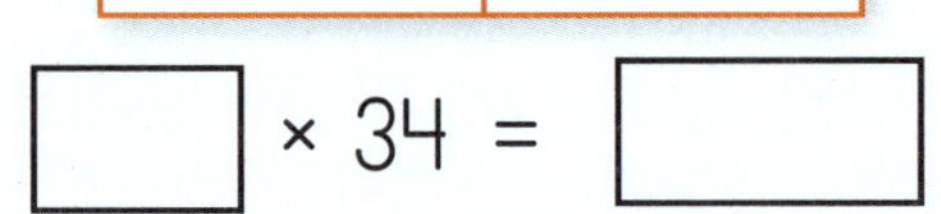 [ ] × 34 = [ ]	[ ] × 34 = [ ]
[ ] × 42 = [ ]	[ ] × 42 = [ ]
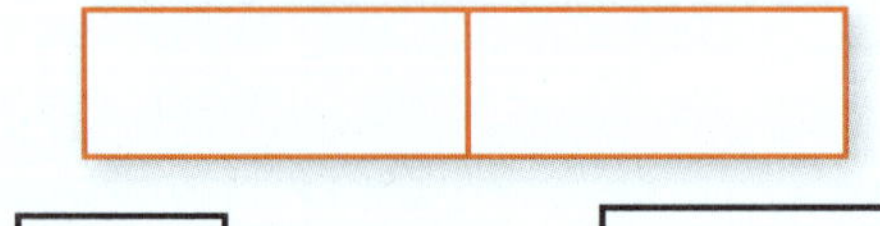 [ ] × 91 = [ ]	[ ] × 91 = [ ]

Practice

Complete the boxes to find the product.

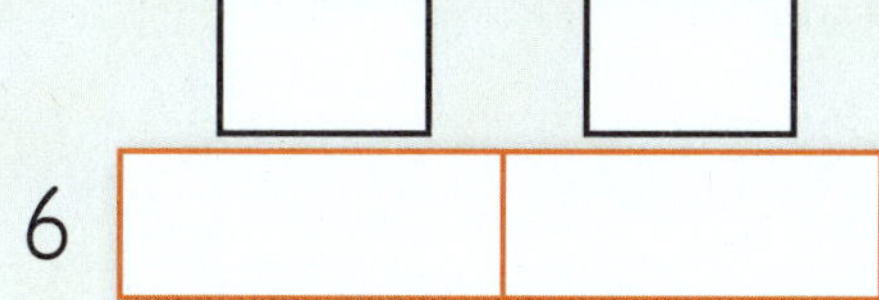

	10	8
3		

3 × 18 = ☐

	20	2
9		

9 × 22 = ☐

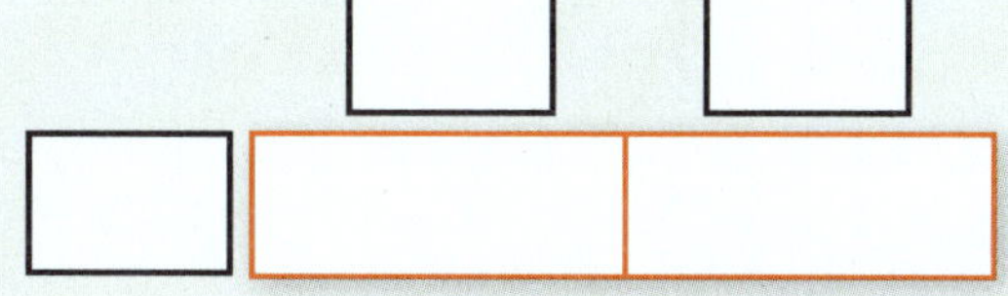

6 × 36 = ☐

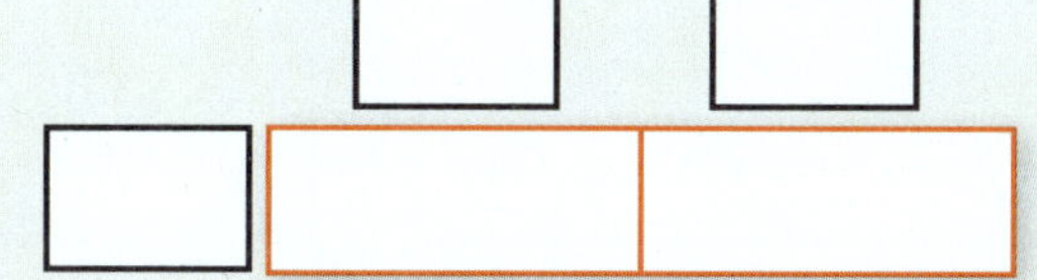

8 × 47 = ☐

7 × 56 = ☐

9 × 99 = ☐

Find the missing numbers.

	70	4
6	420	24

☐ × ☐ = 444

5	50	20

5 × ☐ = 70

	30	☐
7		14

7 × ☐ = ☐

	☐	5
3	240	

☐ × ☐ = ☐

Review

Complete.

3 × 11 = ☐   6 × 11 = ☐   2 × 11 = ☐

7 × 11 = ☐   4 × 11 = ☐   8 × 11 = ☐

5 × 11 = ☐   1 × 11 = ☐   9 × 11 = ☐

Write the word that describes all the shapes in each group.

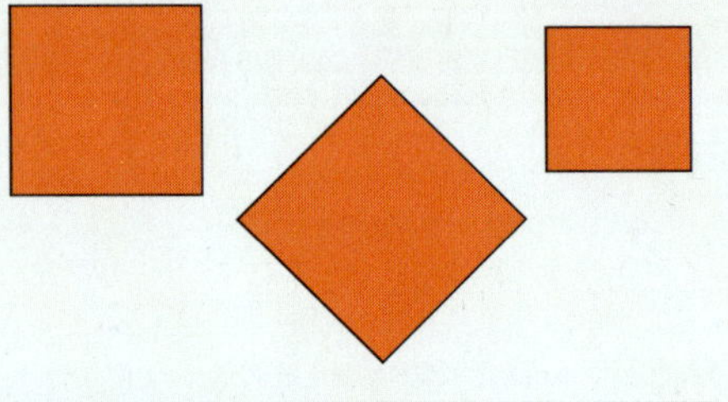

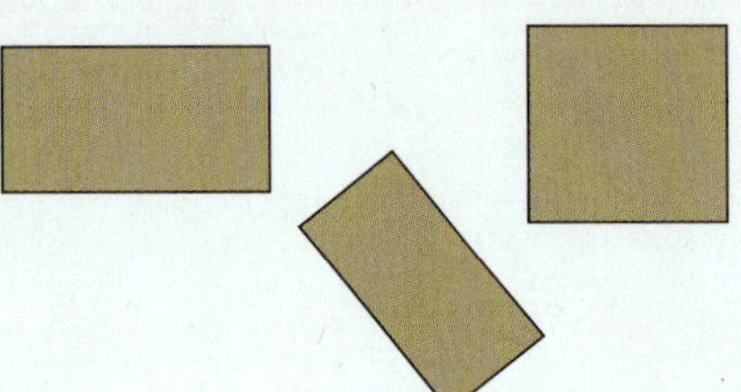

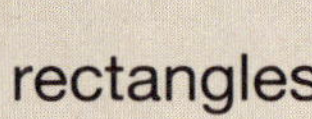

Solve. Write the equations you use.

Truett has saved $12. Luke has saved 4 times as much money as Truett. How much money has Luke saved?

Sophie has saved $50. She has saved 5 times as much as Ellie. How much has Ellie saved?

Lesson Activities

A

20   3

6

$6 \times 23 = $ [ ]

$5 \times 42 = $ [ ]

$4 \times 71 = $ [ ]

$9 \times 84 = $ [ ]

B

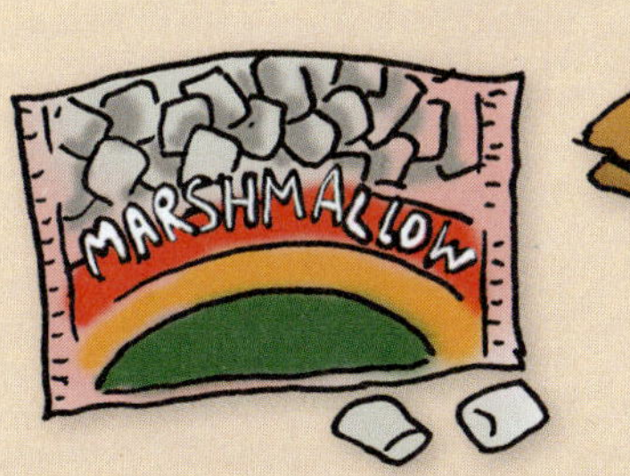

You buy 3 bags of marshmallows to roast at the bonfire.
There are 38 marshmallows in each bag.
How many marshmallows do you buy?

[ ] × [ ] = [ ]

You buy 5 boxes of graham crackers.
Each box has 27 crackers.
How many crackers do you buy?

[ ] × [ ] = [ ]

You buy 36 chocolate bars.
Each bar has 4 pieces of chocolate.
How many pieces of chocolate do you buy?

[ ] × [ ] = [ ]

Practice  Complete the boxes to solve the problems.

Ethan buys 6 boxes of cookies.
Each box has 24 cookies.
How many cookies does he buy?

6 × 24 =

June earns $27 per hour.
She works for 7 hours.
How much money does she earn?

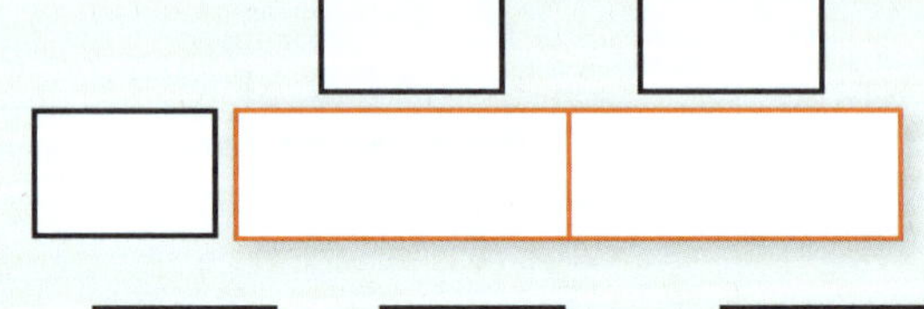

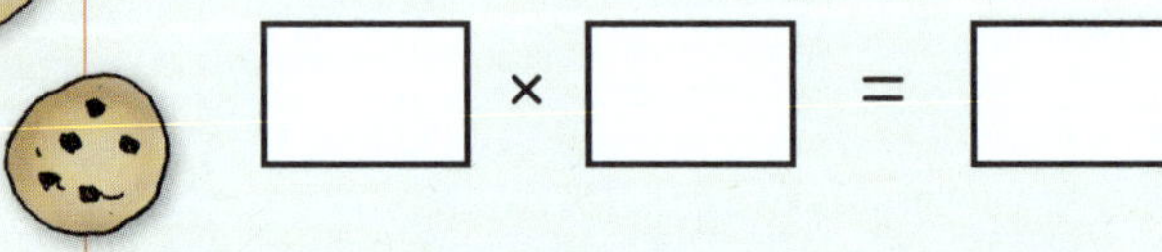

☐ × ☐ = ☐

On Monday, Benjamin reads 48 pages in
his book. On Tuesday, he reads 4 times as
many pages as on Monday.
How many pages does he read on Tuesday?

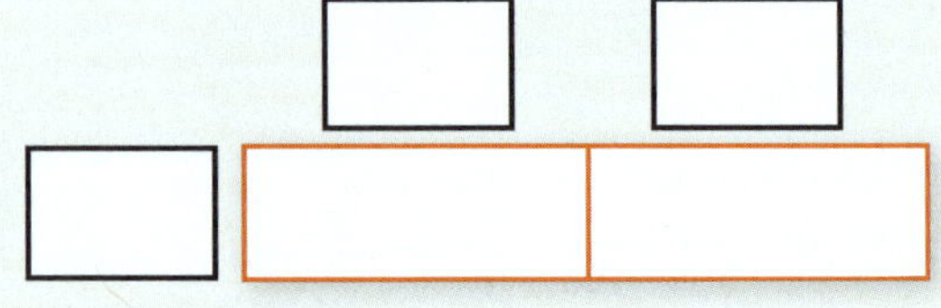

☐ × ☐ = ☐

The chairs at the concert are arranged in
6 rows. There are 48 chairs in each row.
How many chairs are there in all?

☐ × ☐ = ☐

Complete the boxes to find the area.

28 m

7 m

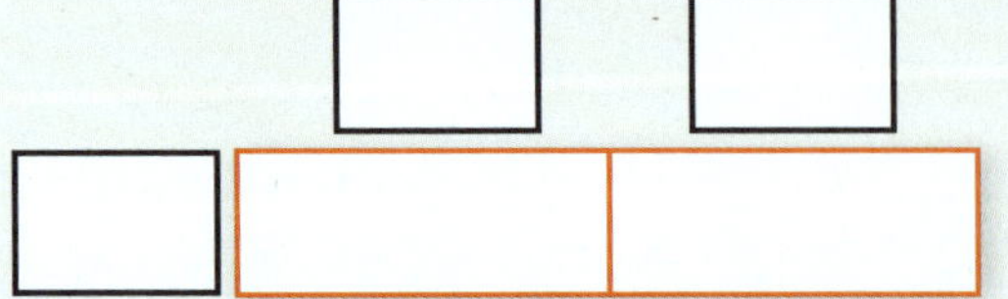

☐ × ☐ = ☐

16 yd.

8 yd.

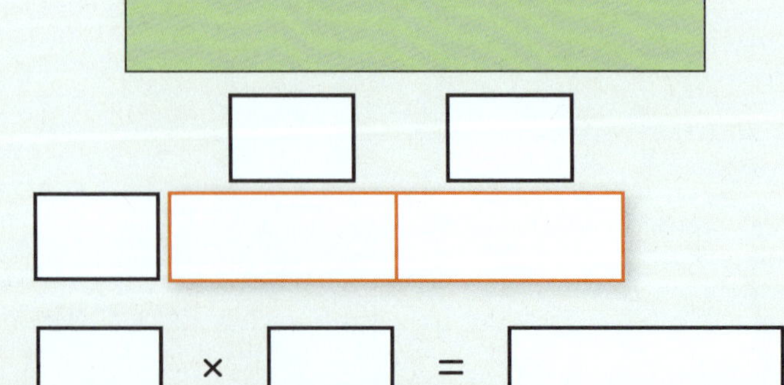

☐ × ☐ = ☐

Review

Complete.

4 × 12 = ☐   2 × 12 = ☐   9 × 12 = ☐

6 × 12 = ☐   5 × 12 = ☐   3 × 12 = ☐

1 × 12 = ☐   8 × 12 = ☐   7 × 12 = ☐

Use a ruler to measure.

Match each number to its dot on the number line.

| 137,419 | 137,250 | 137,806 | 137,723 |

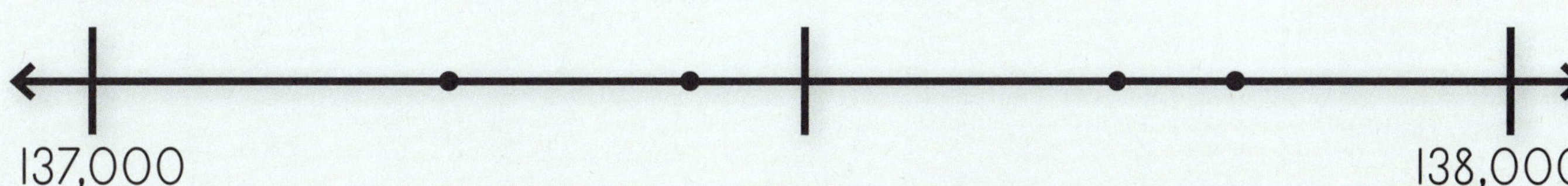

137,000   138,000

Solve. Write the equations you use.

Ella buys 8 packs of pencils.
Each pack has 12 pencils.
How many pencils does she buy?

Nathan buys 9 packs of pens. Each pack
has 10 black pens and 1 red pen.
How many pens does he buy?

Unit Wrap-Up

Madison made a bar graph to show how long she practiced her flute each day. Use the clues to complete her graph.

- Madison practiced 20 minutes on Monday.

- She practiced 10 minutes less on Tuesday than Monday.

- She practiced 5 times as long on Wednesday as she did on Tuesday.

- She practiced 3 times as long on Thursday as she did on Monday.

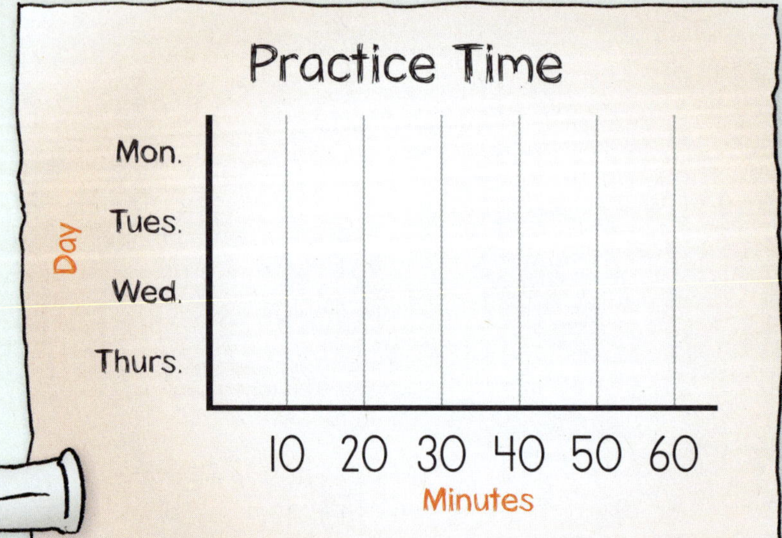

Complete.

$7 \times 11 =$ ☐ $5 \times 12 =$ ☐ $9 \times 11 =$ ☐

$8 \times 12 =$ ☐ $8 \times 11 =$ ☐ $7 \times 12 =$ ☐

$6 \times 11 =$ ☐ $9 \times 12 =$ ☐ $6 \times 12 =$ ☐

Color the problems that equal the number in the star.

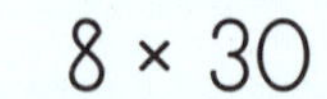

240	400	1,200	1,800
8×30	2×200	4×30	9×200
5×60	8×50	4×300	4×500
6×40	4×10	6×200	6×300
60×40	20×20	40×30	20×90

Unit Wrap-Up

Complete.

$70 - (9 \times 7) =$ ⬚

$(6 \times 5) + 18 =$ ⬚

$(9 \times 8) + (1 \times 8) =$ ⬚

$(9 + 1) \times 8 =$ ⬚

Complete the boxes to solve.

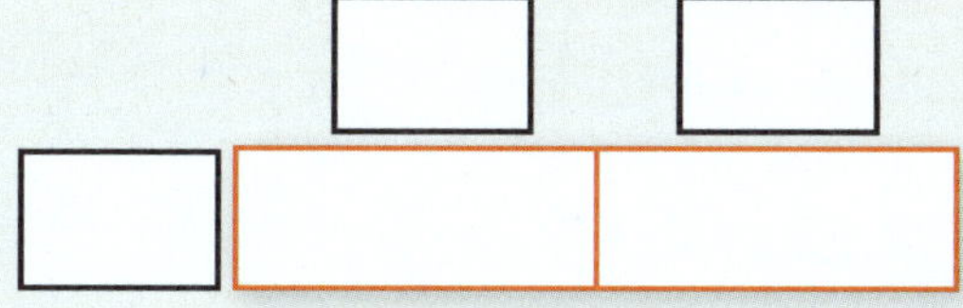

$6 \times 45 =$ ⬚

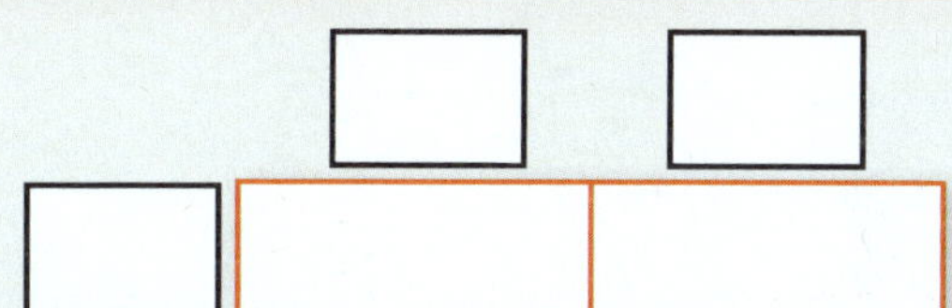

$4 \times 91 =$ ⬚

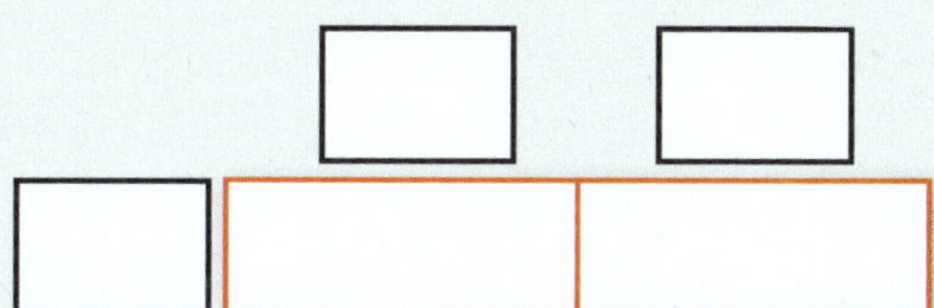

$5 \times 87 =$ ⬚

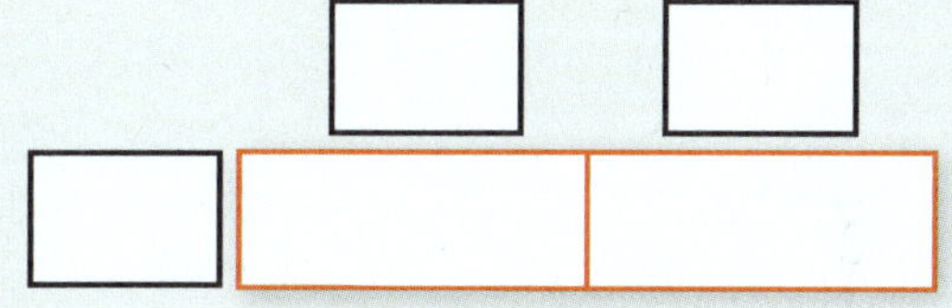

$7 \times 21 =$ ⬚

Solve. Write the equations you use.

Gavin has 4 balls of purple clay and
5 balls of green clay.
Each ball weighs 8 ounces.
How many ounces of clay does he have?

Jerome has played the violin for 4 years.
How many months has he played the violin?

Lesson Activities

$\frac{0}{2}$ $\frac{1}{2}$ $\frac{2}{2}$

0   1

0   1

0   1

0   1

0   1

Practice

Match pairs of fractions that equal 1 whole.

 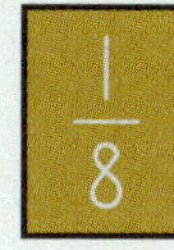 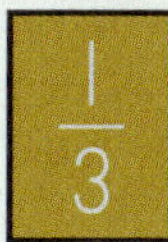  

$\frac{1}{6}$ $\frac{1}{8}$ $\frac{1}{3}$ $\frac{1}{4}$ $\frac{1}{2}$

$\frac{2}{3}$ $\frac{5}{6}$ $\frac{7}{8}$ $\frac{1}{2}$ $\frac{3}{4}$

Label the missing fractions on the number lines.
Then, use the number lines to complete the circles with <, >, or =.

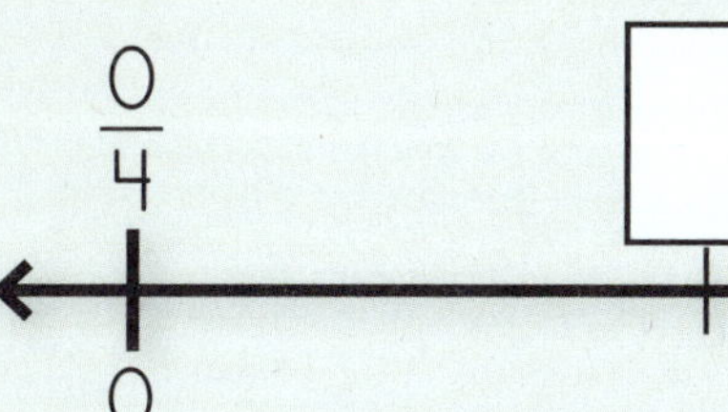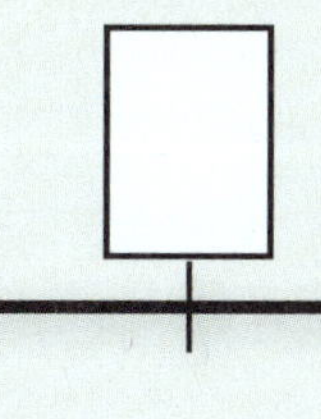

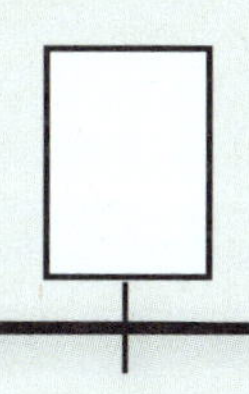

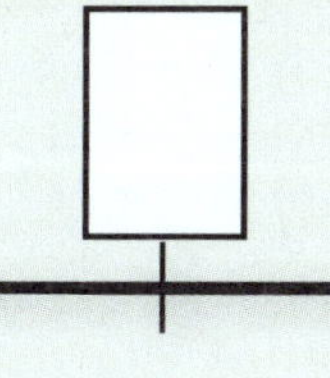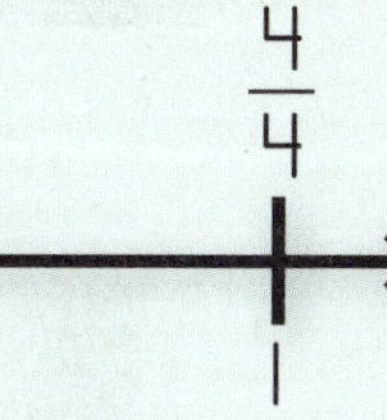

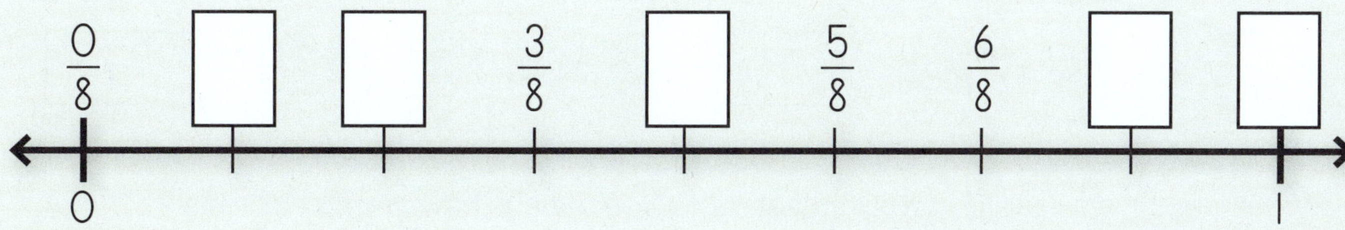

$\frac{1}{4}$ ◯ $\frac{1}{8}$ $\frac{3}{8}$ ◯ $\frac{4}{8}$ $\frac{4}{4}$ ◯ $\frac{8}{8}$

$\frac{1}{4}$ ◯ $\frac{0}{4}$ $\frac{2}{4}$ ◯ $\frac{4}{8}$ $\frac{7}{8}$ ◯ $\frac{3}{4}$

Review 👤

Complete.

8 × 11 = [ ]   8 × 12 = [ ]

7 × 11 = [ ]   7 × 12 = [ ]

5 × 11 = [ ]   5 × 12 = [ ]

9 × 11 = [ ]   9 × 12 = [ ]

Complete with <, >, or =.

275,346 ◯ 25,346

408,752 ◯ 409,752

382,070 ◯ 382,700

974,206 ◯ 974,206

Complete. All times are a.m.

[8:00] ← 1 hr. [9:00]

[ ] ← 2 hr. [9:00]

[ ] ← 4 hr. [9:00]

[ ] ← 8 hr. [9:00]

[ ] ← 9 hr. [9:00]

Complete.

2,500 + 500 = [ ]

4,500 + 1,500 = [ ]

3,500 + 4,500 = [ ]

7,500 + 2,500 = [ ]

9,500 + 3,500 = [ ]

Solve. Write the equations you use.

George keeps his baseball cards in plastic sleeves. 9 cards fit in each sleeve.
If he buys 63 baseball cards, how many sleeves will he fill?

Four friends have a lemonade stand.
They earn $32 in all.
If they split the money evenly, how much does each person get?

Lesson Activities

Mixed Number

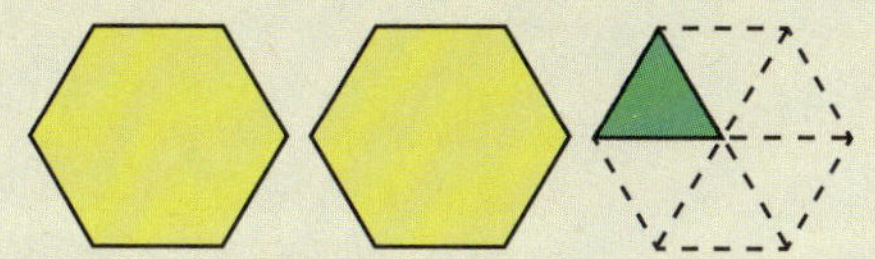

$$2 + \frac{1}{6} = 2\frac{1}{6}$$

Whole Number $\qquad$ Fraction

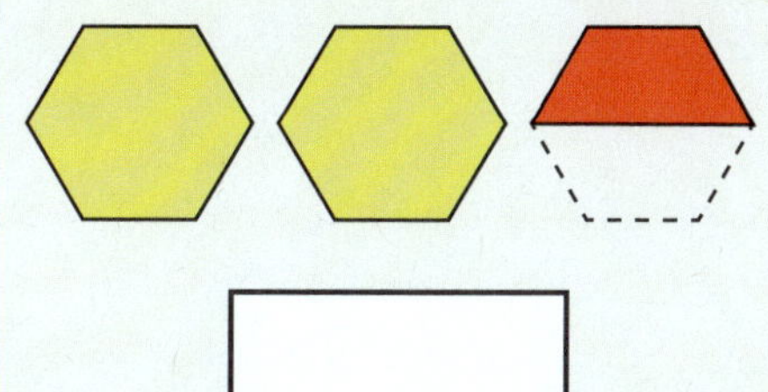

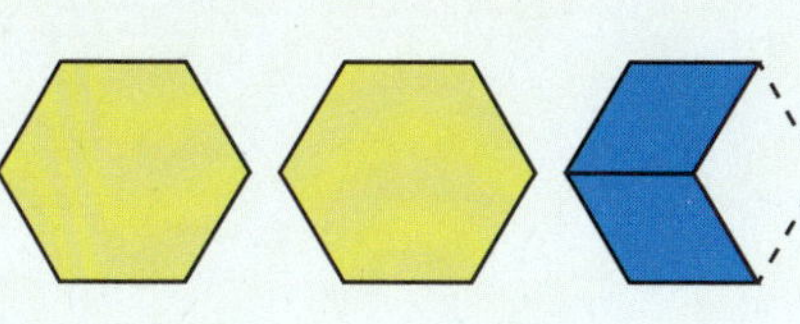

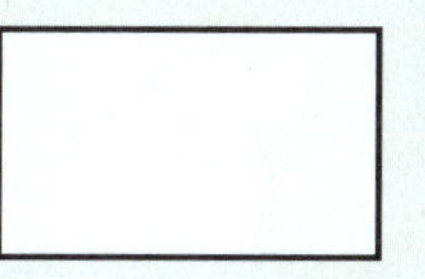

B

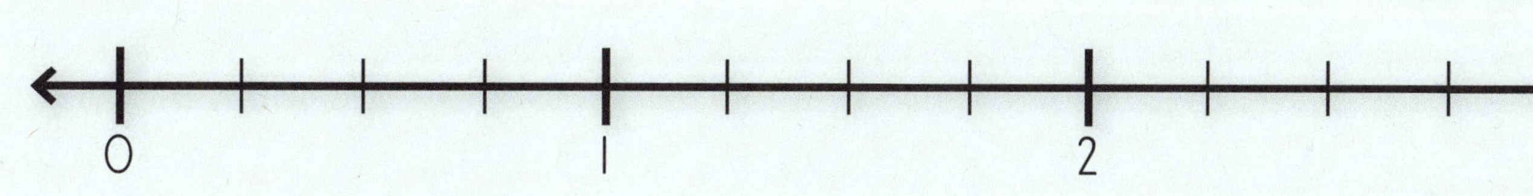

C

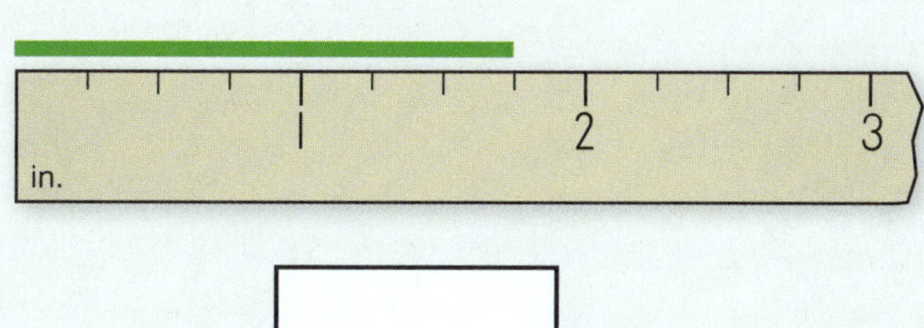

in.

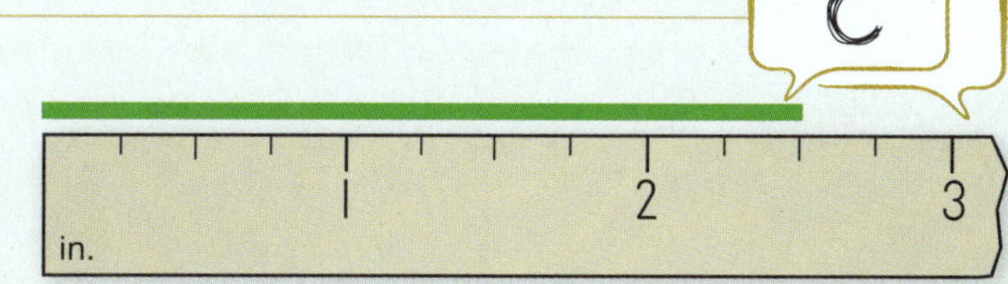

in.

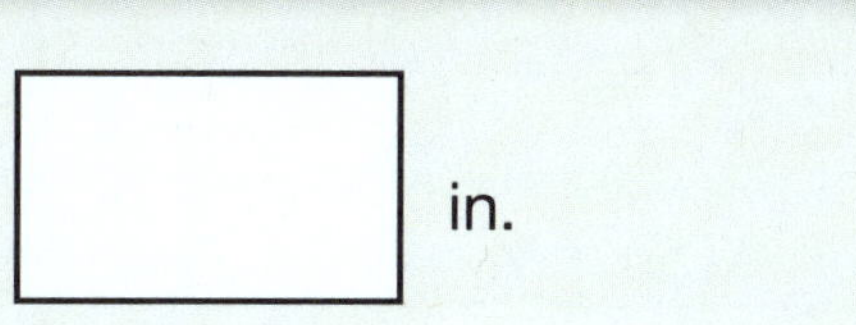

cm

cm

Practice

Match each fraction or mixed number to its place on the number line.

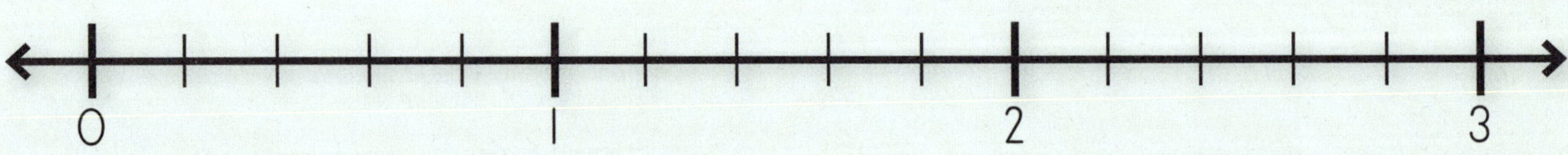

$$1\frac{1}{5} \qquad \frac{3}{5} \qquad 1\frac{3}{5} \qquad 2\frac{4}{5} \qquad 2\frac{2}{5}$$

0　　　1　　　2　　　3

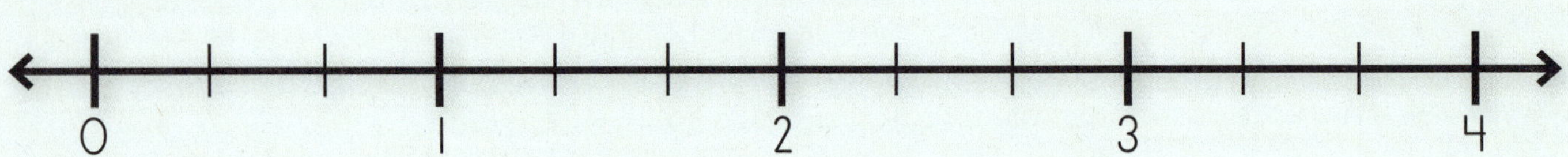

$$1\frac{2}{3} \qquad 2\frac{1}{3} \qquad 1\frac{1}{3} \qquad 3\frac{1}{3} \qquad 2\frac{2}{3}$$

0　　　1　　　2　　　3　　　4

Write each length as a mixed number.

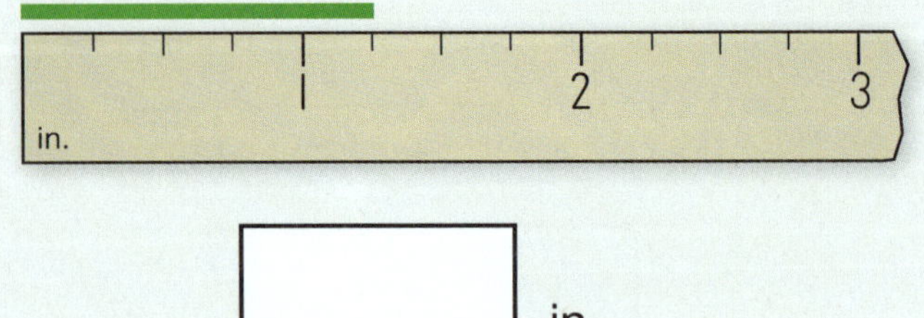

___ in.

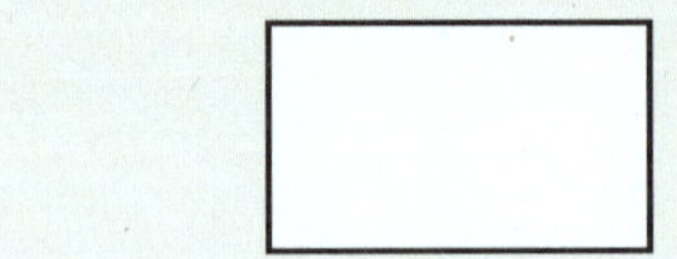

___ in.

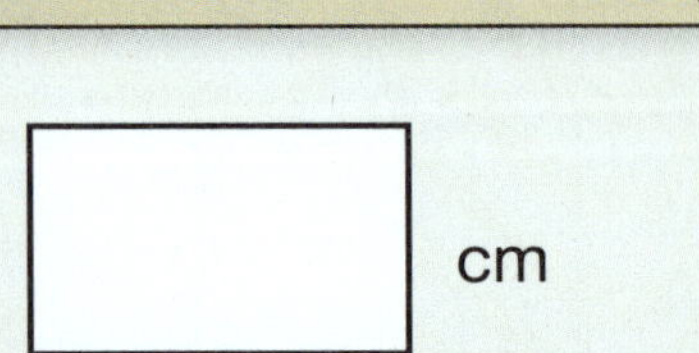

___ cm

___ cm

Review 

Complete the boxes to find the product.

30	8
5		

$5 \times 38 =$ ☐

$4 \times 73 =$ ☐

$7 \times 81 =$ ☐

$9 \times 64 =$ ☐

Copy the triangles.

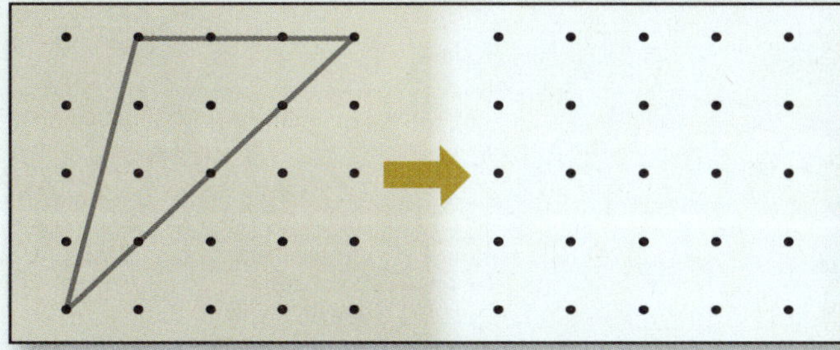

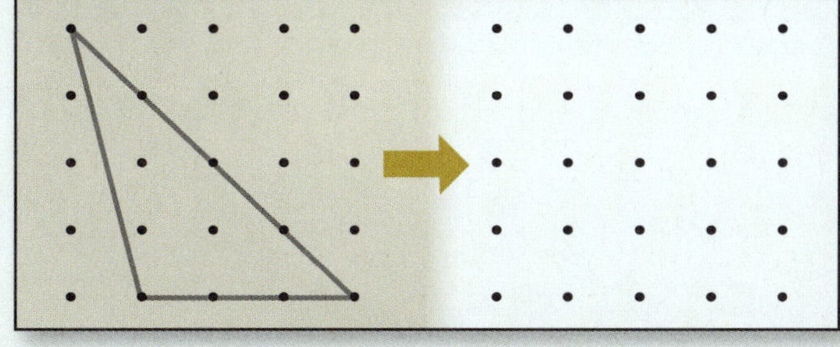

Complete.

$10 \div 3 =$ ☐ 3 R1

$11 \div 3 =$ ☐

$12 \div 3 =$ ☐

$13 \div 3 =$ ☐

$14 \div 3 =$ ☐

$15 \div 3 =$ ☐

Solve. Write the equations you use.

Chloe collects stuffed bears.
She has 3 polar bears. She has 6 times as many panda bears as polar bears.
How many panda bears does she have?

Sullivan collects coins.
He has 30 European coins. He has 5 times as many European coins as Asian coins.
How many Asian coins does he have?

Lesson Activities

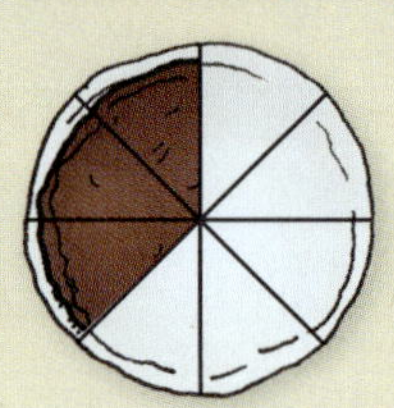

Mixed Number   Improper Fraction

$1\frac{3}{8}$ = $\frac{11}{8}$

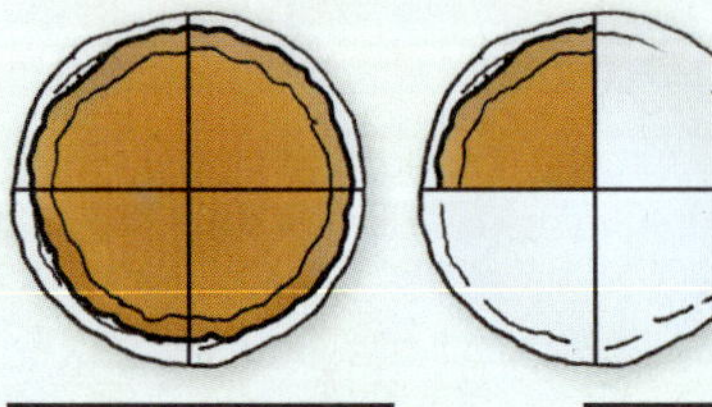

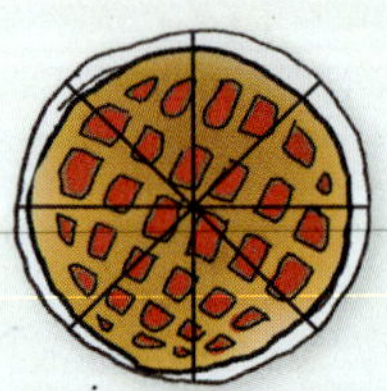

$\boxed{}$ = $\boxed{}$ $\boxed{}$ = $\boxed{}$ $\boxed{}$ = $\boxed{}$

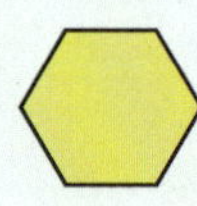 $\frac{}{2}$ $\frac{}{3}$ $\frac{}{6}$

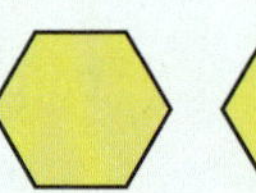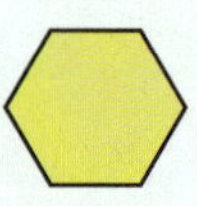 $\frac{}{2}$ $\frac{}{3}$ $\frac{}{6}$

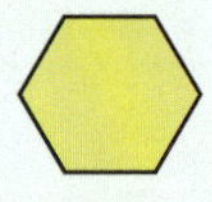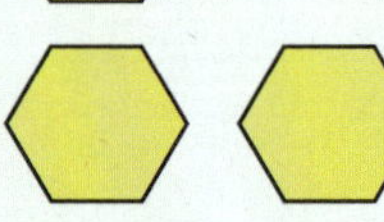 $\frac{}{2}$ $\frac{}{3}$ $\frac{}{6}$

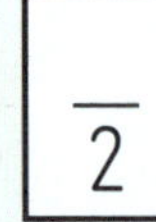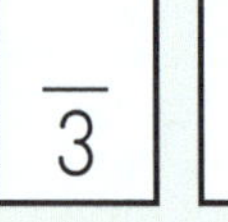 $\frac{}{2}$ $\frac{}{3}$ $\frac{}{6}$

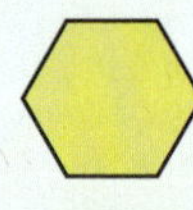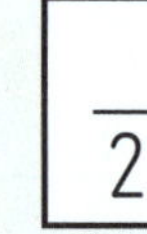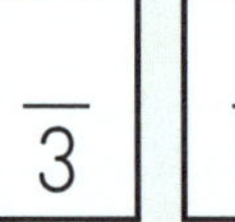

Fraction Crash

$\frac{12}{6}$	$\frac{6}{2}$	$\frac{12}{3}$	$\frac{3}{3}$	$\frac{4}{2}$	$\frac{6}{6}$
$\frac{6}{3}$	$\frac{24}{6}$	$\frac{2}{2}$	$\frac{18}{6}$	$\frac{9}{3}$	$\frac{8}{2}$

Practice

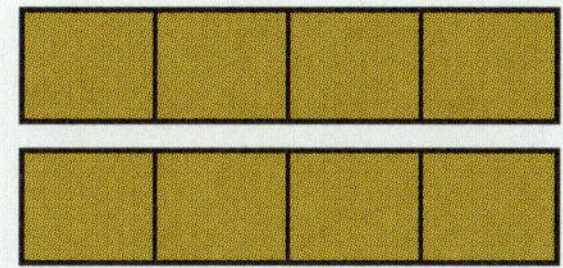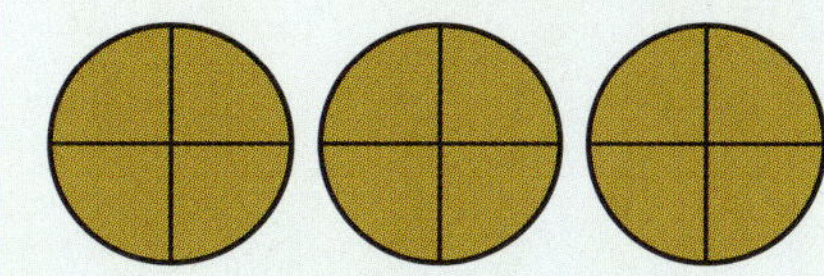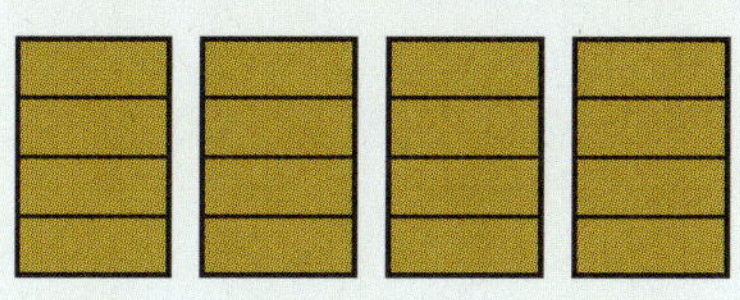

Complete with a fraction.

2 wholes = [ ] fourths

$2 = \dfrac{}{4}$

3 wholes = [ ] fourths

$3 = \dfrac{}{4}$

4 wholes = [ ] fourths

$4 = \dfrac{}{4}$

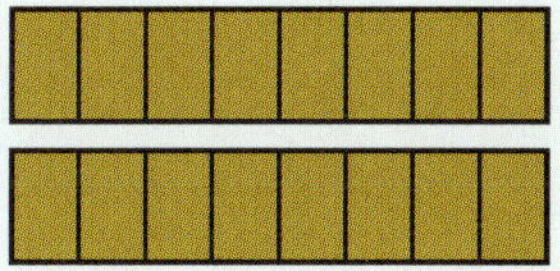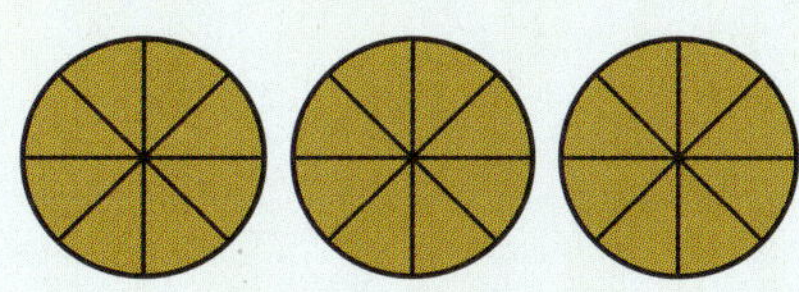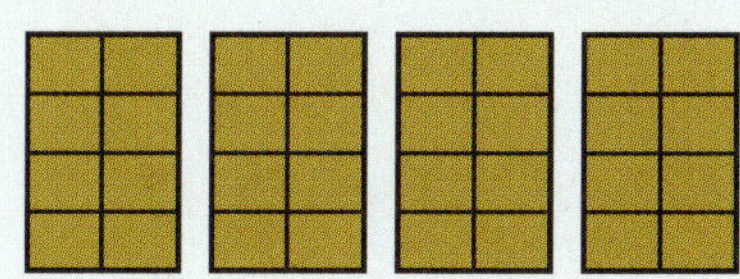

$2 = \dfrac{}{8}$

$3 = \dfrac{}{8}$

$4 = \dfrac{}{8}$

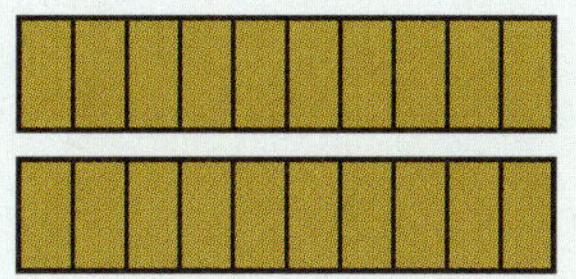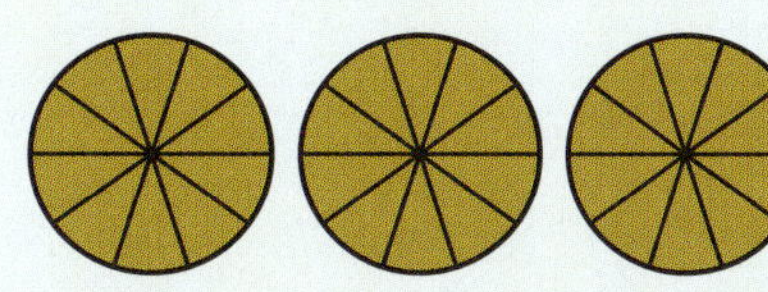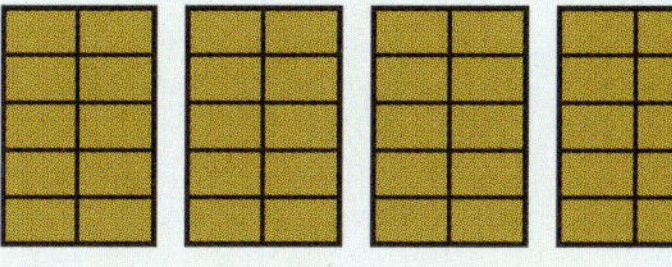

$2 = \dfrac{}{10}$

$3 = \dfrac{}{10}$

$4 = \dfrac{}{10}$

Solve.

Brandon has 2 chocolate bars.
He breaks each chocolate bar into eighths.
How many pieces does he have?

Gabriel makes 3 loaves of banana bread.
He cuts each loaf into sixths. How many
slices of banana bread does he have?

Review

Complete. Follow the steps.

1. Divide
2. Multiply
3. Subtract

3 | 2 9   4 | 2 9   5 | 2 9   6 | 2 9

Round to the underlined place.

47,9_65 ≈

32,_753 ≈

9_8,564 ≈

20_5,499 ≈

356,_078 ≈

Complete.

9 × 40 =

8 × 600 =

7 × 7,000 =

90 × 80 =

6 × 9,000 =

Find the perimeter and area.

12 m
5 m

6 yd.
11 yd.

9 cm
9 cm

Perimeter: ____ m

Area: ____ sq. m

Perimeter: ____ yd.

Area: ____ sq. yd.

Perimeter: ____ cm

Area: ____ sq. cm

Lesson Activities 👥

$\dfrac{}{4}$ $\dfrac{}{5}$ $\dfrac{}{8}$ $\dfrac{}{10}$ $\dfrac{}{12}$

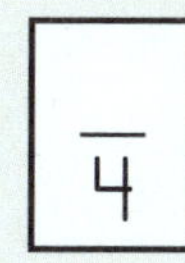

Fraction	$\dfrac{1}{3}$	$\dfrac{2}{3}$	$\dfrac{3}{3}$	$\dfrac{4}{3}$	$\dfrac{5}{3}$	$\dfrac{6}{3}$	$\dfrac{7}{3}$	$\dfrac{8}{3}$	$\dfrac{9}{3}$
Whole or Mixed Number									

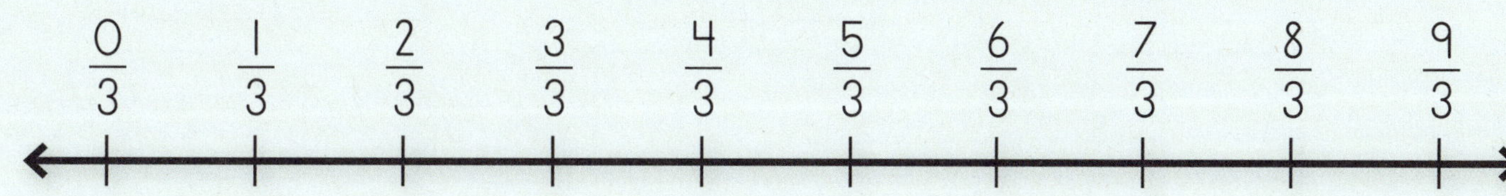

Pizza Roll

   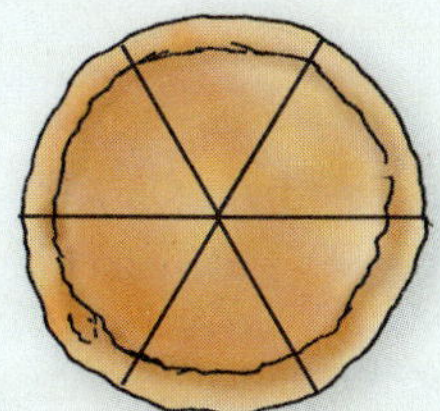

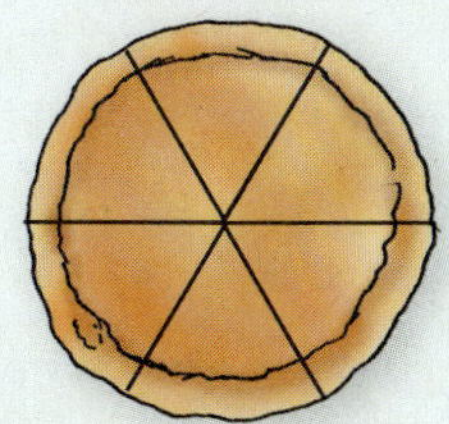 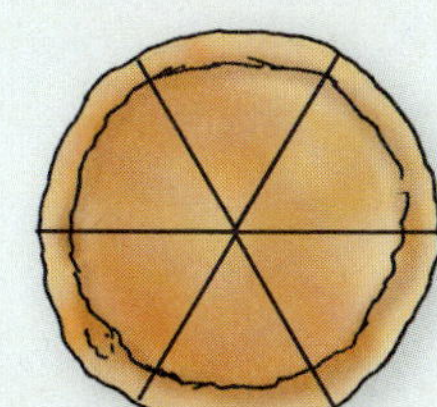 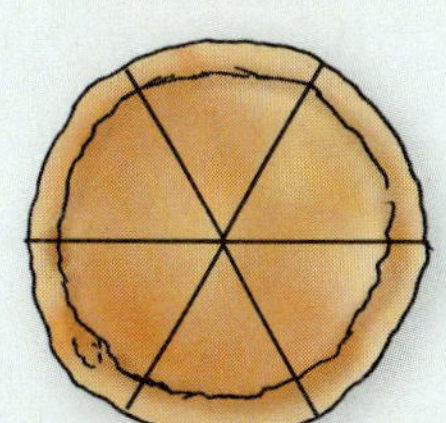 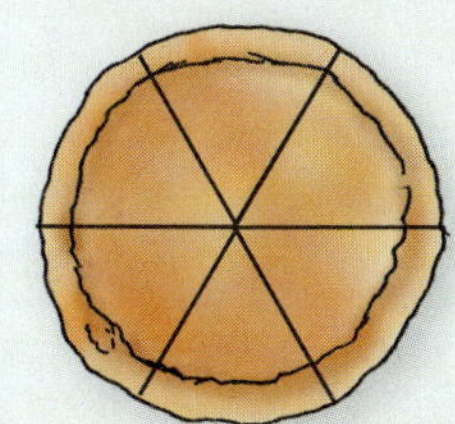

Practice

Color the bars to match the mixed numbers. Then, write each mixed number as a fraction.

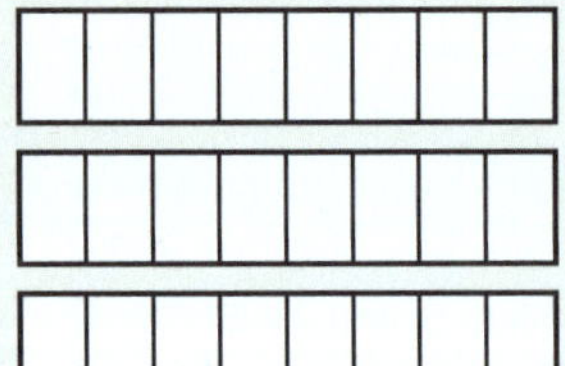

$2\frac{1}{8} = \boxed{}$

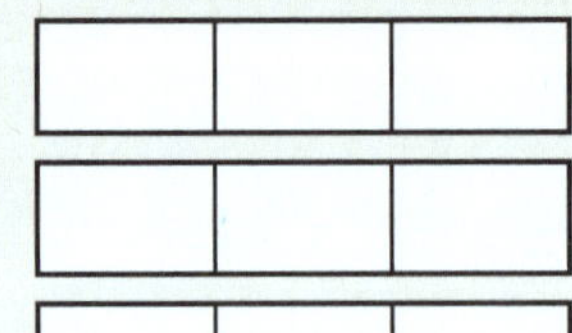

$2\frac{2}{3} = \boxed{}$

$2\frac{4}{5} = \boxed{}$

Color the bars to match the fractions. Then, write each fraction as a mixed number or whole number.

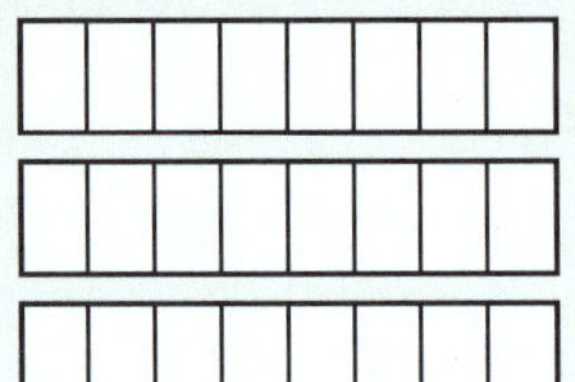

$\frac{20}{8} = \boxed{}$

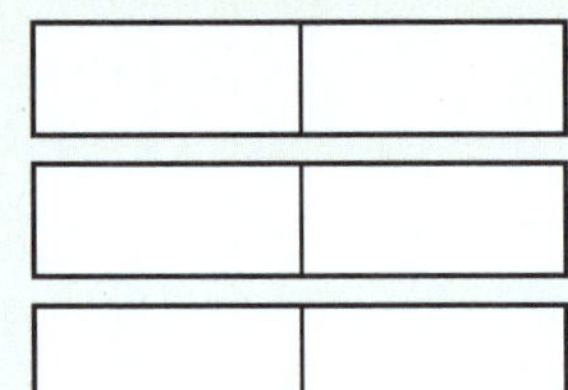

$\frac{6}{2} = \boxed{}$

$\frac{14}{6} = \boxed{}$

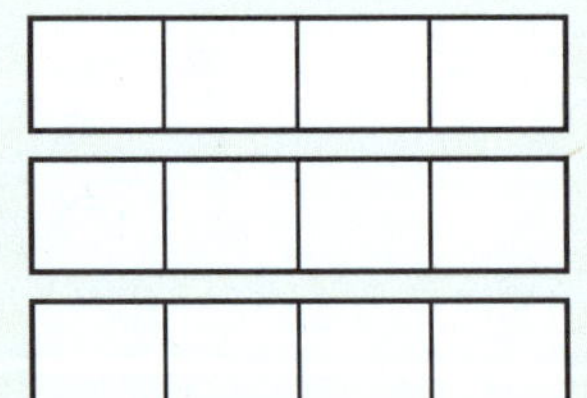

$\frac{12}{4} = \boxed{}$

$\frac{7}{3} = \boxed{}$

$\frac{15}{5} = \boxed{}$

Solve.

Fiona has $2\frac{1}{2}$ sandwiches. How many halves of a sandwich does she have?

Steven's family has $2\frac{5}{6}$ pies. Each pie is cut in sixths. How many slices do they have?

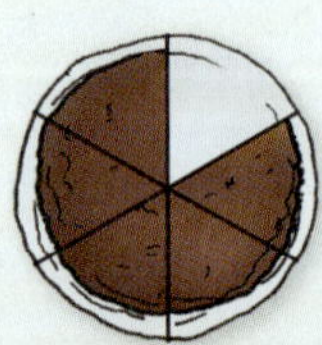

Review

Complete.

$42 \div 6 =$ ☐

$42 \div 7 =$ ☐

$56 \div 8 =$ ☐

$56 \div 7 =$ ☐

Complete.

$(7 + 4) \times 11 =$ ☐

$(3 \times 9) + (7 \times 9) =$ ☐

$60 - (8 \times 7) =$ ☐

$(6 \times 6) + (8 \times 8) =$ ☐

Write the time.

Draw the missing halves for the symmetric shapes.

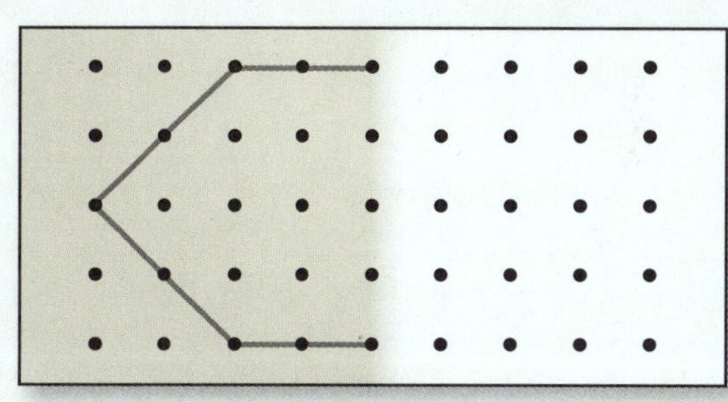

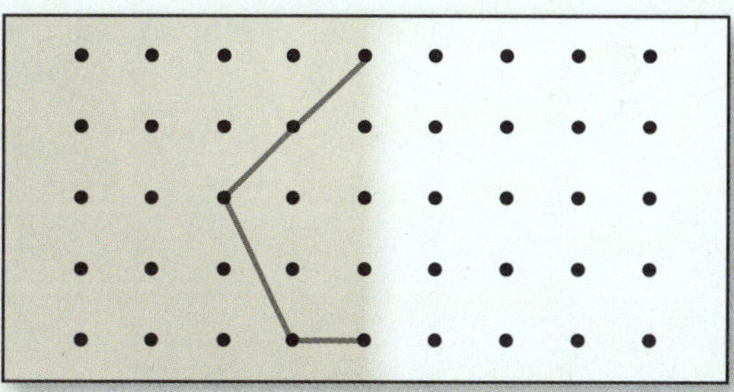

Solve. Write the equations you use.

Maria has 78 trading cards.
Then, she buys 4 new packs.
Each pack has 8 cards.
How many trading cards does she have now?

Sam buys 9 packs of trading cards.
Each pack has 8 cards.
Then, he gives 17 of the cards to a friend.
How many trading cards does he have now?

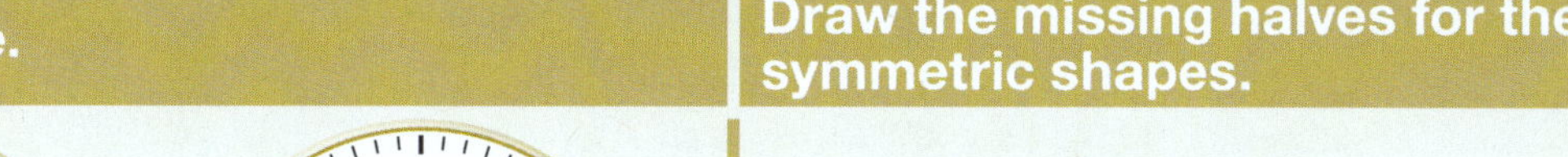

Lesson Activities 👥

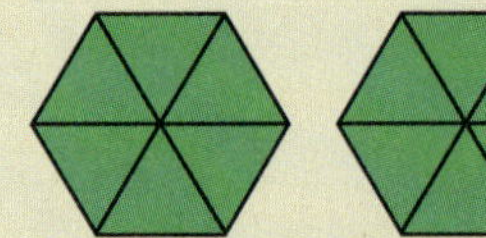

A

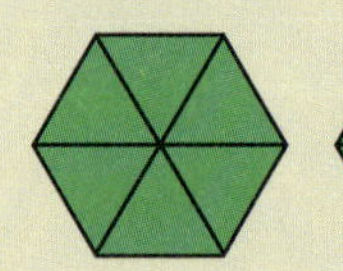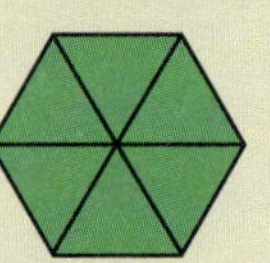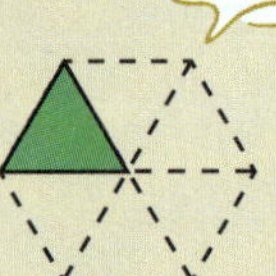

$2 = \dfrac{}{6}$

$2 \times 6 = \boxed{}$

$2\dfrac{1}{6} = \dfrac{}{6}$

$(2 \times 6) + 1 = \boxed{}$

$3 = \dfrac{}{2}$

$3\dfrac{1}{2} = \dfrac{}{2}$

$2 = \dfrac{}{3}$

$2\dfrac{2}{3} = \dfrac{}{3}$

$3 = \dfrac{}{4}$

$3\dfrac{1}{4} = \dfrac{}{4}$

B

Fraction Three in a Row

Player 1 START	$5\dfrac{1}{2}$	$1\dfrac{7}{8}$	$5\dfrac{3}{4}$	$4\dfrac{1}{3}$	$3\dfrac{5}{8}$
$4\dfrac{1}{6}$	$\dfrac{17}{6}$	$\dfrac{11}{3}$	$\dfrac{29}{8}$	$\dfrac{13}{3}$	$1\dfrac{3}{10}$
$3\dfrac{2}{3}$	$\dfrac{19}{8}$	$\dfrac{15}{8}$	$\dfrac{25}{6}$	$\dfrac{13}{5}$	$2\dfrac{5}{6}$
$3\dfrac{1}{4}$	$\dfrac{15}{4}$	$\dfrac{13}{4}$	$\dfrac{11}{2}$	$\dfrac{17}{3}$	$5\dfrac{2}{3}$
	$\dfrac{11}{6}$	$\dfrac{23}{4}$	$\dfrac{19}{4}$	$\dfrac{13}{10}$	
$1\dfrac{5}{6}$	$2\dfrac{3}{5}$	$2\dfrac{3}{8}$	$3\dfrac{3}{4}$	$4\dfrac{3}{4}$	Player 2 START

Practice 

**Color the bars to match each whole number or mixed number.
Then, convert the number to a fraction.**

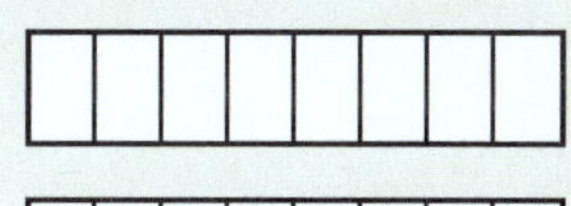

$1\frac{3}{8}$ = ☐

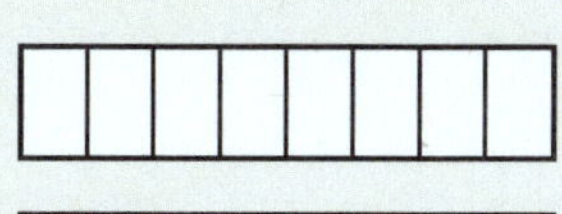

2 = ☐

2 $\frac{7}{8}$ = ☐

$1\frac{2}{5}$ = ☐

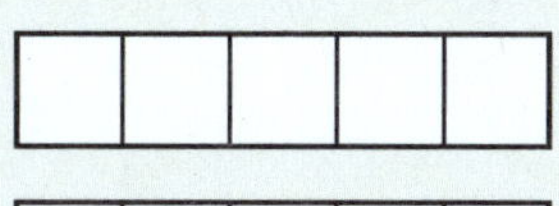

2 = ☐

$2\frac{3}{5}$ = ☐

Write each mixed number as a fraction.

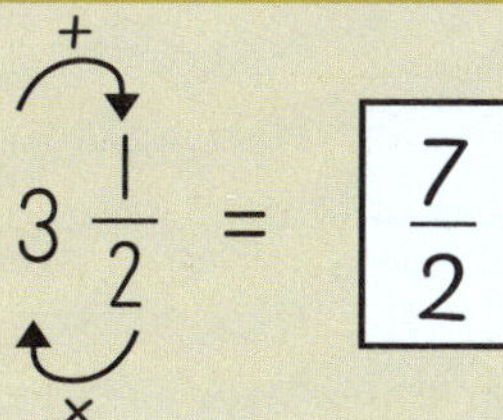

$3\frac{1}{2}$ = $\boxed{\dfrac{7}{2}}$

$4\frac{1}{2}$ = ☐

$7\frac{1}{2}$ = ☐

$2\frac{1}{4}$ = ☐

$3\frac{3}{4}$ = ☐

$5\frac{1}{4}$ = ☐

$2\frac{1}{6}$ = ☐

$4\frac{5}{6}$ = ☐

$5\frac{2}{6}$ = ☐

Review   Complete the missing fractions on the number lines.

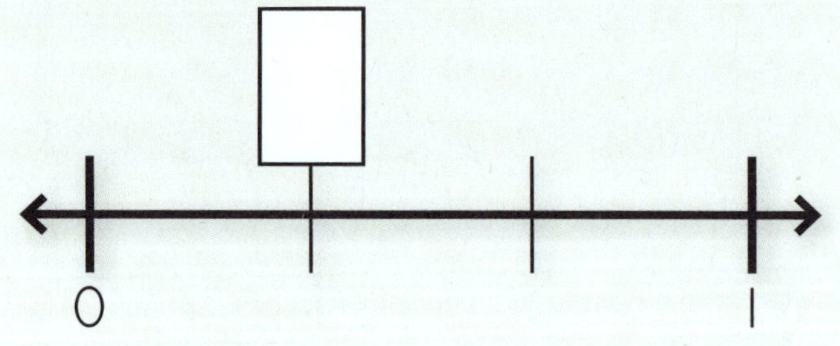

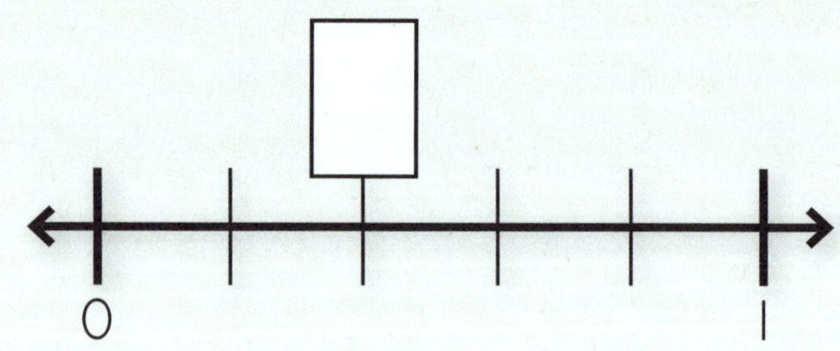

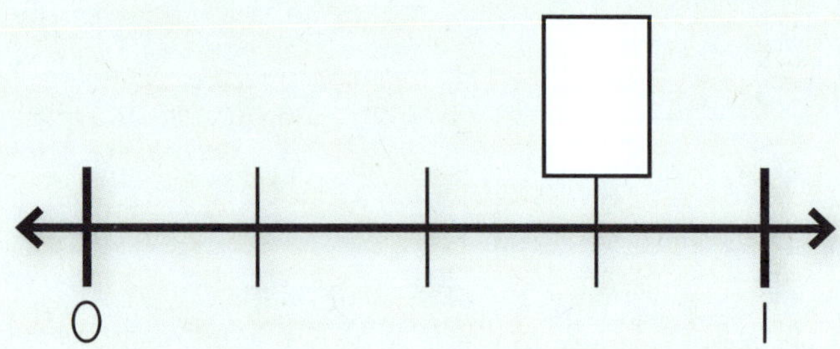

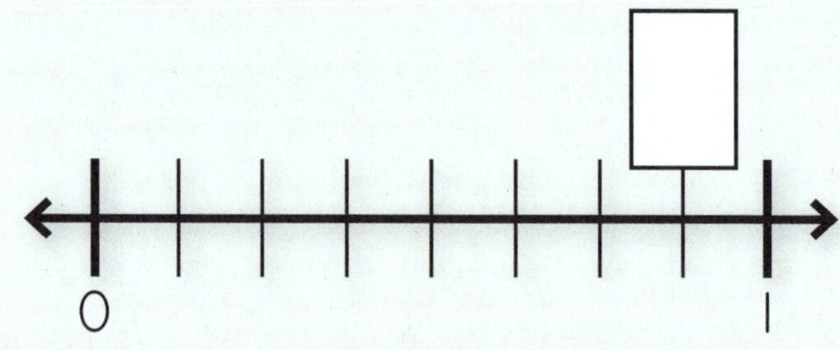

Complete the boxes to find the product.

30   8

8

$8 \times 38 =$

$7 \times 65 =$

Solve. Write the equations you use.

Charis' family picks 56 apples.
They put 8 apples in each bag.
How many bags do they fill?

Carson's family buys 3 boxes of donuts.
There are 12 donuts in each box.
How many donuts do they buy?

Lesson Activities

$$\frac{6}{3} = \boxed{}$$

$6 \div 3 = \boxed{}$

$$\frac{7}{3} = \boxed{}$$

$7 \div 3 = \boxed{}$

A

$$\frac{11}{3} = \boxed{} \qquad \frac{13}{6} = \boxed{} \qquad \frac{8}{2} = \boxed{}$$

$$\frac{9}{4} = \boxed{} \qquad \frac{19}{8} = \boxed{} \qquad \frac{8}{5} = \boxed{}$$

B

Fraction Three in a Row

Player 1 START	$\frac{27}{10}$	$\frac{11}{8}$	$\frac{6}{6}$	$\frac{9}{5}$	$\frac{13}{4}$
$\frac{5}{2}$	$3\frac{1}{3}$	$1\frac{4}{5}$	2	$1\frac{3}{10}$	$\frac{5}{3}$
$\frac{10}{3}$	1	$3\frac{1}{4}$	$2\frac{1}{6}$	4	$\frac{8}{2}$
$\frac{9}{4}$	$3\frac{1}{8}$	$2\frac{7}{10}$	$1\frac{3}{8}$	$1\frac{5}{6}$	$\frac{11}{6}$
$\frac{15}{5}$	$2\frac{1}{2}$	3	$2\frac{1}{4}$	$1\frac{2}{3}$	
	$\frac{13}{6}$	$\frac{25}{8}$	$\frac{13}{10}$	$\frac{8}{4}$	Player 2 START

Practice

Color the bars to match each fraction.
Then, write the fraction as a whole number or mixed number.

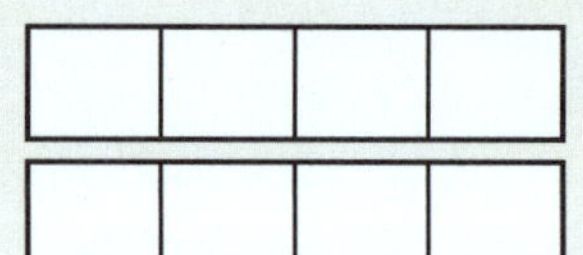

$$\frac{7}{4} = \boxed{}$$

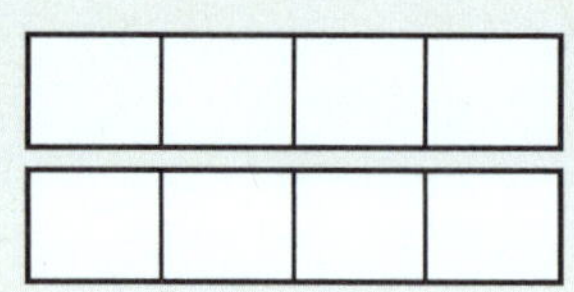

$$\frac{8}{4} = \boxed{}$$

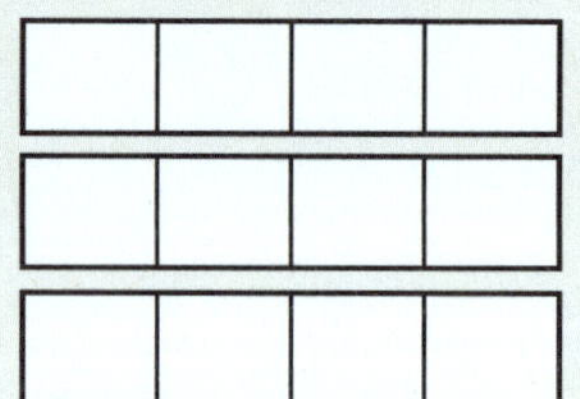

$$\frac{9}{4} = \boxed{}$$

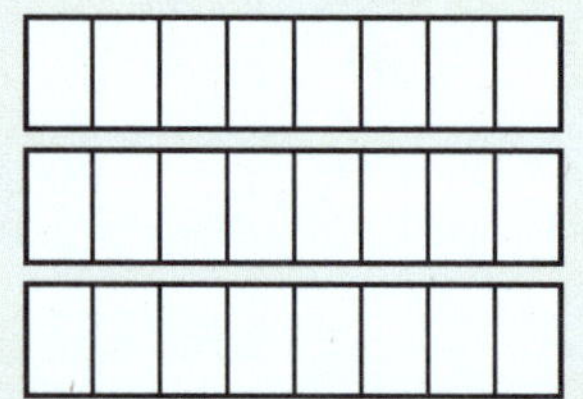

$$\frac{17}{8} = \boxed{}$$

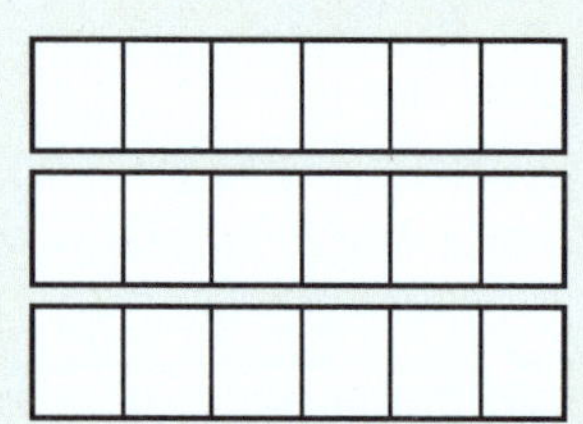

$$\frac{15}{6} = \boxed{}$$

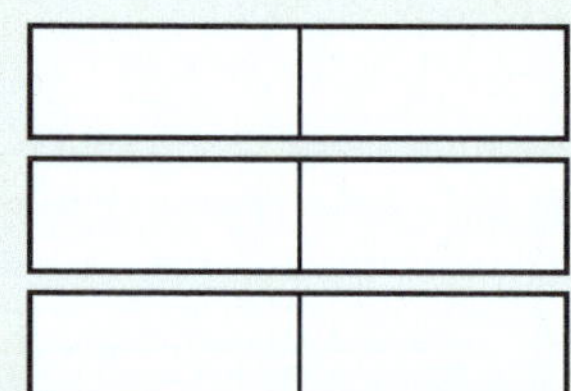

$$\frac{5}{2} = \boxed{}$$

Write each fraction as a whole number or mixed number.

$$\div \frac{9}{8} = \boxed{1\frac{1}{8}}$$

$$\frac{5}{4} = \boxed{}$$

$$\frac{12}{6} = \boxed{}$$

$$\frac{11}{5} = \boxed{}$$

$$\frac{7}{2} = \boxed{}$$

$$\frac{8}{3} = \boxed{}$$

$$\frac{11}{4} = \boxed{}$$

$$\frac{18}{3} = \boxed{}$$

$$\frac{13}{8} = \boxed{}$$

Review

Match the fractions and mixed numbers to their places on the number line.

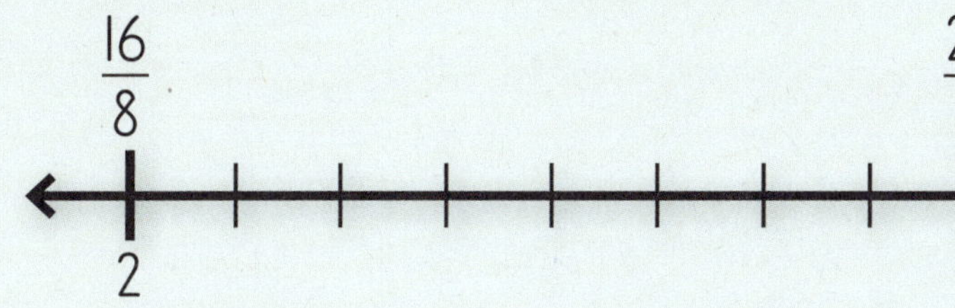

$$\frac{20}{8} \qquad \frac{23}{8} \qquad \frac{29}{8} \qquad \frac{25}{8}$$

$$2\frac{7}{8} \qquad 3\frac{1}{8} \qquad 2\frac{4}{8} \qquad 3\frac{5}{8}$$

Complete.

$49 \div 7 = $	$48 \div 8 = $	$81 \div 9 = $
$42 \div 7 = $	$64 \div 8 = $	$54 \div 9 = $
$56 \div 7 = $	$56 \div 8 = $	$72 \div 9 = $
$63 \div 7 = $	$72 \div 8 = $	$63 \div 9 = $

Complete.

4 weeks = ____ days   35 days = ____ weeks

4 weeks, 2 days = ____ days   38 days = ____ weeks, ____ days

12 weeks = ____ days   42 days = ____ weeks

12 weeks, 1 day = ____ days   45 days = ____ weeks, ____ days

Lesson Activities 

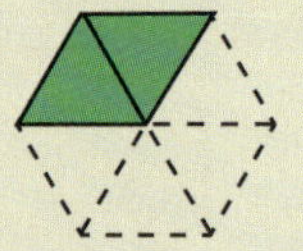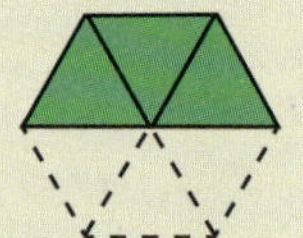

$$\frac{2}{6} + \frac{3}{6} = \boxed{}$$

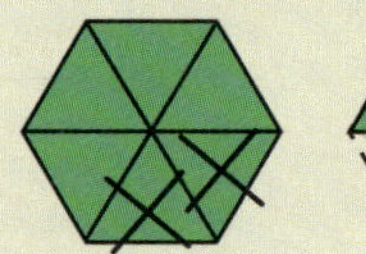

$$\frac{7}{6} - \frac{3}{6} = \boxed{}$$

$$\frac{5}{3} + \frac{2}{3} = \boxed{}$$

$$\frac{3}{8} + \frac{4}{8} = \boxed{}$$

$$\frac{4}{2} - \frac{1}{2} = \boxed{}$$

$$\frac{6}{4} - \frac{3}{4} = \boxed{}$$

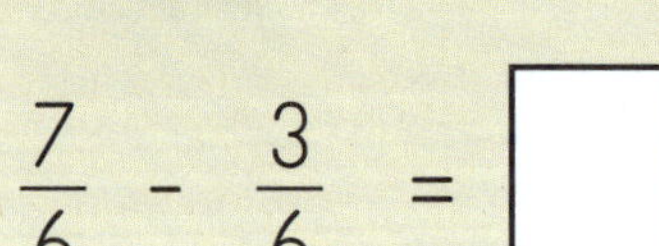

Climb and Slide

Practice

Complete with a fraction. Color the bars to match.

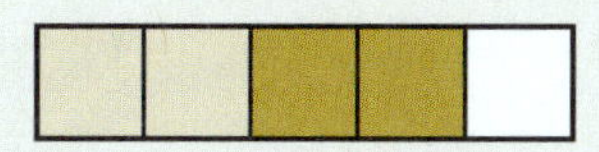

$$\frac{2}{5} + \frac{2}{5} = \boxed{}$$

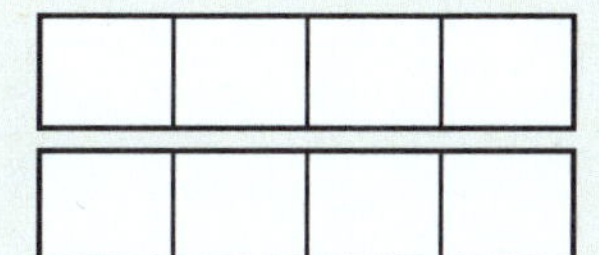

$$\frac{5}{8} + \frac{3}{8} = \boxed{}$$

$$\frac{1}{6} + \frac{4}{6} = \boxed{}$$

$$\frac{2}{3} + \frac{2}{3} = \boxed{}$$

$$\frac{5}{4} + \frac{3}{4} = \boxed{}$$

$$\frac{8}{8} + \frac{7}{8} = \boxed{}$$

Complete with a fraction. X the bars to match.

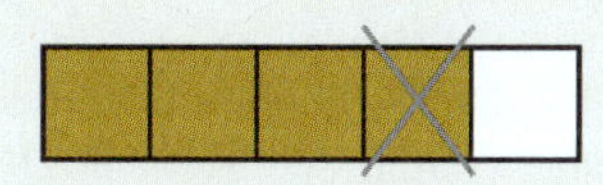

$$\frac{4}{5} - \frac{1}{5} = \boxed{}$$

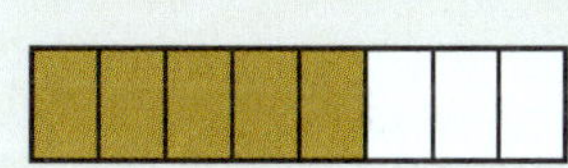

$$\frac{5}{8} - \frac{2}{8} = \boxed{}$$

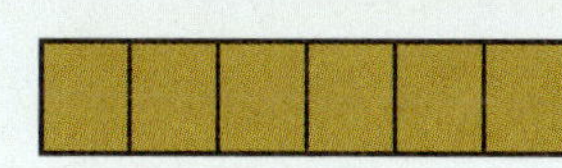

$$\frac{6}{6} - \frac{6}{6} = \boxed{}$$

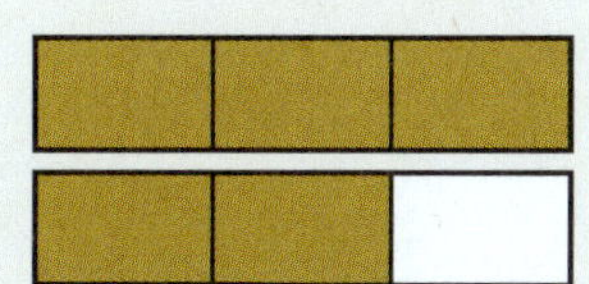

$$\frac{5}{3} - \frac{3}{3} = \boxed{}$$

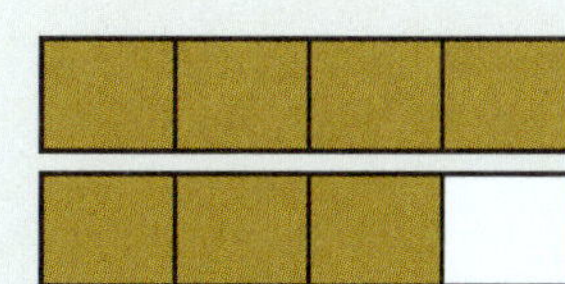

$$\frac{7}{4} - \frac{5}{4} = \boxed{}$$

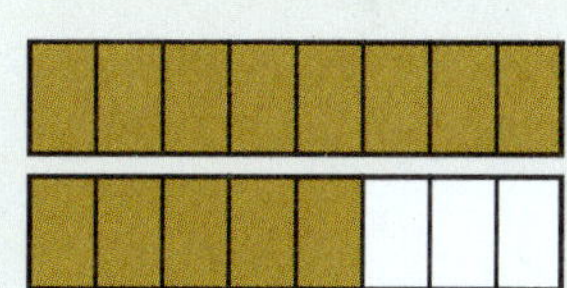

$$\frac{13}{8} - \frac{5}{8} = \boxed{}$$

Complete.

Jacob runs around the track 5 times. Each lap is $\frac{1}{4}$ of a mile.

- Write how far Jacob runs as a fraction.

- Write how far Jacob runs as a mixed number.

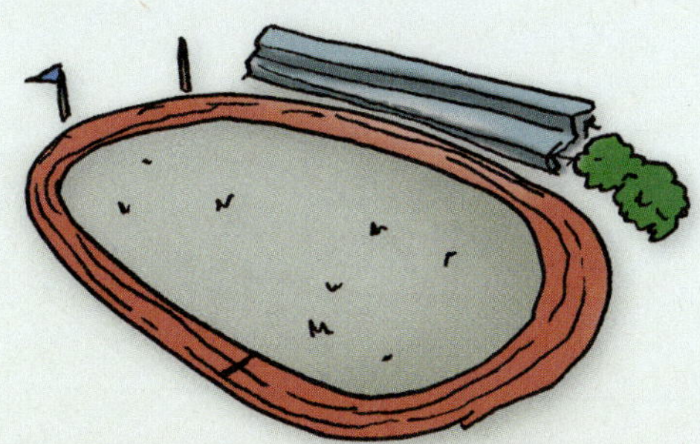

Review

Convert the mixed numbers to fractions.
Convert the fractions to mixed numbers or whole numbers.

$5\frac{1}{2} =$ ☐ $3\frac{2}{3} =$ ☐ $5\frac{3}{4} =$ ☐

$\frac{17}{5} =$ ☐ $\frac{25}{6} =$ ☐ $\frac{16}{5} =$ ☐

Write a fraction or mixed number for each length.

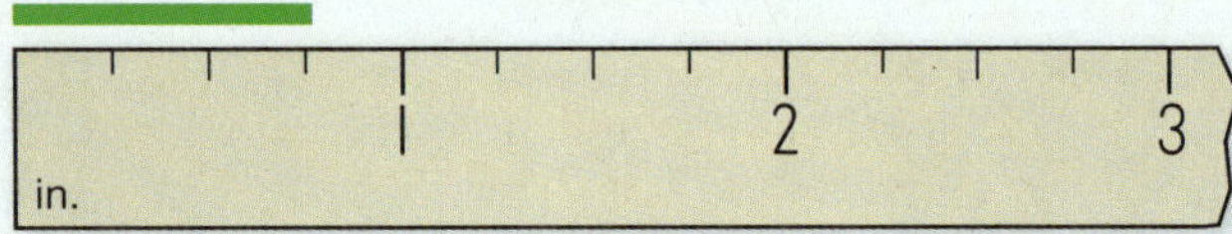

☐ in.

☐ in.

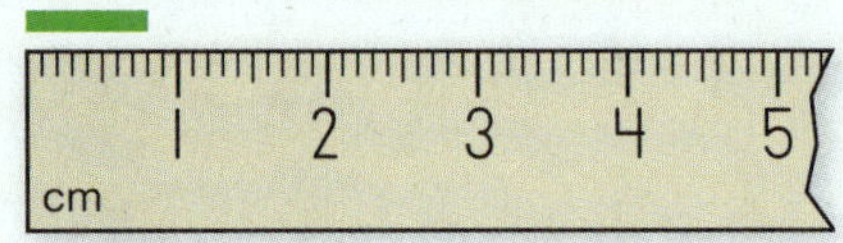

☐ cm

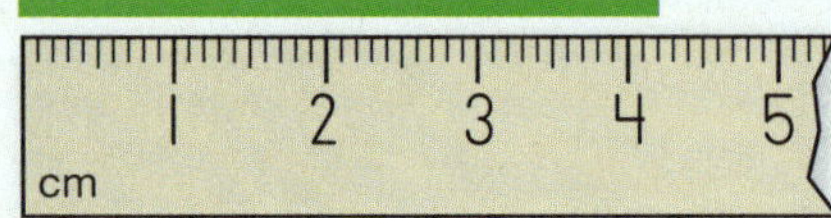

☐ cm

Solve. Write the equations you use.

Josephine's family is buying a new car. The car costs $35,789, plus $2,147 in sales tax. How much does the car cost in all?

The art museum is raising money for a new exhibit. The goal is $50,000. So far, they have raised $27,900. How much more money do they need?

Lesson Activities

Repeated Addition 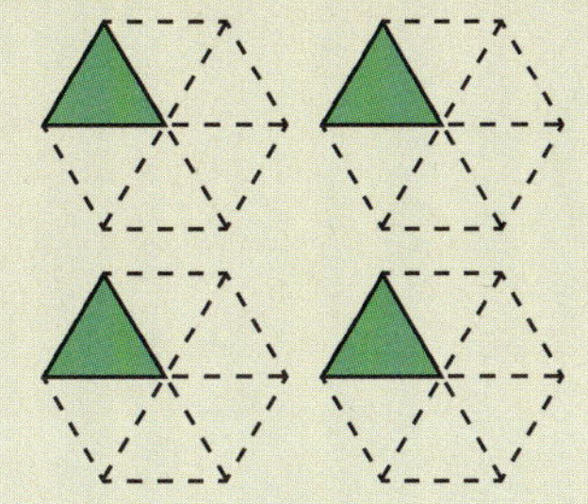 Multiplication

$$\frac{1}{6} + \frac{1}{6} + \frac{1}{6} + \frac{1}{6} = \boxed{}$$

$$4 \times \frac{1}{6} = \boxed{}$$

$$2 \times \frac{1}{3} = \boxed{}$$

$$5 \times \frac{1}{6} = \boxed{}$$

$$3 \times \frac{1}{4} = \boxed{}$$

$$4 \times \frac{2}{6} = \boxed{} = \boxed{}$$

$$3 \times \frac{1}{2} = \boxed{} = \boxed{}$$

$$3 \times \frac{3}{8} = \boxed{} = \boxed{}$$

Roll and Multiply

Player 1	Player 2
$\boxed{} \times \frac{1}{6} = \boxed{} = \boxed{}$	$\boxed{} \times \frac{1}{6} = \boxed{} = \boxed{}$
$\boxed{} \times \frac{1}{3} = \boxed{} = \boxed{}$	$\boxed{} \times \frac{1}{3} = \boxed{} = \boxed{}$
$\boxed{} \times \frac{1}{2} = \boxed{} = \boxed{}$	$\boxed{} \times \frac{1}{2} = \boxed{} = \boxed{}$
$\boxed{} \times \frac{2}{3} = \boxed{} = \boxed{}$	$\boxed{} \times \frac{2}{3} = \boxed{} = \boxed{}$
$\boxed{} \times \frac{3}{2} = \boxed{} = \boxed{}$	$\boxed{} \times \frac{3}{2} = \boxed{} = \boxed{}$

Practice 👤 Write a fraction to complete each equation.

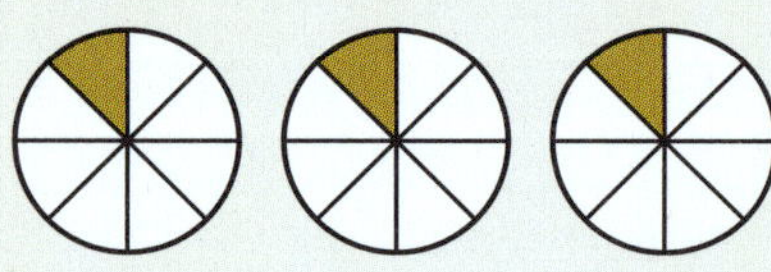

$$3 \times \frac{1}{8} = \boxed{}$$

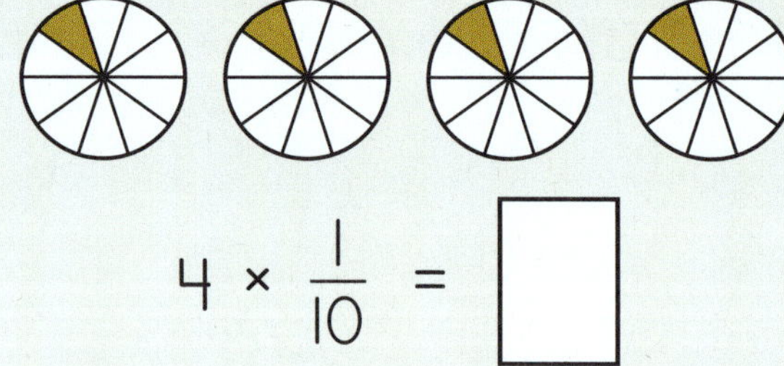

$$4 \times \frac{1}{10} = \boxed{}$$

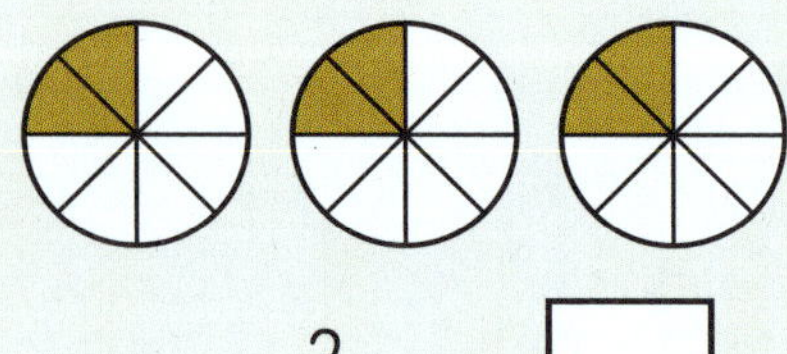

$$3 \times \frac{2}{8} = \boxed{}$$

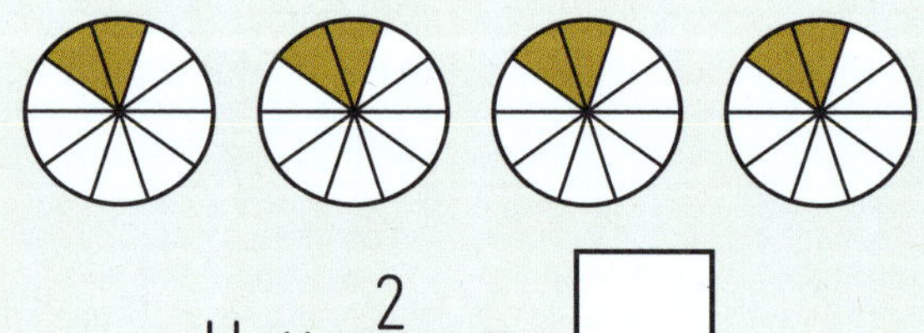

$$4 \times \frac{2}{10} = \boxed{}$$

**Write a fraction to complete each equation.
Then, convert the fraction to a mixed number or a whole number.**

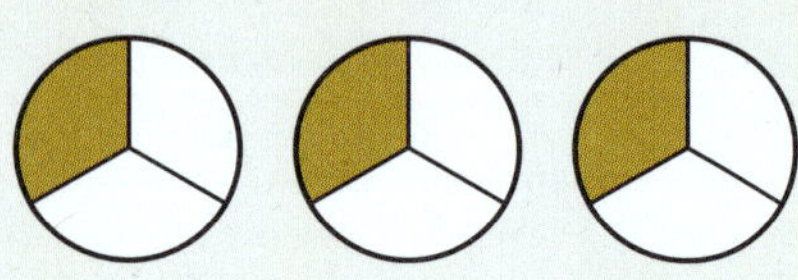

$$3 \times \frac{1}{3} = \boxed{} = \boxed{}$$

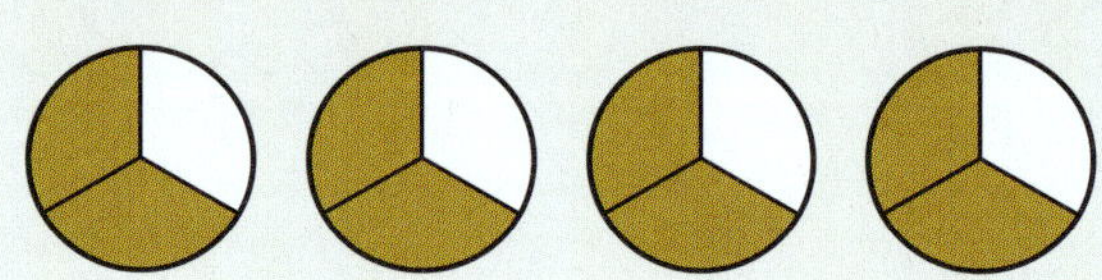

$$4 \times \frac{2}{3} = \boxed{} = \boxed{}$$

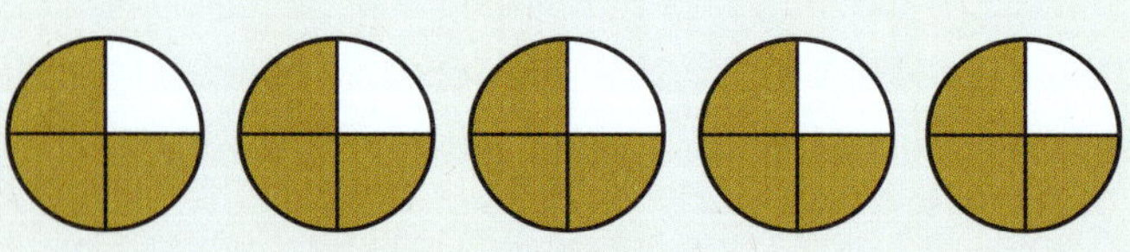

$$5 \times \frac{3}{4} = \boxed{} = \boxed{}$$

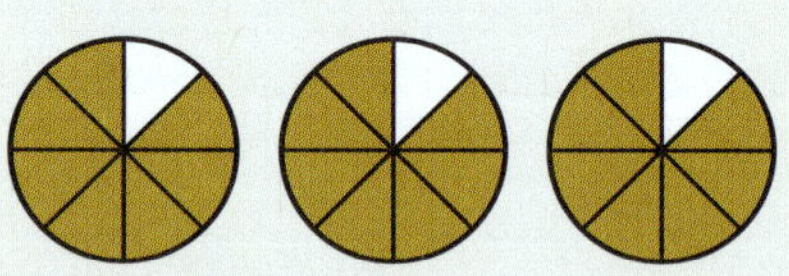

$$3 \times \frac{7}{8} = \boxed{} = \boxed{}$$

$$2 \times \frac{5}{6} = \boxed{} = \boxed{}$$

$$8 \times \frac{1}{2} = \boxed{} = \boxed{}$$

Review Complete.

```
  2 9 0 , 6 8 4        8 7 6 , 9 8 5
+ 3 4 5 , 1 2 5      - 6 8 4 , 9 2 0
```

Choose the more sensible unit for each item.

Weight of an egg

| 2 oz. | 2 lb. |

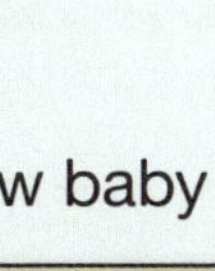

Weight of a new baby

| 7 oz. | 7 lb. |

Weight of a dumbbell

| 8 g | 8 kg |

Capacity of an aquarium

| 8 c. | 8 gal. |

Capacity of a bathtub

| 50 c. | 50 gal. |

Capacity of a watering can

| 6 mL | 6 L |

Complete with a fraction.

$$\frac{2}{3} + \frac{5}{3} = \boxed{}$$

$$\frac{4}{8} + \frac{5}{8} = \boxed{}$$

$$\frac{10}{10} - \frac{3}{10} = \boxed{}$$

Complete.

$7 \times 11 = \boxed{}$ $7 \times 12 = \boxed{}$

$4 \times 11 = \boxed{}$ $4 \times 12 = \boxed{}$

$6 \times 11 = \boxed{}$ $6 \times 12 = \boxed{}$

$8 \times 11 = \boxed{}$ $8 \times 12 = \boxed{}$

Lesson Activities

A

Mixed Number Addition Algorithm

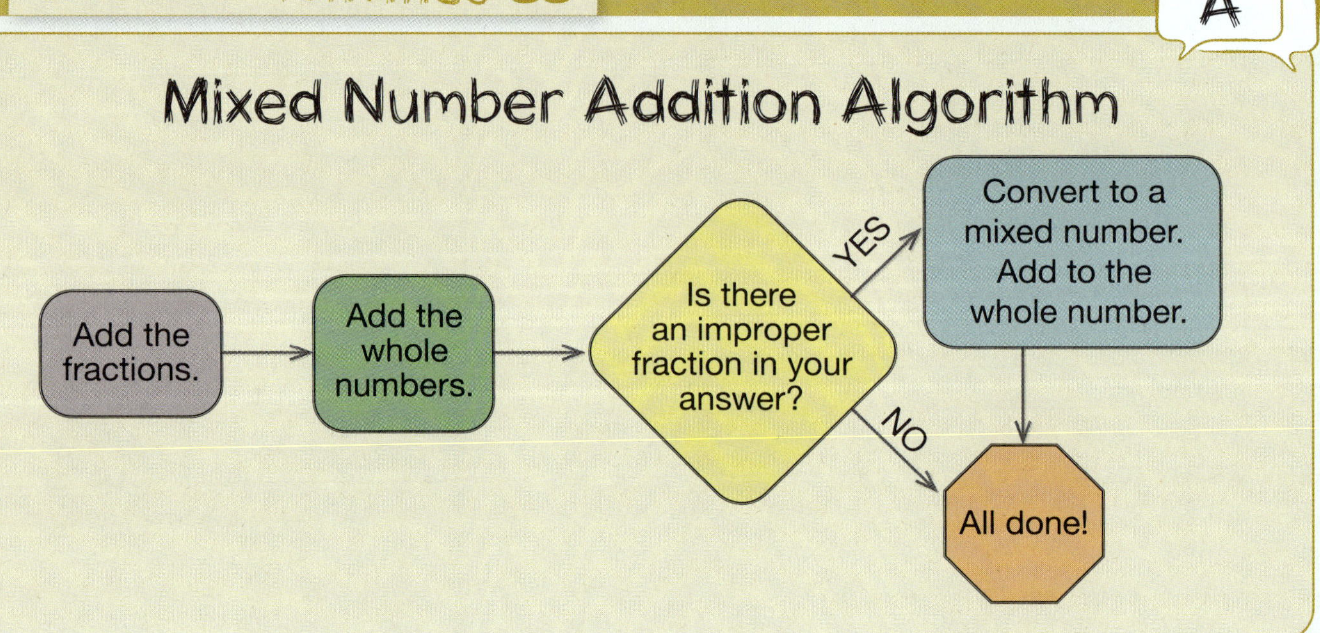

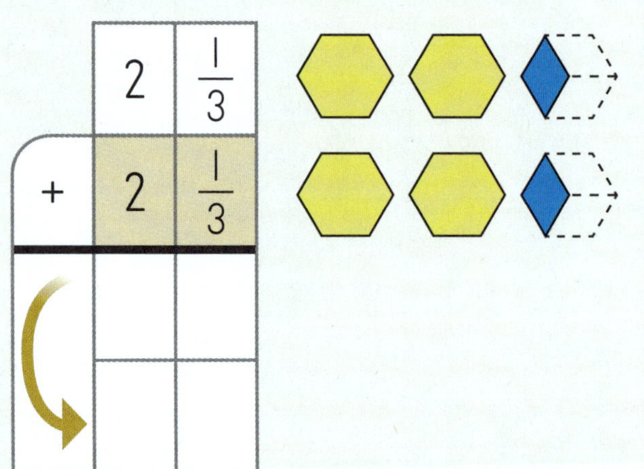

SPIN TO WIN!

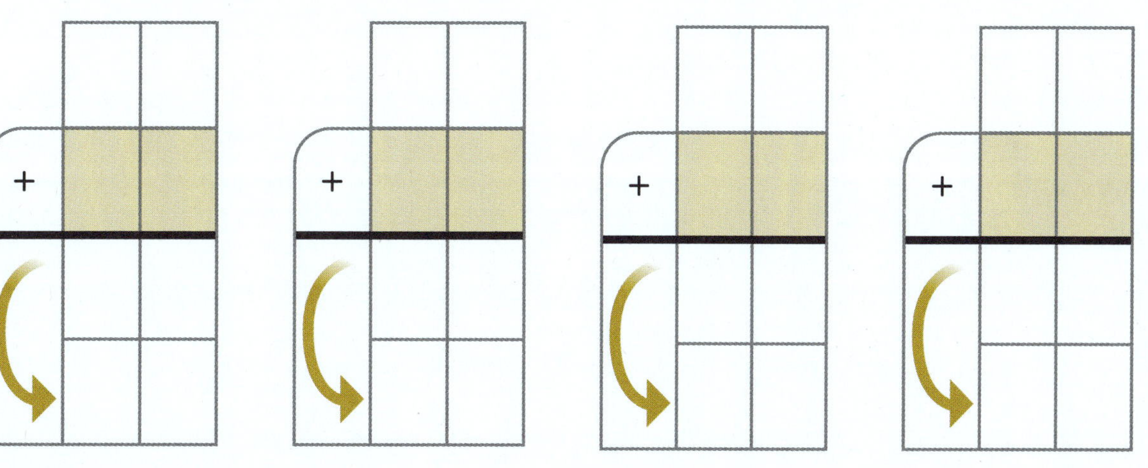

Practice Complete.

	2	$\frac{3}{8}$
+	4	$\frac{7}{8}$

	2	$\frac{7}{10}$
+	1	$\frac{2}{10}$

	6	$\frac{3}{4}$
+	2	$\frac{2}{4}$

	3	$\frac{3}{5}$
+	2	$\frac{2}{5}$

Review Write a fraction to complete each equation. Then, convert the fraction to a mixed number or whole number.

$4 \times \frac{2}{5} = \boxed{\frac{8}{5}} = \boxed{1\frac{3}{5}}$

$2 \times \frac{4}{6} = \boxed{} = \boxed{}$

$3 \times \frac{3}{8} = \boxed{} = \boxed{}$

$6 \times \frac{2}{3} = \boxed{} = \boxed{}$

Use the clues to find the secret number.

- The number has 6 digits.
- There is a 5 in the thousands place.
- There is a 6 in the ten thousands place.
- The sum of the digit in the tens place and the digit in the thousands place is 8.
- The product of the digit in the tens place and the digit in the ones place is 27.
- The digit in the ones place is the same as the digit in the hundreds place.
- The number is greater than 400,000 and less than 500,000.

Secret Number: | | | | | | |

Lesson Activities 👥

A

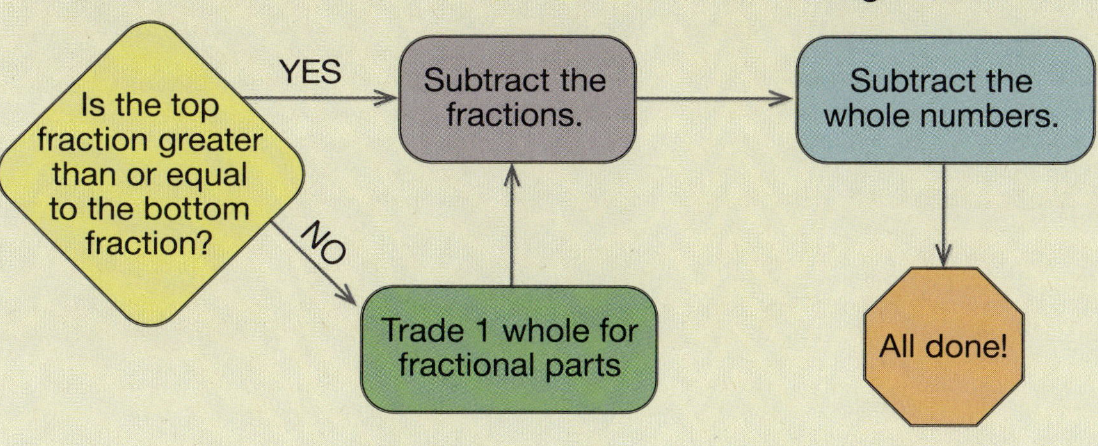

$$2\ \frac{5}{6}$$
$$-\ 1\ \frac{1}{6}$$

$$3$$
$$-\ 1\ \frac{2}{3}$$

$$2\ \frac{1}{6}$$
$$-\ \ \ \frac{5}{6}$$

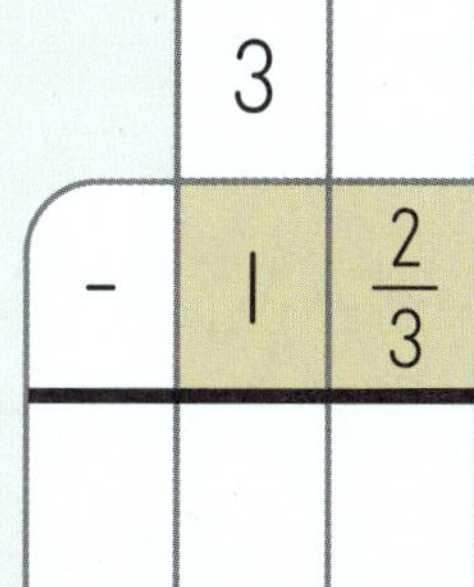

$$5\ \frac{1}{4}$$
$$-\ 2\ \frac{3}{4}$$

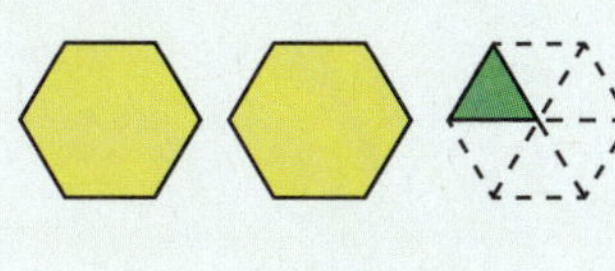

SPIN TO WIN!

B

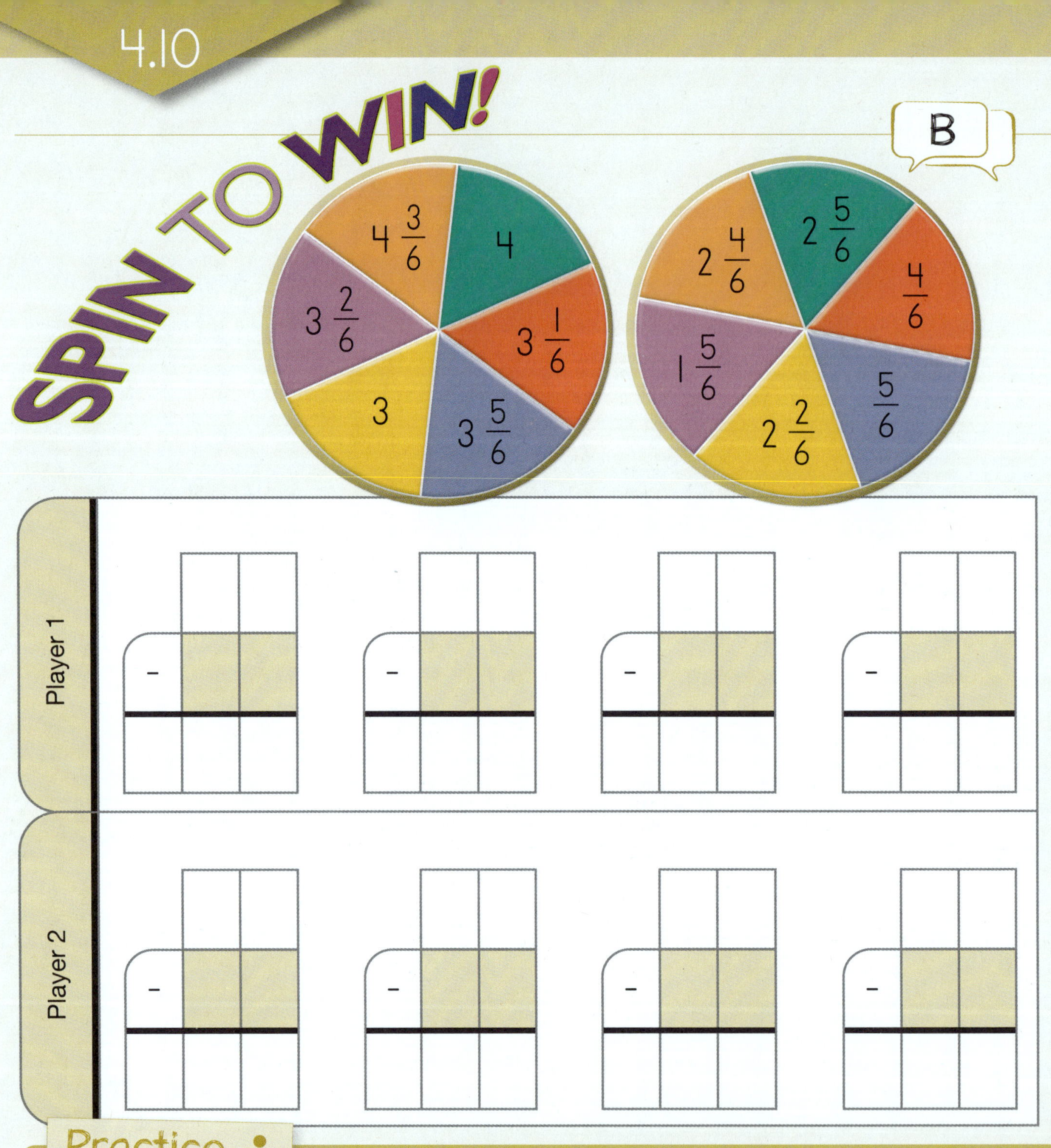

Player 1

Player 2

Practice

Complete.

Review 

Color the multiples in order from Start to End.

Multiples of 11

Start →

11	22	33	36	40
17	24	44	45	42
21	48	55	66	72
30	56	60	77	110
36	63	72	88	99

END

Multiples of 12

Start →

24	36	42	64	80
12	48	60	72	77
8	56	54	84	92
4	16	40	96	108
6	20	28	110	120

END

Complete.

400,000 + 27,000 = ____________

125,000 + 125,000 = ____________

76,000 + 4,000 = ____________

100,000 – 10,000 = ____________

500,000 – 50,000 = ____________

$8 \times 3,000 =$ ____________

$7 \times 6,000 =$ ____________

$8 \times 8,000 =$ ____________

$4 \times 5,000 =$ ____________

$9 \times 10,000 =$ ____________

Complete the missing mixed numbers.

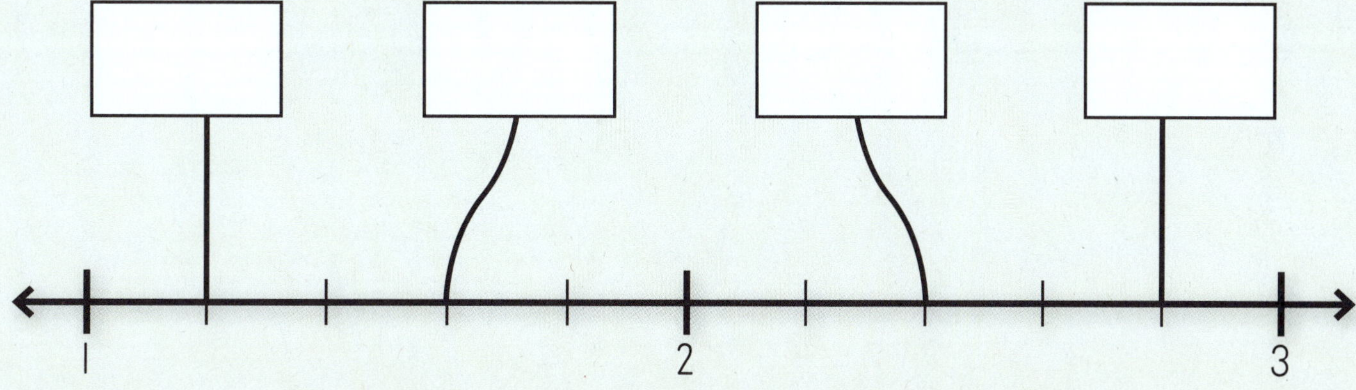

Lesson Activities

$4 = \dfrac{\square}{5}$ $2\dfrac{1}{8} = \square$ $\dfrac{11}{4} = \square$

$5 \times \dfrac{3}{4} = \square = \square$

Emmett's mom uses $3\dfrac{1}{8}$ pounds of red apples and $1\dfrac{6}{8}$ pounds of green apples to make applesauce. How many pounds of apples does she use in all?

Stella uses $\dfrac{1}{4}$ meter of ribbon for each bow. How many meters of ribbon does she need to make 9 bows?

Jai has 4 quarts of juice. He uses $2\dfrac{7}{8}$ quarts to make punch. How much juice is left?

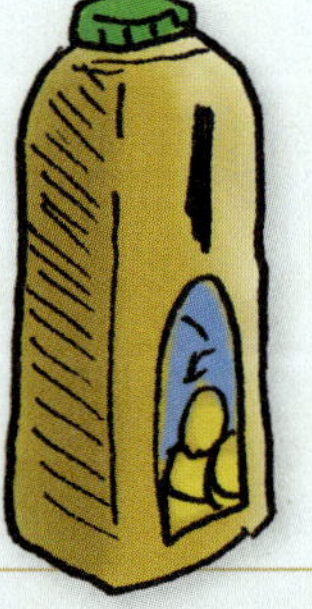

The Meadow hiking trail is $3\dfrac{7}{10}$ kilometers long. The Highlands trail is $2\dfrac{4}{10}$ kilometers long. How much longer is the Meadow trail than the Highlands trail?

Practice

Complete.

$$2\ \frac{3}{8}$$
$$+\ 4\ \frac{7}{8}$$

$$2\ \frac{2}{5}$$
$$+\ 3\ \frac{3}{5}$$

$$5$$
$$-\ 2\ \frac{4}{5}$$

$$3\ \frac{1}{4}$$
$$-\ 1\ \frac{3}{4}$$

Solve. Write the equations you use.

Juniper helps her dad make 3 pizzas.
They put sausage on $1\frac{3}{4}$ pizzas.
They leave the rest plain.
How much is plain?

Zionna uses $2\frac{1}{3}$ cups of white flour and
$1\frac{2}{3}$ cups of whole wheat flour to make bread.
How much flour does she use in all?

Joseph practices piano for $\frac{1}{2}$ hour each day.
How many hours does he practice in 7 days?

 Gideon was $21\frac{1}{2}$ inches long when
he was born. His sister was 2 inches
shorter when she was born. How long
was his sister when she was born?

Review Match.

four hundred thousand seven	4,700
four hundred thousand seventy	40,700
four thousand seven hundred	400,007
forty thousand seventy	40,070
forty thousand seven hundred	400,070

Use the printed ruler to draw a line with the given length.

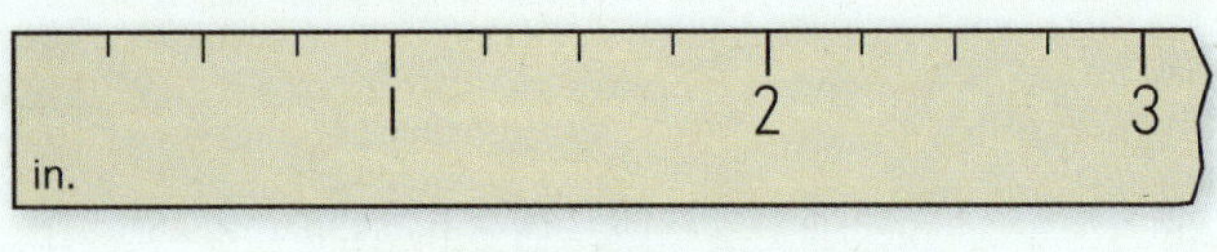

$1\frac{2}{4}$ in.

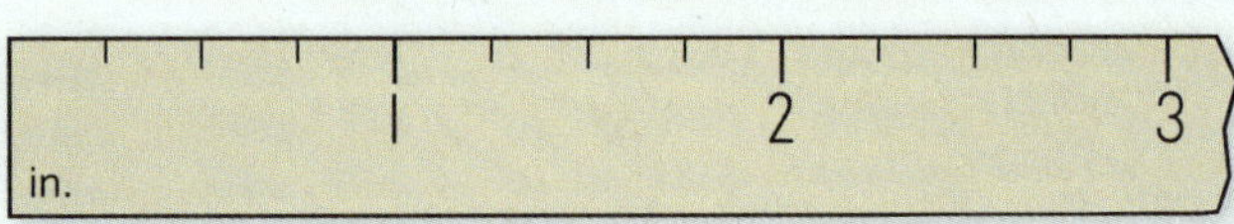

$\frac{3}{4}$ in.

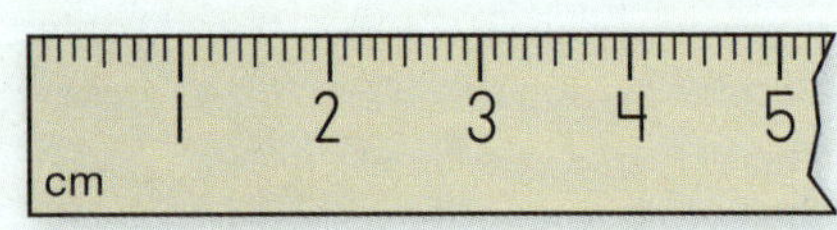

$3\frac{2}{10}$ cm

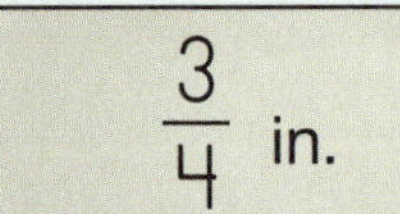

$\frac{8}{10}$ cm

Complete the boxes to find the product.

$8 \times 23 = \boxed{}$

$7 \times 41 = \boxed{}$

Unit Wrap-Up

Connect each number to its place on the number line.

$$\frac{4}{4} \qquad \frac{1}{4} \qquad \frac{5}{4} \qquad \frac{8}{4} \qquad 1\frac{2}{4} \qquad 1\frac{3}{4}$$

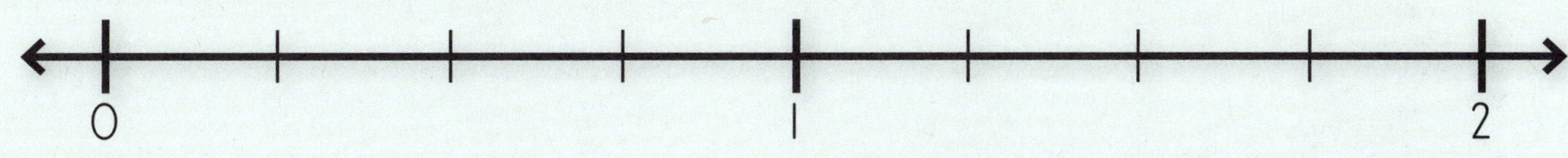

$$0 \qquad\qquad\qquad\qquad 1 \qquad\qquad\qquad\qquad 2$$

Convert the mixed numbers to fractions.

$$2\frac{5}{6} = \boxed{\frac{}{6}} \qquad 1\frac{3}{5} = \boxed{} \qquad 3\frac{1}{4} = \boxed{}$$

$$4\frac{3}{10} = \boxed{} \qquad 6\frac{2}{3} = \boxed{} \qquad 5\frac{7}{8} = \boxed{}$$

Convert the fractions to mixed numbers.

$$\frac{8}{3} = \boxed{} \qquad \frac{12}{4} = \boxed{} \qquad \frac{17}{5} = \boxed{}$$

$$\frac{11}{6} = \boxed{} \qquad \frac{17}{10} = \boxed{} \qquad \frac{31}{8} = \boxed{}$$

Unit Wrap-Up

Write a fraction to complete each equation. Then, convert the fraction to a mixed number or whole number.

$10 \times \dfrac{2}{10} =$ ☐ $=$ ☐ $6 \times \dfrac{2}{5} =$ ☐ $=$ ☐

Complete.

$3\,\dfrac{1}{8}$

$+\ 2\,\dfrac{5}{8}$

$6\,\dfrac{3}{4}$

$+\quad \dfrac{3}{4}$

$4\,\dfrac{1}{2}$

$+\ 2\,\dfrac{1}{2}$

$2\,\dfrac{5}{8}$

$+\ 3$

$2\,\dfrac{9}{10}$

$-\ 1\,\dfrac{3}{10}$

$4\,\dfrac{1}{5}$

$-\ 3$

5

$-\ 2\,\dfrac{2}{5}$

$4\,\dfrac{1}{3}$

$-\ 2\,\dfrac{2}{3}$

Solve. Write the equations you use.

Asher runs $3\,\dfrac{3}{8}$ miles. Lewis runs $1\,\dfrac{5}{8}$ miles farther than Asher.
How far does Lewis run?

Adelaide buys 4 bottles of juice.
Each bottle holds $\dfrac{3}{4}$ liter of juice.
How many liters of juice does she buy?

Lesson Activities

A

Dice Tic-Tac Toe

36 ÷ 9	56 ÷ 7	54 ÷ 9	48 ÷ 8	42 ÷ 7
72 ÷ 8	30 ÷ 6	32 ÷ 8	45 ÷ 9	63 ÷ 9
48 ÷ 6	90 ÷ 9	64 ÷ 8	28 ÷ 7	54 ÷ 6
27 ÷ 9	81 ÷ 9	36 ÷ 6	49 ÷ 7	35 ÷ 7
42 ÷ 6	63 ÷ 7	40 ÷ 8	72 ÷ 9	56 ÷ 8

B

12 ÷ 2 =	12 ÷ 3 =	12 ÷ 4 =
13 ÷ 2 =	13 ÷ 3 =	13 ÷ 4 =
14 ÷ 2 =	14 ÷ 3 =	14 ÷ 4 =
15 ÷ 2 =	15 ÷ 3 =	15 ÷ 4 =
16 ÷ 2 =	16 ÷ 3 =	16 ÷ 4 =

Possible remainders:

Possible remainders:

Possible remainders:

Practice

Complete.

8 48	9 54	7 56	7 42	8 72
9 63	6 36	8 40	8 64	9 36
6 42	9 72	6 48	8 56	7 49
6 54	8 32	7 35	9 81	7 63

Complete.

$25 \div 5 = \boxed{}$ $39 \div 10 = \boxed{}$ $30 \div 8 = \boxed{}$

$26 \div 5 = \boxed{}$ $40 \div 10 = \boxed{}$ $31 \div 8 = \boxed{}$

$27 \div 5 = \boxed{}$ $41 \div 10 = \boxed{}$ $32 \div 8 = \boxed{}$

Solve. Write the equations you use.

Abigail has a 72-inch-long board.
She cuts the board into 8 equal pieces.
How long is each piece?

There are 48 children at dance class.
The teachers divide the students into
6 equal groups.
How many children are in each group?

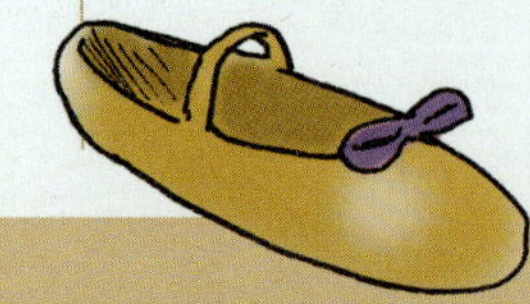

Lesson 5.1

Review

Complete. Use the example to help.

Example (mixed number subtraction with frames):

$$2\tfrac{1}{8} \;(=1\tfrac{9}{8}) \;-\; 1\tfrac{5}{8} \;=\; \tfrac{4}{8}$$

$$4\tfrac{2}{6} \;-\; 1\tfrac{3}{6} \;=\;$$

$$6\tfrac{1}{3} \;-\; 3\tfrac{2}{3} \;=\;$$

$$5\tfrac{1}{4} \;-\; 3\tfrac{3}{4} \;=\;$$

Complete the chart.

Expanded Form	Standard Form
$30{,}000 + 5$	
$30{,}000 + 50$	
$30{,}000 + 500$	
$300{,}000 + 5{,}000$	
$300{,}000 + 50{,}000$	

Complete.

$4 \times 12 =$ ____ $7 \times 12 =$ ____ $5 \times 12 =$ ____

$9 \times 12 =$ ____ $2 \times 12 =$ ____ $10 \times 12 =$ ____

$3 \times 12 =$ ____ $8 \times 12 =$ ____ $6 \times 12 =$ ____

Lesson Activities 

$30 \div 7 = $ ______

$30 \div 8 = $ ______

$30 \div 9 = $ ______

$30 \div 12 = $ ______

Flip and Divide

Player 1		Player 2	
$20 \div$ ___	= ______	$20 \div$ ___	= ______
$30 \div$ ___	= ______	$30 \div$ ___	= ______
$40 \div$ ___	= ______	$40 \div$ ___	= ______
$50 \div$ ___	= ______	$50 \div$ ___	= ______
$60 \div$ ___	= ______	$60 \div$ ___	= ______
Sum of remainders	______	Sum of remainders	______

Practice   **Complete.**

$49 \div 10 = \boxed{}$

$38 \div 5 = \boxed{}$

$34 \div 4 = \boxed{}$

$43 \div 7 = \boxed{}$

$39 \div 6 = \boxed{}$

$50 \div 8 = \boxed{}$

$35 \div 8 = \boxed{}$

$94 \div 9 = \boxed{}$

Solve. Write the equations you use.

Soren has 60 centimeters of yarn.
He cuts the yarn into pieces that are 8 centimeters long.

- How many pieces does he make?

- How much yarn is left over?

Mina has 46 shells.
She puts 9 shells on each shelf.

- How many shelves does she fill?

- How many shells are left over?

Review — Complete. Use the example to help.

Example: 3 $\frac{6}{6}$ − 1 $\frac{4}{6}$ = 1 $\frac{2}{6}$

4 − 1 $\frac{4}{6}$ =

5 − 2 $\frac{1}{3}$ =

3 − 1 $\frac{4}{5}$ =

Complete.

	×12
2	
4	
8	
3	
6	
9	
5	
7	
10	

Match.

kilogram	g
gram	m
liter	kg
milliliter	cm
centimeter	mL
meter	km
kilometer	L

Complete the fact family to match the marbles.

$4 \times 5 =$

$ \times =$

$ \div =$

$ \div =$

Lesson Activities 

21 ÷ 3 = ______

Check: ______

21 ÷ 4 = ______

Check: ______

21 ÷ 2 = ______

Check: ______

21 ÷ 6 = ______

Check: ______

21 ÷ 7 = ______

Check: ______

21 ÷ 8 = ______

Check: ______

19 children play kickball. They make 2 teams. They make the teams as equal as possible. How many children are on each team?

19 children are at tennis practice. The coach splits them into pairs. How many pairs does he make?

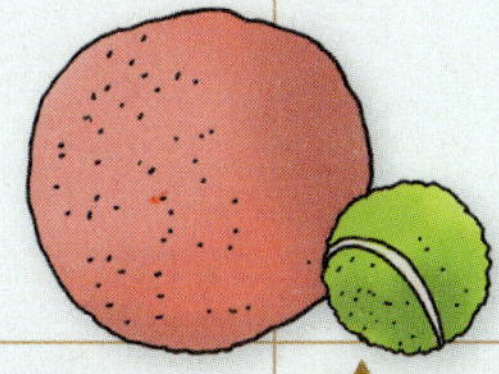

Trevor has 19 yards of fabric for costumes for the play. He needs 2 yards for each costume. If he makes as many costumes as possible, how much fabric will be left over?

 2 friends have a lemonade stand. They earn $19 and split the money equally. How much does each friend get?

Practice

Solve the division problems. Then, match them with the problem you could use to check your answer.

$42 \div 4 = \boxed{}$

$(9 \times 4) + 6$

$42 \div 8 = \boxed{}$

$(8 \times 5) + 2$

$42 \div 7 = \boxed{}$

7×6

$42 \div 9 = \boxed{}$

$(4 \times 10) + 2$

Solve. Write the equations you use.

There are 29 children at tae kwon do lessons. They split into 3 groups and make the groups as equal as possible. How many children are in each group?

Nikola bakes 43 cupcakes for the bake sale. He puts 6 cupcakes in each box and fills as many boxes as possible. How many cupcakes does he have left over?

38 children carpool to the nature center. 6 children fit in each minivan. How many minivans do they need to fit all the children?

Lenora arranges 45 chairs for the piano recital. She puts 8 chairs in each row. Then, she puts away the extra chairs. How many rows does she make?

Review

Complete. Use the example to help.

Connect each number to its dot on the number line.

| 249,628 | 249,130 | 250,325 | 250,050 |

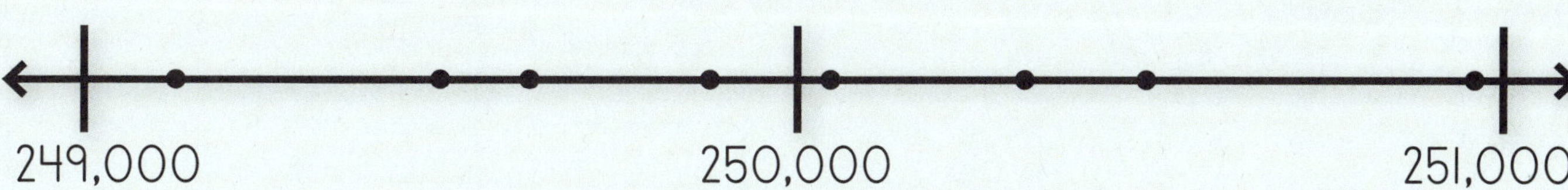

249,000   250,000   251,000

| 249,500 | 249,879 | 250,501 | 250,964 |

Round each number to the underlined place. Use the number line (above) to help.

249,628 ≈ [ ]   250,325 ≈ [ ]

249,130 ≈ [ ]   250,050 ≈ [ ]

249,879 ≈ [ ]   250,964 ≈ [ ]

249,500 ≈ [ ]   250,501 ≈ [ ]

Lesson Activities 

Multiplication Crash

24	84	36	60	120
108	72	12	96	48

$48 \div 12 = \boxed{}$

$\boxed{} \times 12 = 48$

$24 \div 12 = \boxed{}$ $60 \div 12 = \boxed{}$ $120 \div 12 = \boxed{}$

$12 \div 12 = \boxed{}$ $108 \div 12 = \boxed{}$ $84 \div 12 = \boxed{}$

$36 \div 12 = \boxed{}$ $96 \div 12 = \boxed{}$ $72 \div 12 = \boxed{}$

$55 \div 11 = \boxed{}$

$\boxed{} \times 11 = 55$

$33 \div 11 = \boxed{}$ $66 \div 11 = \boxed{}$ $99 \div 11 = \boxed{}$

$22 \div 11 = \boxed{}$ $44 \div 11 = \boxed{}$ $88 \div 11 = \boxed{}$

$11 \div 11 = \boxed{}$ $77 \div 11 = \boxed{}$ $110 \div 11 = \boxed{}$

Practice

Complete.

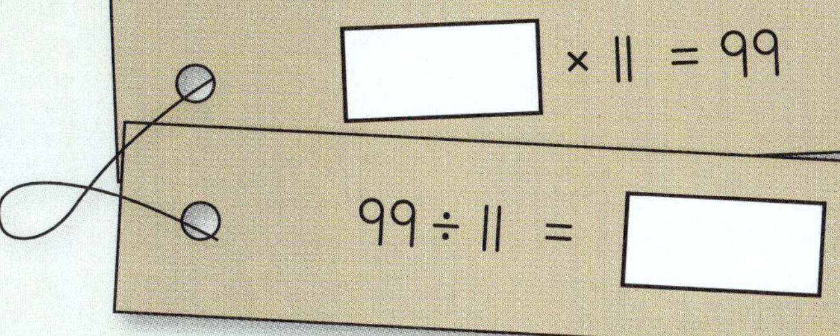

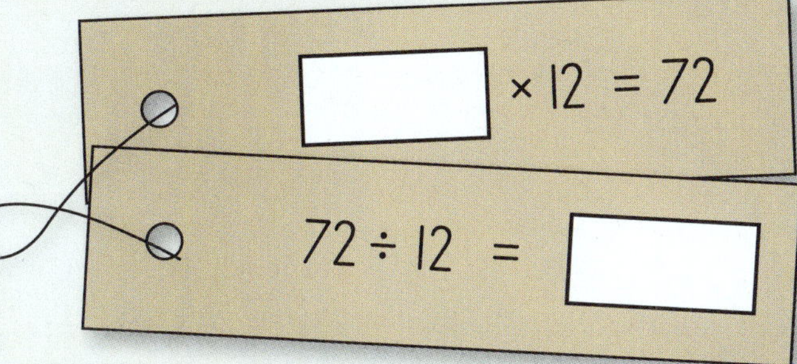

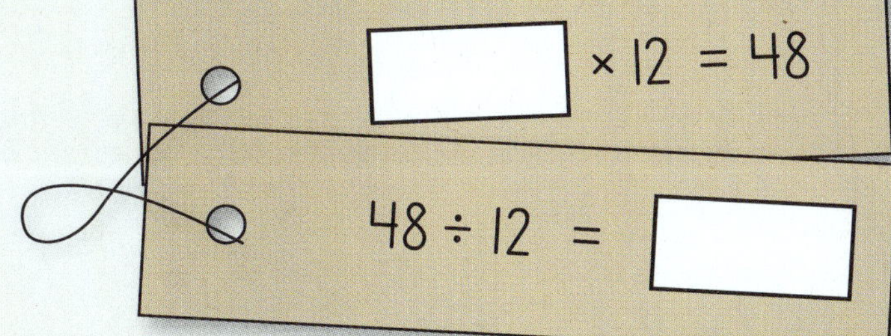

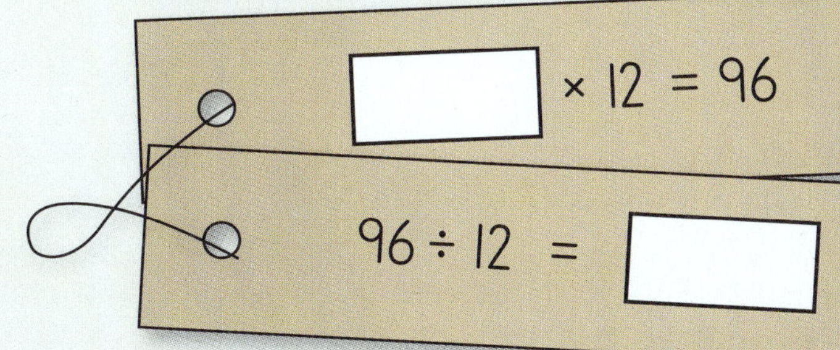

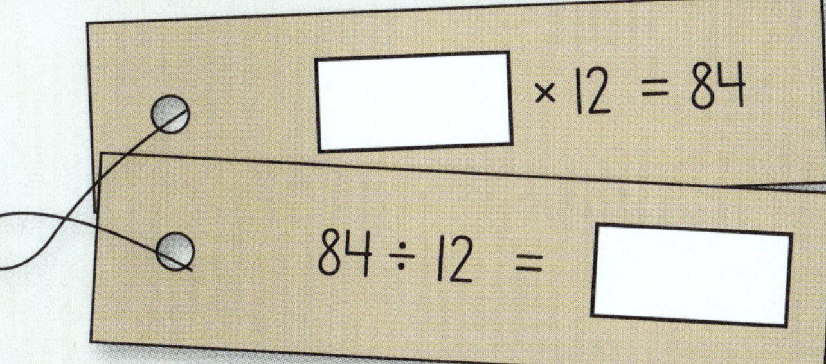

Solve. Write the equations you use.

Pompoms come in packs of 12.
Willow needs 60 pompoms for a craft.
How many packs should she buy?

Each movie ticket costs $11.
Charlie's dad paid $77.
How many tickets did he buy?

5.4

Convert the mixed numbers to fractions. Use the example to help.

$2\frac{1}{4} = \boxed{\dfrac{9}{4}}$

$3\frac{5}{6} = \boxed{}$

$4\frac{3}{5} = \boxed{}$

Convert the fractions to mixed numbers or whole numbers. Use the example to help.

$\div\ \dfrac{12}{4} = \boxed{3}$

$\dfrac{15}{6} = \boxed{}$

$\dfrac{19}{8} = \boxed{}$

Complete. Follow the steps.

1. Divide
2. Multiply
3. Subtract

Complete. All times are a.m.

10:30	→ 30 min.	$\boxed{}$
10:40	→ 30 min.	$\boxed{}$
10:50	→ 30 min.	$\boxed{}$
11:00	→ 30 min.	$\boxed{}$

Complete.

$8 \times 7 = \boxed{}$

$8 \times 70 = \boxed{}$

$8 \times 700 = \boxed{}$

$8 \times 7{,}000 = \boxed{}$

Lesson Activities

$80 \div 4 =$ ☐

8 tens $\div 4 =$ ☐ tens

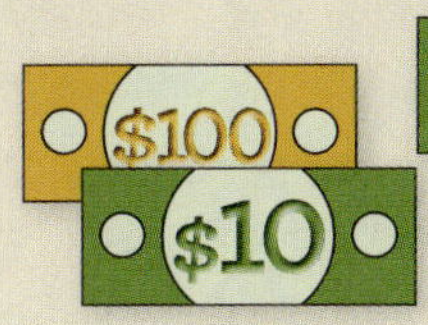
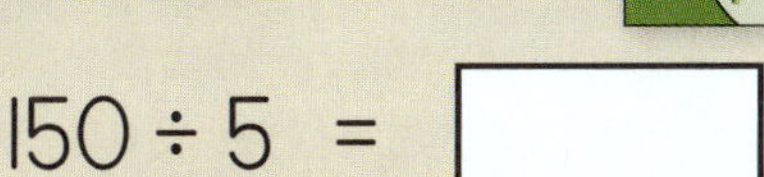

A

$150 \div 5 =$ ☐

15 tens $\div 5 =$ ☐ tens

$90 \div 3 =$ ☐

$60 \div 2 =$ ☐

$100 \div 5 =$ ☐

$160 \div 8 =$ ☐

$180 \div 6 =$ ☐

$240 \div 4 =$ ☐

B

MENTAL MATH ARCADE

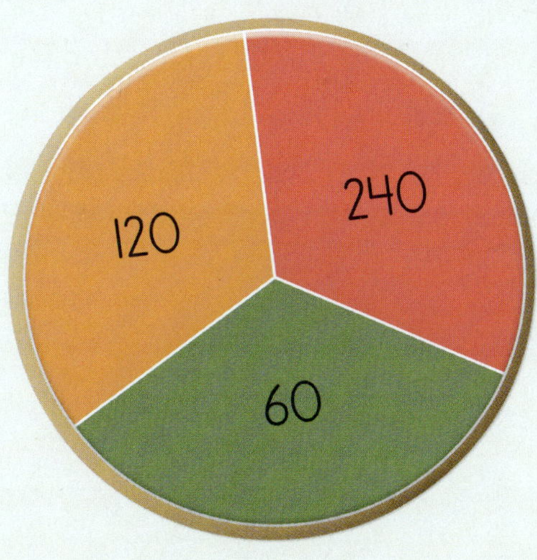

Practice

Color the problems that equal the number in the star.

20

| 80 ÷ 4 |
| 90 ÷ 3 |
| 60 ÷ 3 |

30

| 80 ÷ 4 |
| 60 ÷ 2 |
| 90 ÷ 3 |

40

| 80 ÷ 2 |
| 120 ÷ 3 |
| 80 ÷ 4 |

50

| 200 ÷ 2 |
| 100 ÷ 2 |
| 200 ÷ 4 |

Match.

180 ÷ 3	50	420 ÷ 6
320 ÷ 4	60	400 ÷ 8
210 ÷ 3	70	540 ÷ 6
250 ÷ 5	80	360 ÷ 6
360 ÷ 4	90	400 ÷ 5

Solve. Write the equations you use.

Oscar has 90 building blocks. He uses all the blocks to build 3 identical towers. How many blocks are in each tower?

Raya has 80 feet of rope. She cuts the rope into 4-foot-long pieces. How many pieces does she make?

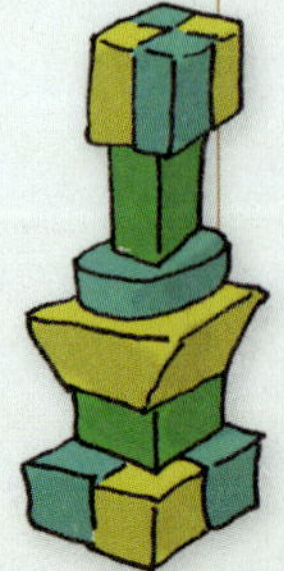

Review

Write a fraction to complete each equation. Convert the fraction to a whole number or mixed number if possible.

$$6 \times \frac{1}{5} = \boxed{\frac{6}{5}} = \boxed{1\frac{1}{5}}$$

$$12 \times \frac{1}{4} = \boxed{} = \boxed{}$$

$$9 \times \frac{2}{10} = \boxed{} = \boxed{}$$

$$10 \times \frac{7}{10} = \boxed{} = \boxed{}$$

Match.

7 thousands	70	70 tens
7 tens	700	70 ones
7 hundreds	7,000	70 thousands
7 ten thousands	70,000	70 hundreds

Complete.

```
  6 8 , 0 9 4
+ 5 1 , 6 2 8
─────────────
```

```
  6 8 , 0 9 4
- 5 1 , 6 2 8
─────────────
```

Complete.

$$(10 \times 8) + (2 \times 8) = \boxed{}$$

$$(7 \times 8) + (5 \times 8) = \boxed{}$$

$$(6 \times 8) + (6 \times 8) = \boxed{}$$

$$(8 \times 8) + (4 \times 8) = \boxed{}$$

Lesson Activities 

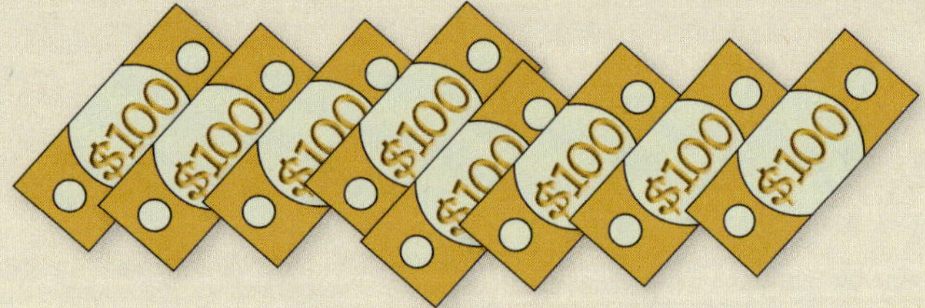

$800 \div 4 =$ ☐

8 hundreds $\div 4 =$ ☐ hundreds

$200 \div 4 =$ ☐

20 tens $\div 4 =$ ☐ tens

$400 \div 2 =$ ☐

$400 \div 4 =$ ☐

$400 \div 5 =$ ☐

$300 \div 3 =$ ☐

$300 \div 5 =$ ☐

$300 \div 6 =$ ☐

$6{,}000 \div 3 =$ ☐

6 thousands $\div 3 =$ ☐ thousands

$2{,}000 \div 4 =$ ☐

20 hundreds $\div 4 =$ ☐ hundreds

$4{,}000 \div 2 =$ ☐

$6{,}000 \div 2 =$ ☐

$8{,}000 \div 2 =$ ☐

$3{,}000 \div 5 =$ ☐

$4{,}000 \div 5 =$ ☐

$5{,}000 \div 5 =$ ☐

Flip and Divide

Player 1		Player 2	
180 ÷ ☐ = ☐		180 ÷ ☐ = ☐	
300 ÷ ☐ = ☐		300 ÷ ☐ = ☐	
600 ÷ ☐ = ☐		600 ÷ ☐ = ☐	
3,000 ÷ ☐ = ☐		3,000 ÷ ☐ = ☐	
6,000 ÷ ☐ = ☐		6,000 ÷ ☐ = ☐	
Sum of quotients ☐		Sum of quotients ☐	

Practice

Match.

2,400 ÷ 4	400	1,200 ÷ 3
800 ÷ 2	500	4,000 ÷ 8
1,000 ÷ 2	600	1,200 ÷ 2

6,000 ÷ 3	2,000	9,000 ÷ 3
15,000 ÷ 5	3,000	8,000 ÷ 2
12,000 ÷ 3	4,000	10,000 ÷ 5

Review

Find the perimeter and area.

7 ft.

11 ft.

Perimeter: ___ ft.

Area: ___ sq. ft.

8 in.

8 in.

Perimeter: ___ in.

Area: ___ sq. in.

12 km

4 km

Perimeter: ___ km

Area: ___ sq. km

Complete with <, >, or =.

17,400 ◯ 17,004

80,000 ◯ 79,999

65,246 ◯ 56,264

108,000 ◯ 180,000

Write the time.

___

___

Solve. Write the equations you use.

Taylor uses 2 pieces of rope to make a rope ladder. Each piece is $4\frac{6}{10}$ m long. How much rope does he use in all?

Jude has 3 boards. He cuts each board into fourths to make steps. How many steps does he make?

Unit Wrap-Up

Match.

55 ÷ 11	4	72 ÷ 12
77 ÷ 11	5	48 ÷ 12
88 ÷ 11	6	60 ÷ 12
44 ÷ 11	7	96 ÷ 12
66 ÷ 11	8	84 ÷ 12

Complete.

32 ÷ 8 = [ ]

33 ÷ 8 = [ ]

56 ÷ 7 = [ ]

60 ÷ 7 = [ ]

49 ÷ 7 = [ ]

51 ÷ 7 = [ ]

72 ÷ 9 = [ ]

75 ÷ 9 = [ ]

33 ÷ 6 = [ ]

43 ÷ 5 = [ ]

51 ÷ 5 = [ ]

83 ÷ 9 = [ ]

Unit Wrap-Up

Complete.

$80 \div 4 =$ ☐

$800 \div 4 =$ ☐

$8{,}000 \div 4 =$ ☐

$60 \div 2 =$ ☐

$600 \div 2 =$ ☐

$6{,}000 \div 2 =$ ☐

$240 \div 6 =$ ☐

$2{,}400 \div 6 =$ ☐

⭐ $24{,}000 \div 6 =$ ☐

$300 \div 5 =$ ☐

$3{,}000 \div 5 =$ ☐

⭐ $30{,}000 \div 5 =$ ☐

Complete.

23 people are coming for a holiday meal at McKenzee's house.
Each table seats 8 people.
How many tables do they need?

Quintin needs 6 feathers for each craft.
He has 50 feathers.
How many crafts can he make?

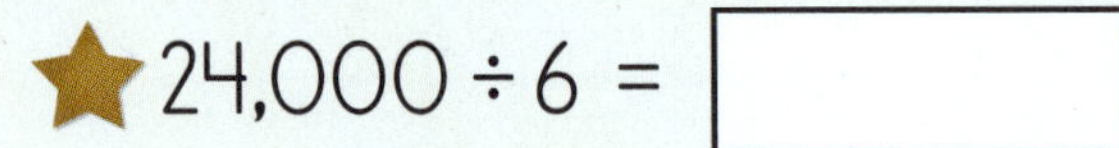

Rock climbing class costs $140 for 7 lessons.
How much does each lesson cost?

3 friends work together to earn $600.
They split the money equally.
How much money does each friend get?

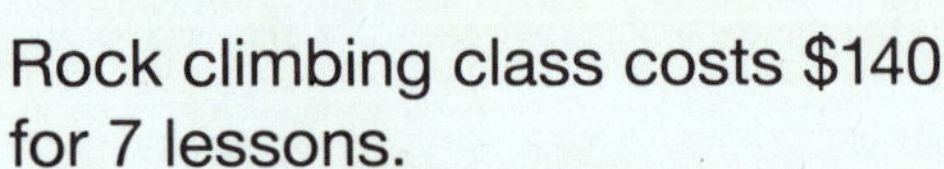

Lesson Activities 👥

Perimeter

The distance around the outside edge

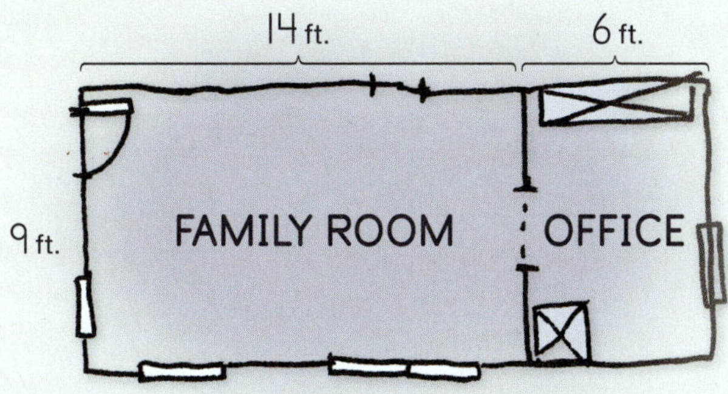

What is the perimeter of the family room?

What is the perimeter of the office?

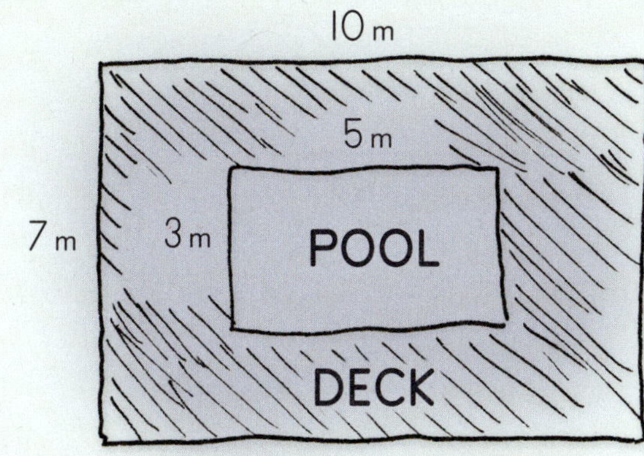

What is the perimeter of the deck?

What is the perimeter of the pool?

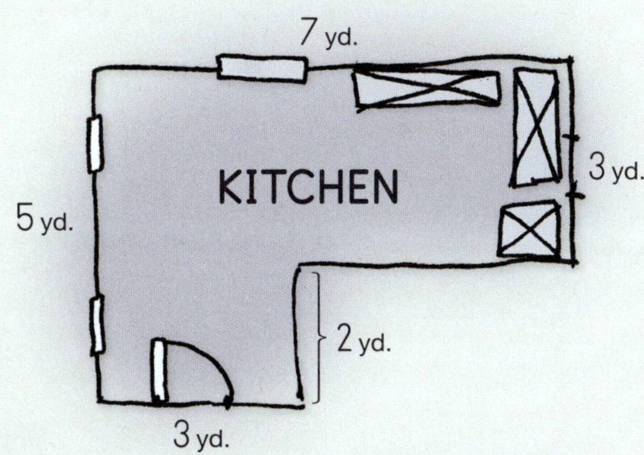

What is the perimeter of the kitchen?

B

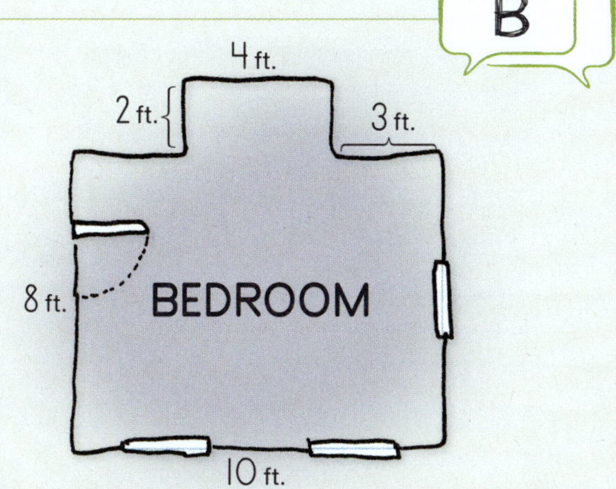

What is the perimeter of the bedroom?

Practice

Find the perimeter of each shape. Include the correct units.

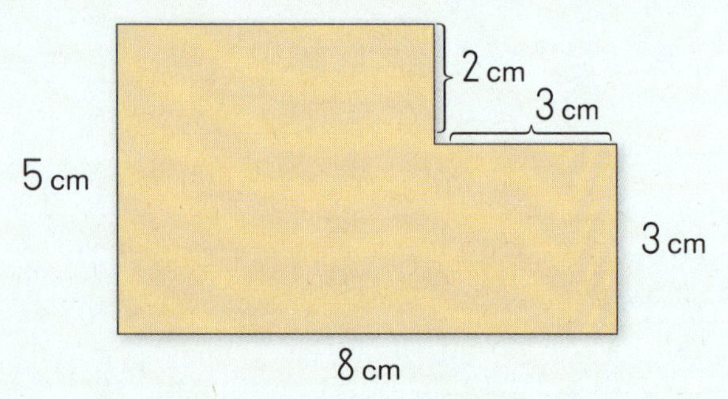

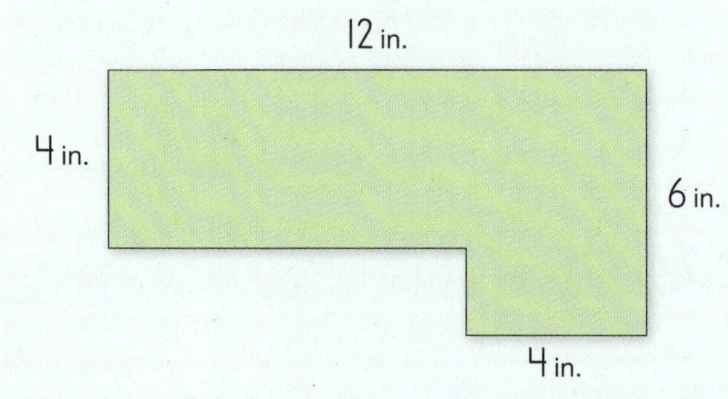

Perimeter: __________

Perimeter: __________

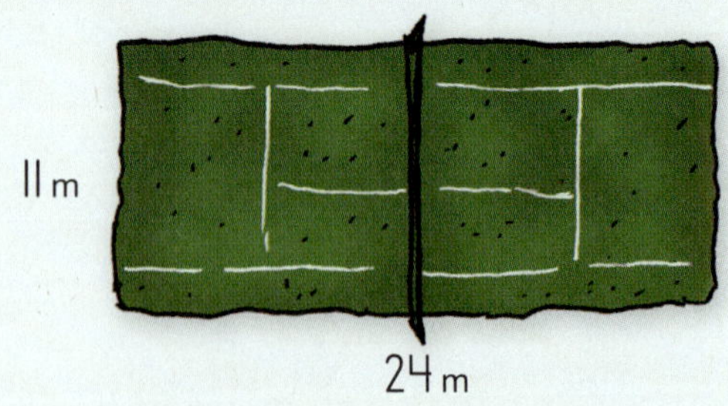

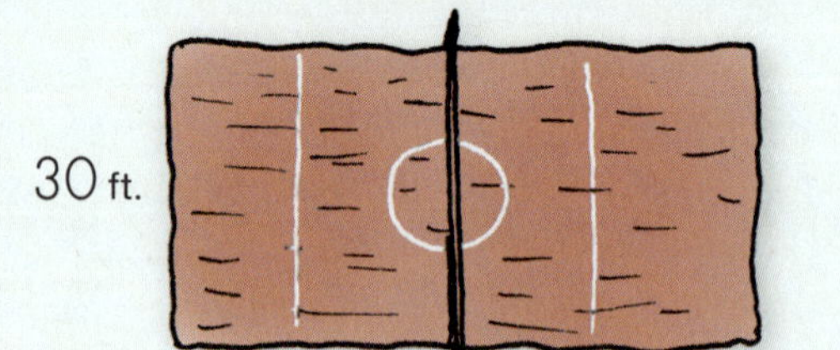

Perimeter: __________

Perimeter: __________

Solve. Write the equations you use.

What is the perimeter of the tennis court?

What is the perimeter of the volleyball court?

Review  Complete.

	3	$\frac{4}{5}$
+	2	$\frac{2}{5}$

	5	$\frac{5}{8}$
+	2	$\frac{5}{8}$

	6	$\frac{1}{3}$
−	2	$\frac{2}{3}$

	4	$\frac{3}{10}$
−	2	$\frac{8}{10}$

Choose the more sensible unit for each item.

Weight of a feather

1 gram	1 kilogram

Weight of a chicken

3 grams	3 kilograms

Weight of an ostrich

145 grams	145 kilograms

Complete.

$80 \div 2 = \boxed{}$

$400 \div 2 = \boxed{}$

$60 \div 3 = \boxed{}$

$320 \div 4 = \boxed{}$

$100 \div 2 = \boxed{}$

$600 \div 3 = \boxed{}$

$90 \div 3 = \boxed{}$

$640 \div 8 = \boxed{}$

Lesson Activities

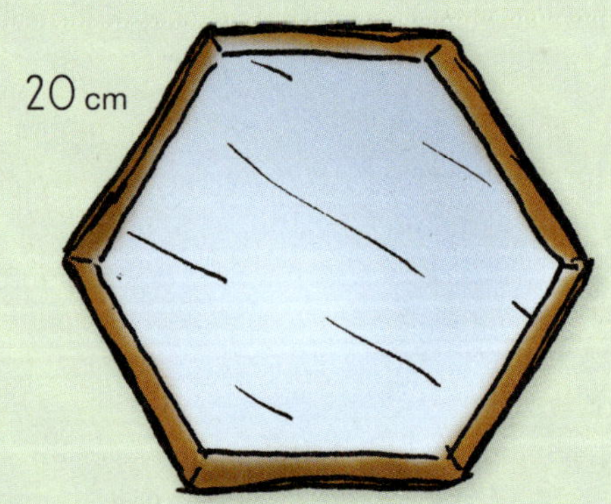

20 cm

2 Ways to Find the Perimeter of a Shape with All Equal Sides

Add up all the sides

Multiply the number of sides times the length of each side

A

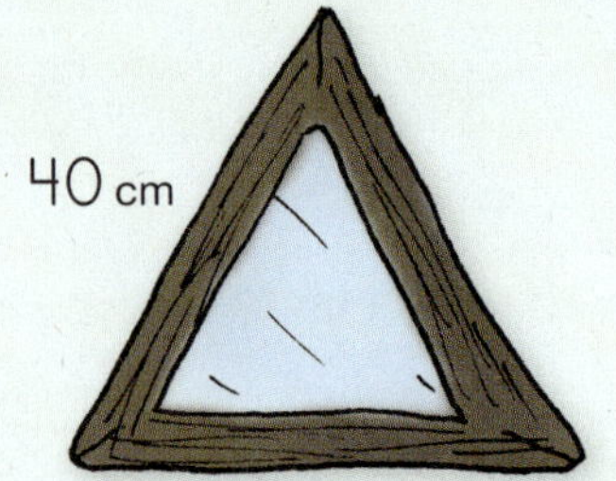

40 cm

12 cm

50 cm

Perimeter: ______

Perimeter: ______

Perimeter: ______

B

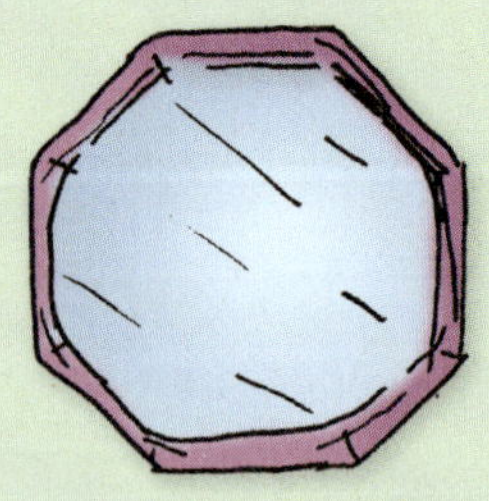

The perimeter of the mirror is 80 in.
How long is each side?

The perimeter of the mirror is 60 in.
How long is each side?

The perimeter of the mirror is 160 in.
How long is each side?

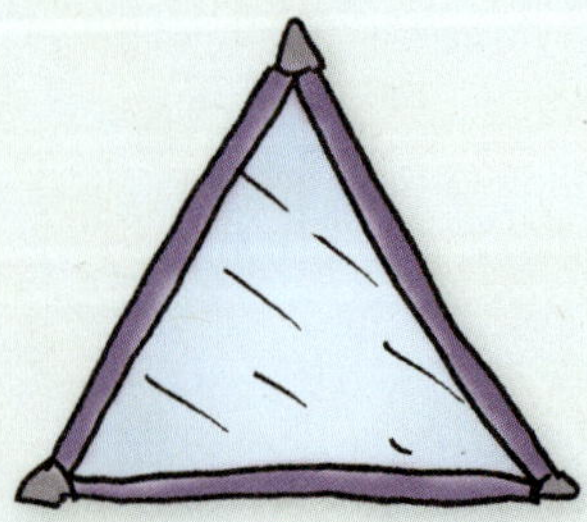

Practice

Find the perimeter of each shape.
All the sides of each shape are equal.

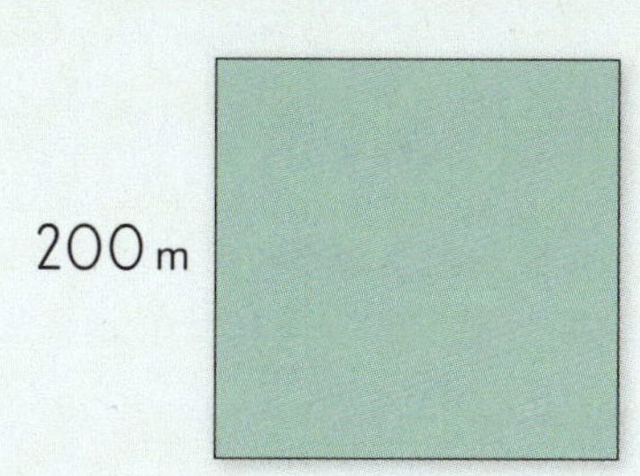

200 m

Perimeter: [ ]

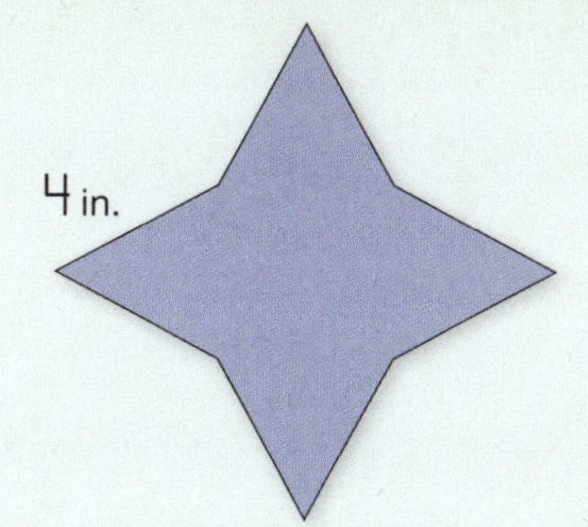

4 in.

Perimeter: [ ]

6 cm

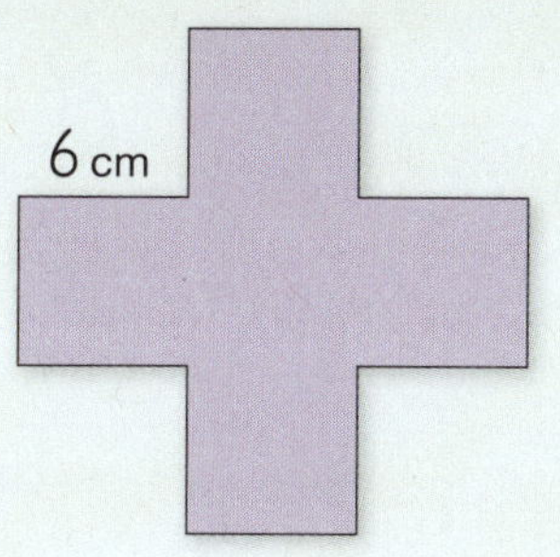

Perimeter: [ ]

Complete the missing numbers in the chart.

Number of sides	Length of each side (inches)	Perimeter of shape with equal sides (inches)
6	30	
10	7	
4		24
8		160
★	20	100

Solve. Write the equations you use.

Harper makes a star craft with 10 equal sides. Each side is 6 inches long. What is the perimeter of the craft?

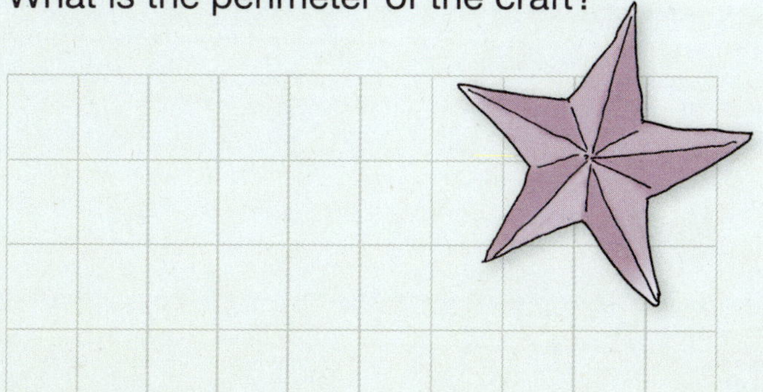

Brayden builds a garden bed with 5 equal sides. He uses 150 feet of edging to surround the bed. How long is each side?

Review

Convert the mixed numbers to fractions.
Convert the fractions to whole numbers or mixed numbers.

$2\dfrac{7}{8} = \boxed{}$

$5\dfrac{1}{10} = \boxed{}$

$6\dfrac{5}{6} = \boxed{}$

$\dfrac{19}{6} = \boxed{}$

$\dfrac{28}{4} = \boxed{}$

$\dfrac{67}{10} = \boxed{}$

Complete.

$9 \times 300 = \boxed{}$

$9 \times 7{,}000 = \boxed{}$

$8 \times 700 = \boxed{}$

$6 \times 8{,}000 = \boxed{}$

$12 \times 300 = \boxed{}$

$11 \times 9{,}000 = \boxed{}$

$11 \times 400 = \boxed{}$

$12 \times 4{,}000 = \boxed{}$

$10 \times 500 = \boxed{}$

$10 \times 10{,}000 = \boxed{}$

Solve. Write the equations you use.

Poppy has 20 flowers to plant.
She plants them in 3 groups. She makes
the groups as equal as possible.
How many flowers are in each group?

Amrut's family has 2 pizzas.
They eat $1\dfrac{3}{8}$ pizzas.
What fraction of a pizza is left?

LANDSCAPING HELP DESK

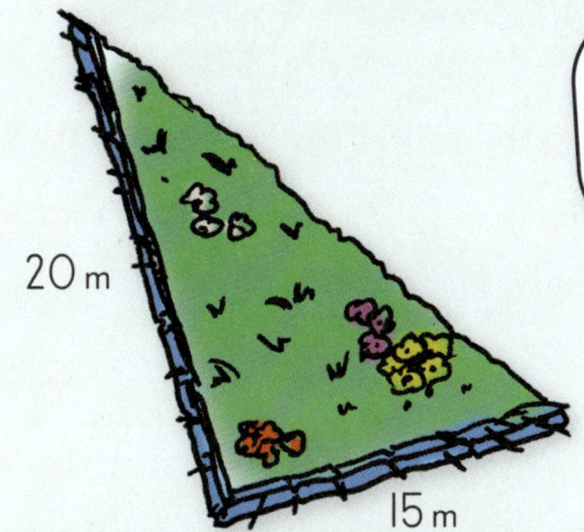

The perimeter of my yard is 60 m. I've already built a fence around 2 sides. How much more fencing do I need to fully surround the yard?

B

I'd like to make 3 garden beds like this one. How many feet of fence will I need to enclose all 3 beds?

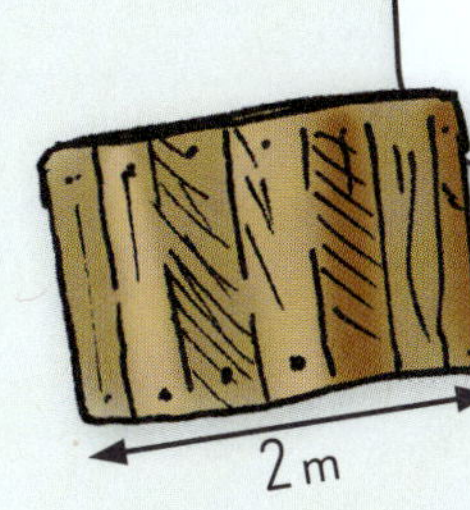

I want to build a fence around my yard. Each fence panel is 2 meters wide. How many do I need?

Each side of the garden is 5 feet long. I'd like to edge the garden with 1-foot bricks. Each brick costs $2. How much will it cost to buy enough bricks to enclose the garden?

Practice

Find the length of the missing sides.

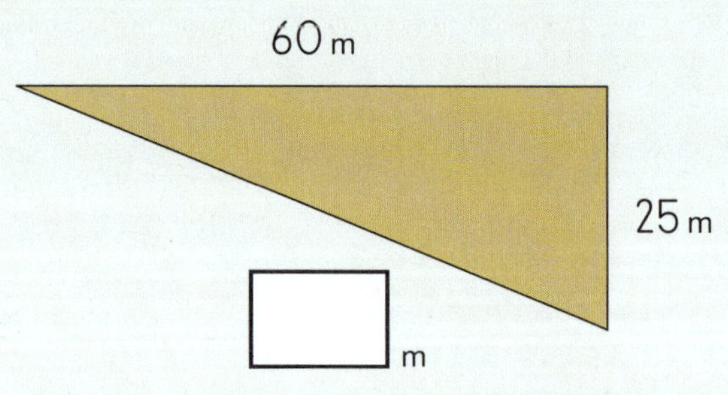

Perimeter: 150 m

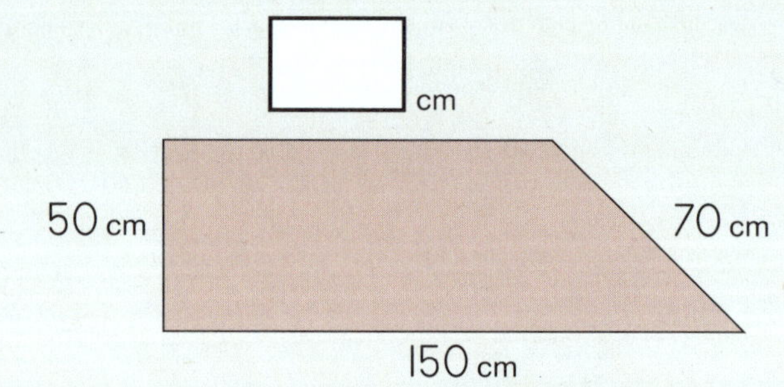

Perimeter: 370 cm

All sides are equal.

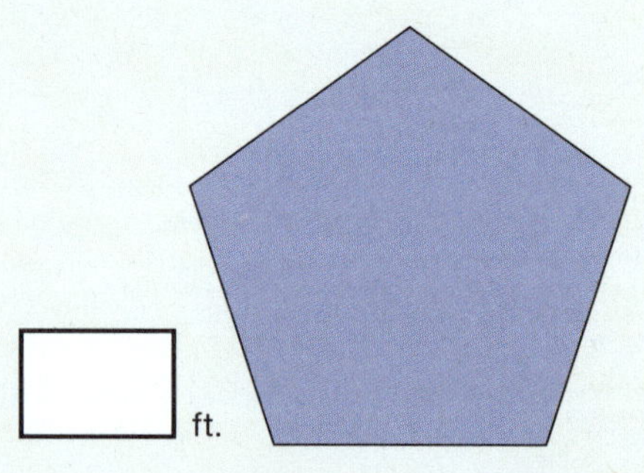

Perimeter: 40 ft.

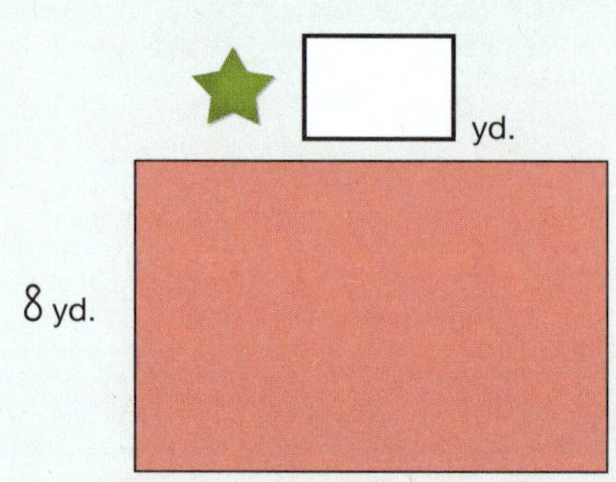

Perimeter: 40 yd.

Solve. Write the equations you use.

Porter wants to build 4 pens for chickens.
Each pen is 8 feet long and 6 feet wide.
How much fencing does he need?

Emilia wants to build a horse paddock
50 feet long and 40 feet wide.
She already has 30 feet of fencing.
How much more fencing does she need?

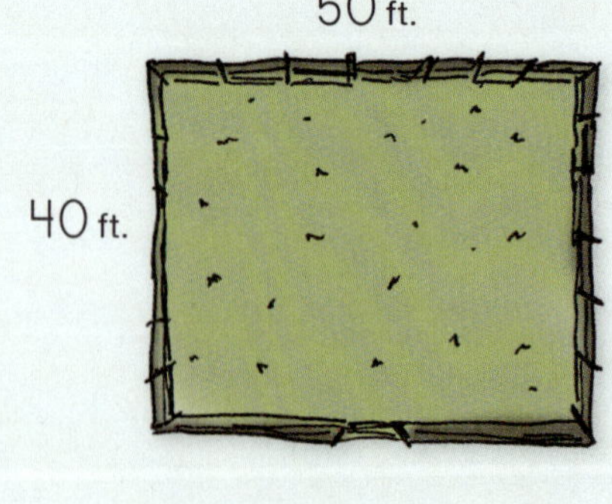

Review   Complete.

4 × 12 = [ ]   8 × 12 = [ ]   7 × 12 = [ ]

2 × 12 = [ ]   3 × 12 = [ ]   10 × 12 = [ ]

5 × 12 = [ ]   6 × 12 = [ ]   9 × 12 = [ ]

Complete.

$(2 \times 20) + (3 \times 20) =$ [ ]

$(4 \times 50) + (6 \times 50) =$ [ ]

$(9 \times 80) + (1 \times 80) =$ [ ]

$(2 \times 12) + (2 \times 25) =$ [ ]

Complete. All times are p.m.

3:40 → [20] min. → 4:00

3:40 → [ ] min. → 4:10

3:40 → [ ] min. → 4:20

3:40 → [ ] min. → 4:30

Write a fraction to complete each equation.
Convert the fraction to a mixed number or whole number if possible.

$4 \times \dfrac{3}{5} =$ [ ] = [ ] $16 \times \dfrac{1}{4} =$ [ ] = [ ]

$30 \times \dfrac{1}{8} =$ [ ] = [ ] $10 \times \dfrac{2}{3} =$ [ ] = [ ]

Lesson Activities 👥

A

Area

The amount of space a shape covers

Area: ☐ sq. cm

Area of a Rectangle

length × width

Area: ☐ sq. cm

☐ sq. cm

☐ sq. cm

☐ sq. cm

B

Player 1

Area Capture

Player 2

Strikes: ● ● ●

Strikes: ● ● ●

Practice

Find the area of each shape.

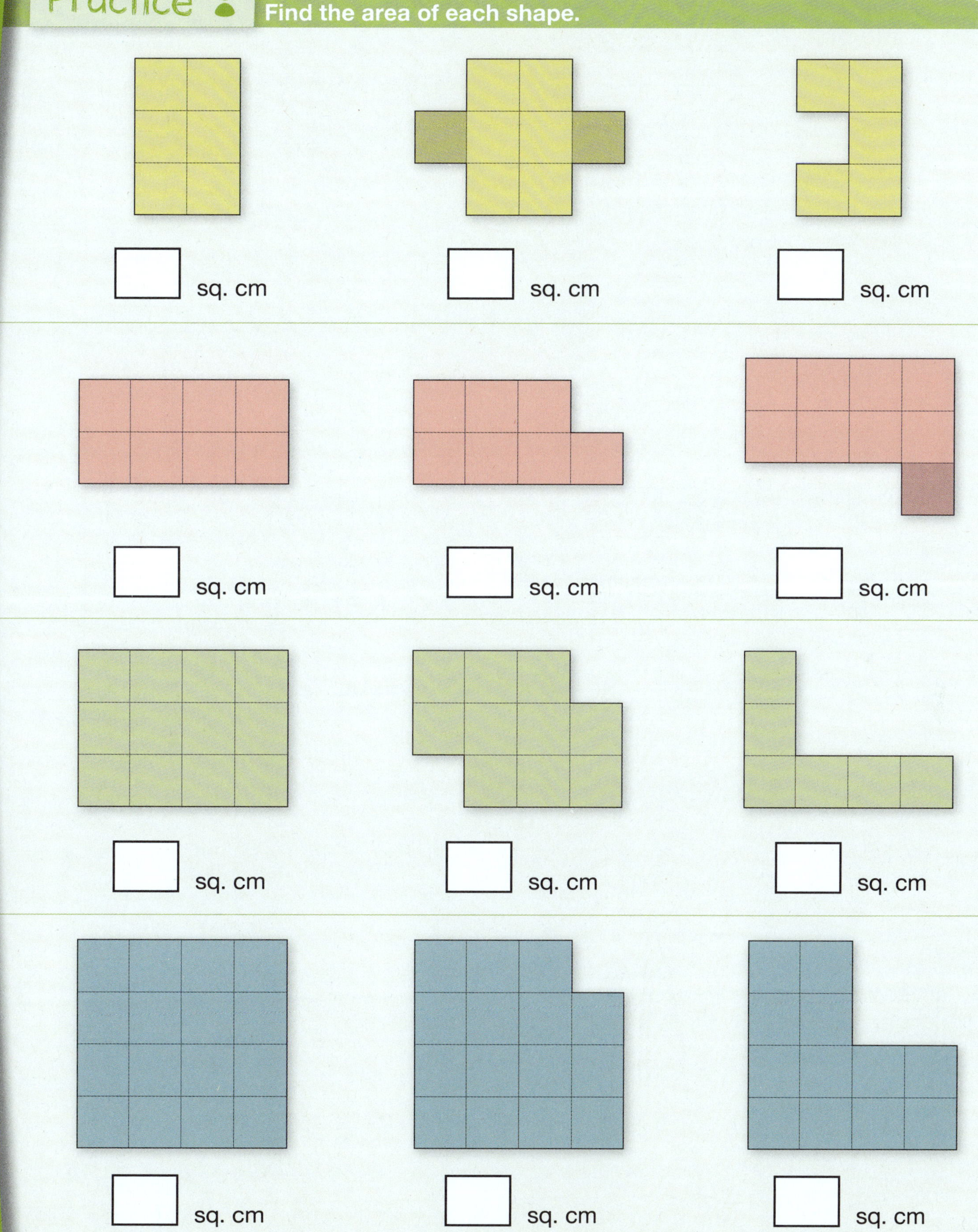

Review 

Complete the boxes to find the product.

	50	5

4 × 55 = [ ]

8 × 33 = [ ]

4 × 44 = [ ]

7 × 77 = [ ]

Complete. All times are p.m.

5:15 → 60 min. → 6:15

5:30 → [ ] min. → 6:15

5:40 → [ ] min. → 6:15

5:55 → [ ] min. → 6:15

Round to the underlined digit.

3,824 ≈ [ ]

7,630 ≈ [ ]

147,899 ≈ [ ]

385,401 ≈ [ ]

Complete with <, >, or =.

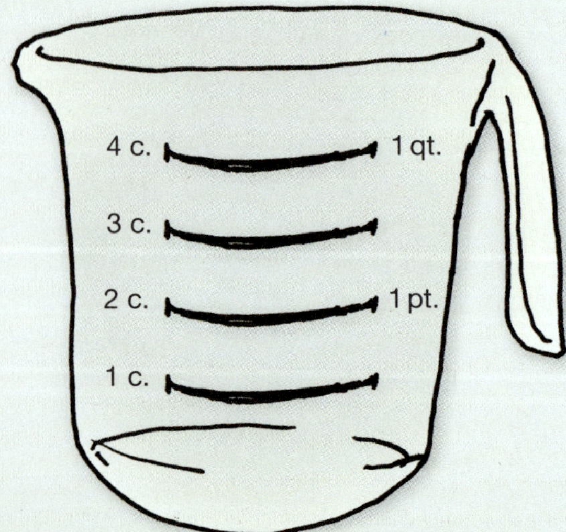

1 c. ◯ 1 pt.   1 pt. ◯ 1 qt.

2 c. ◯ 1 pt.   2 pt. ◯ 1 qt.

3 c. ◯ 2 pt.   ★ 3 pt. ◯ 2 qt.

4 c. ◯ 2 pt.   ★ 4 pt. ◯ 2 qt.

Lesson Activities 👥

A

Perimeter Units	Area Units
inches (in.)	square inches (sq. in.)
feet (ft.)	square feet (sq. ft.)
yards (yd.)	square yards (sq. yd.)
miles (mi.)	square miles (sq. mi.)
centimeters (cm)	square centimeters (sq. cm)
meters (m)	square meters (sq. m)
kilometers (km)	square kilometers (sq. km)

B

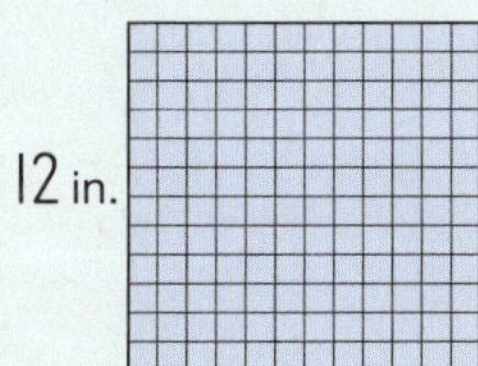

1 sq. ft. = ☐ sq. in.

C

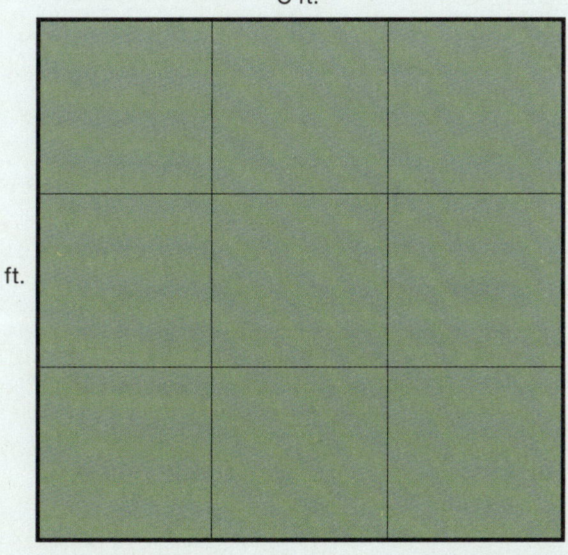

1 sq. yd. = ☐ sq. ft.

1 sq. m = ☐ sq. cm

Practice

Use the paper square foot you made in the lesson to measure the approximate area of each item.

Item	Approximate Area (Square Feet)
Television or computer screen	
Refrigerator door	
Kitchen or dining room table	
Small rug	

Find the area of each object. Include the correct units.

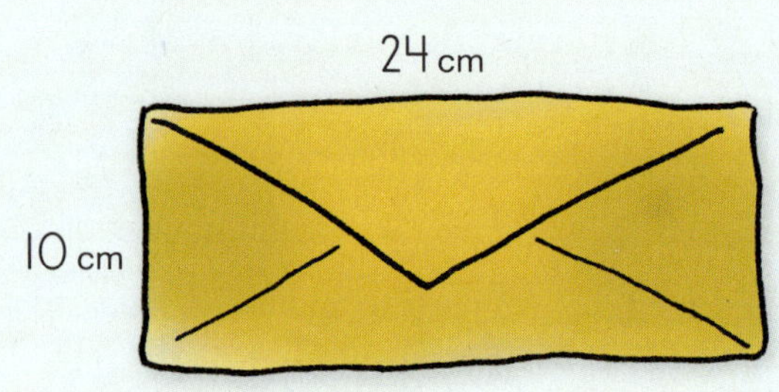

Area:

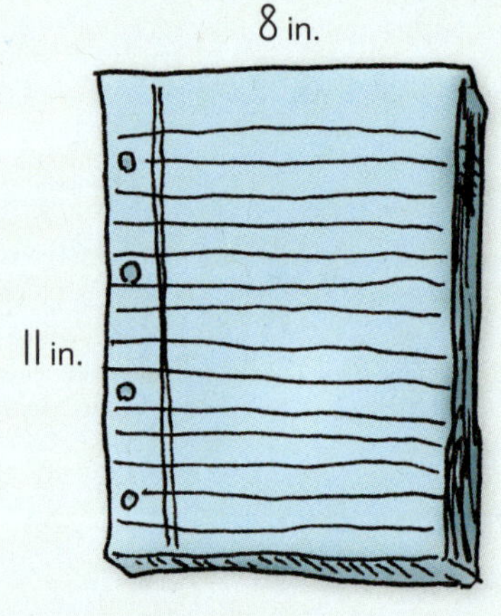

Area:

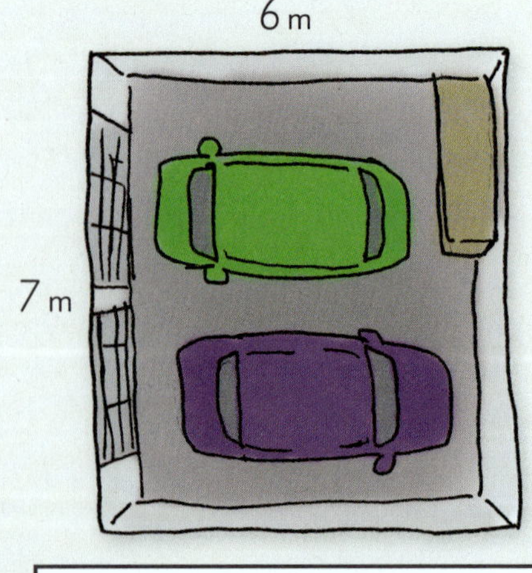

Area:

Area:

Review

Label the mixed numbers on the number line.

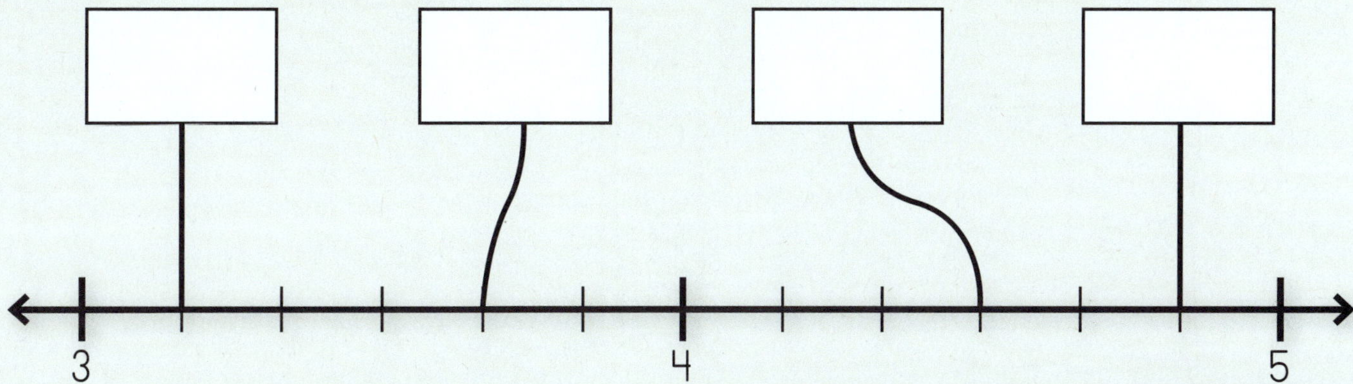

Complete.

$(4 \times 7) + 3 =$ ____

$(6 \times 5) + 4 =$ ____

$(9 \times 3) + 1 =$ ____

$(6 \times 7) + 3 =$ ____

$(8 \times 9) + 2 =$ ____

Complete.

$36 \div 12 =$ ____ $12 \div 12 =$ ____

$60 \div 12 =$ ____ $72 \div 12 =$ ____

$24 \div 12 =$ ____ $96 \div 12 =$ ____

$108 \div 12 =$ ____ $48 \div 12 =$ ____

$84 \div 12 =$ ____ $120 \div 12 =$ ____

Solve. Write the equations you use.

The Fresh Loaf Bakery earned $17,864 in October. It earned $25,041 in November. How much more did it earn in November than October?

The Fresh Loaf Bakery makes 300 loaves of bread each day. How many loaves does it make each week?

Lesson Activities

Practice

Find the area of the shaded part of each shape.

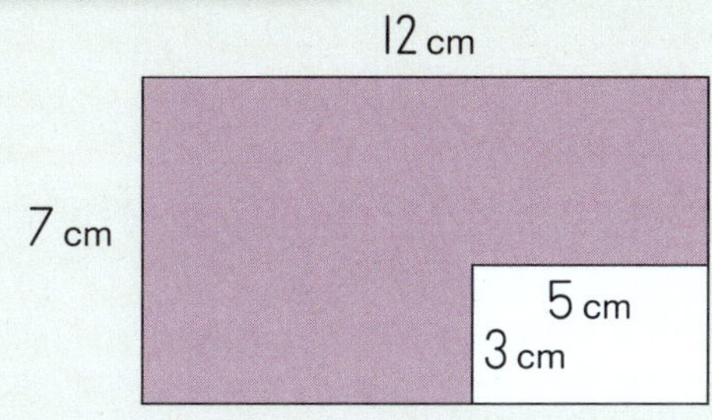

Area: ☐ sq. cm

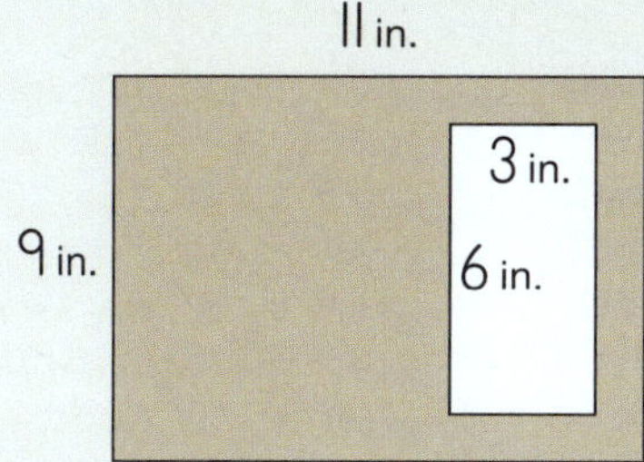

Area: ☐ sq. in.

Match each shape with the equation that tells its area.
Then, complete the equation. All measurements are in meters.

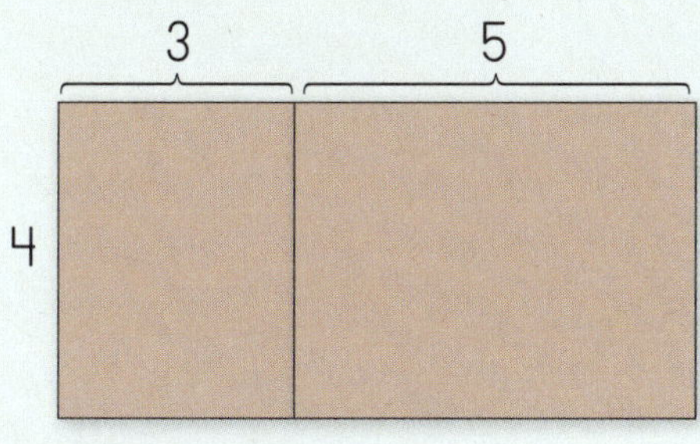

$(4 \times 5) + (2 \times 2) =$ ☐

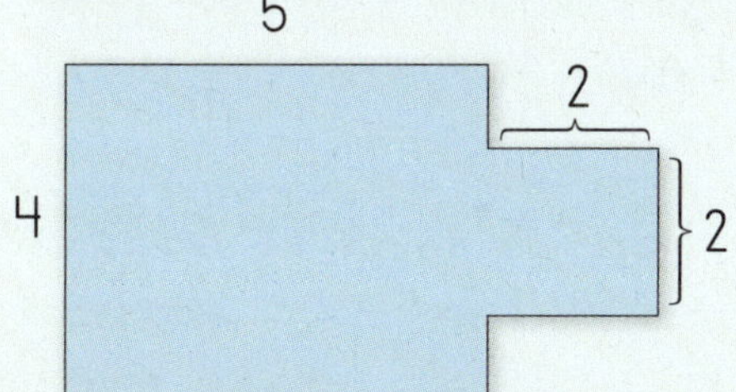

$(4 \times 4) + (2 \times 2) =$ ☐

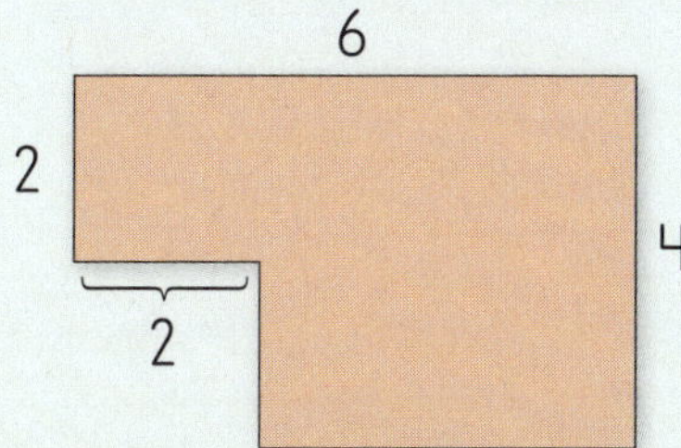

$4 \times (3 + 5) =$ ☐

$(6 \times 5) - (2 \times 2) =$ ☐

Review — Complete.

$44 \div 11 =$ ☐ $66 \div 11 =$ ☐ $33 \div 11 =$ ☐

$77 \div 11 =$ ☐ $88 \div 11 =$ ☐ $110 \div 11 =$ ☐

$55 \div 11 =$ ☐ $22 \div 11 =$ ☐ $99 \div 11 =$ ☐

Find the weight of each item. Include the correct unit.

Complete.

$40 \times 5 =$ ☐

$400 \times 5 =$ ☐

$4,000 \times 5 =$ ☐

$60 \times 8 =$ ☐

$600 \times 8 =$ ☐

$6,000 \times 8 =$ ☐

Solve. Write the equations you use.

Each batch of brownies requires $\frac{3}{4}$ cup of sugar.
If you make 3 batches,
how much sugar do you need?

Daniel runs $\frac{4}{10}$ of a kilometer.
Miri runs 5 times as far as Daniel.
How far does Miri run?

Lesson Activities

FABRIC STORE HELP DESK

A

The striped fabric is 4 ft. wide. I need 36 sq. ft. to make a shower curtain. How long a piece should I buy?

B

I'd like to buy this fabric to make curtains. Each square yard costs $7. How much does the fabric cost?

I'd like to cut this fabric into 4 equal pieces to make pillows. What will be the area of each piece?

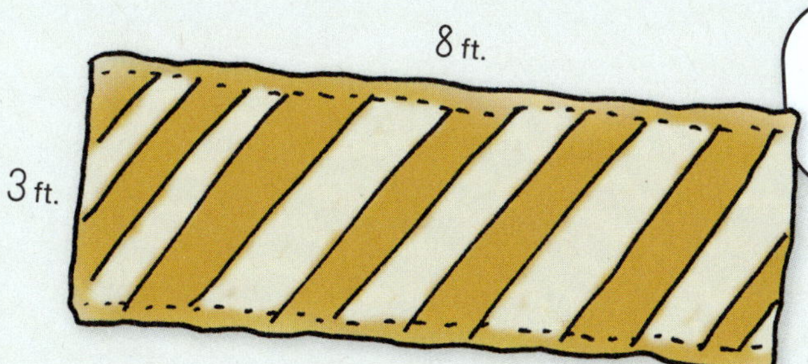

I had a piece of fabric that was 6 ft. by 8 ft. Then, I cut off a piece of fabric that was 2 ft. by 6 ft. How many square feet of fabric do I have left?

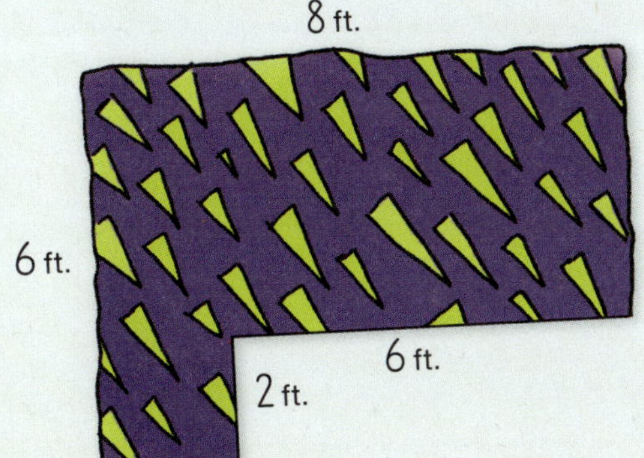

Practice

Find the length of the missing sides.

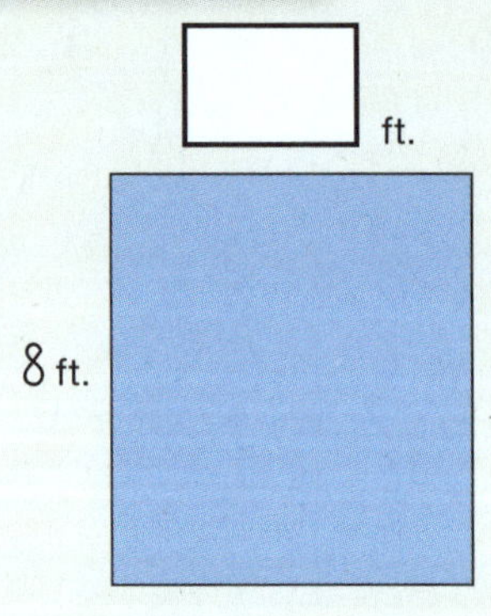
ft.

8 ft.

Area: 56 sq. ft.

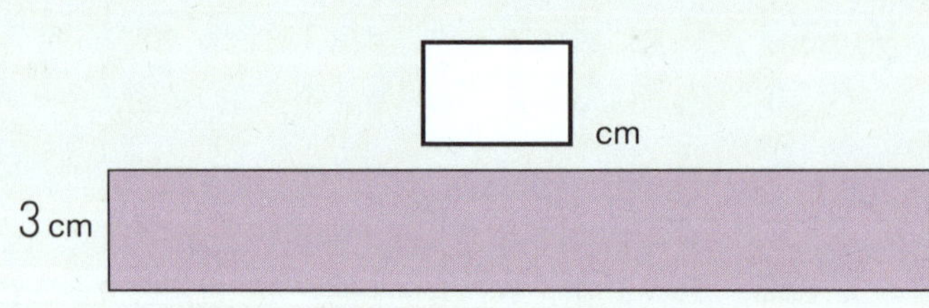
cm

3 cm

Area: 60 sq. cm

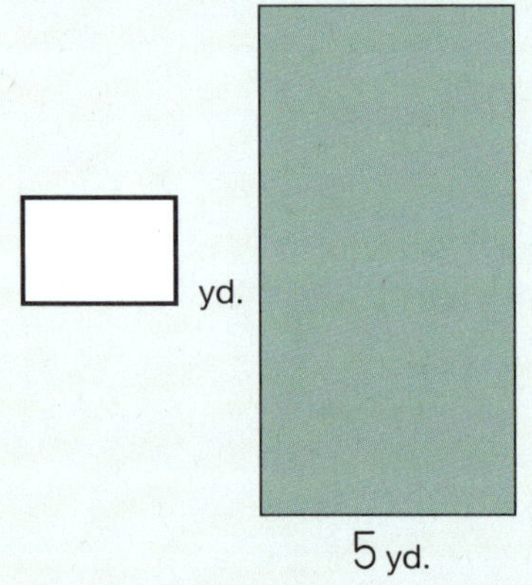
yd.

5 yd.

Area: 50 sq. yd

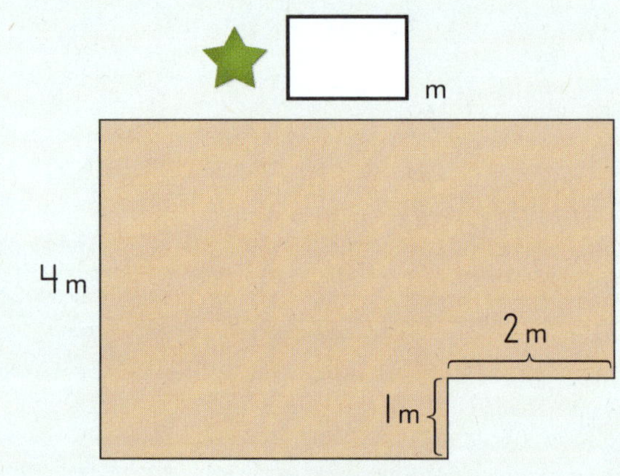
m

4 m

2 m

1 m

Area: 22 sq. m

Solve. Write the equations you use.

Owen finds an old sheet 8 ft. long and 5 ft. wide. He cuts the sheet into 4 equal pieces to make crafts. What is the area of each piece?

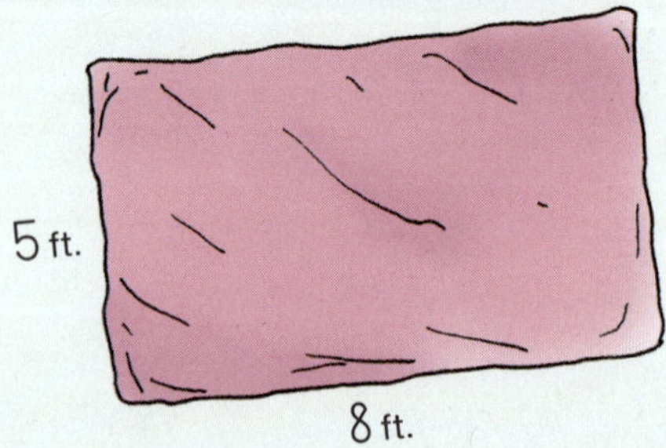

5 ft.

8 ft.

Amelia tapes together 6 sheets of paper to make a banner. Each piece of paper is 8 in. wide and 10 in. long. What is the area of the banner?

Review  Complete the chart.

Words	Standard Form
thirty thousand	
two hundred thousand	
nine thousand six	
fifty thousand four hundred	
four hundred thousand sixty	

Complete.

$360 \div 9 =$ ☐ $\qquad$ $4{,}800 \div 6 =$ ☐

$560 \div 8 =$ ☐ $\qquad$ $3{,}200 \div 8 =$ ☐

$450 \div 5 =$ ☐ $\qquad$ $6{,}300 \div 7 =$ ☐

Write each length as a fraction or mixed number.

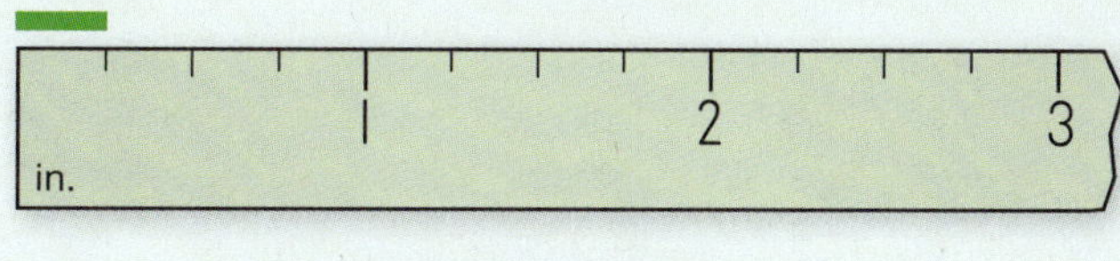

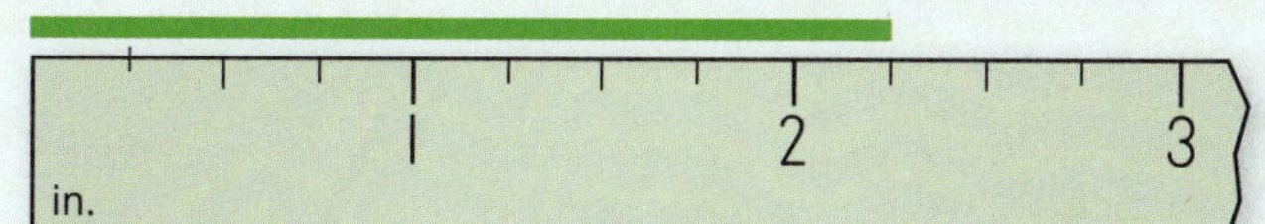

☐ in.

☐ in.

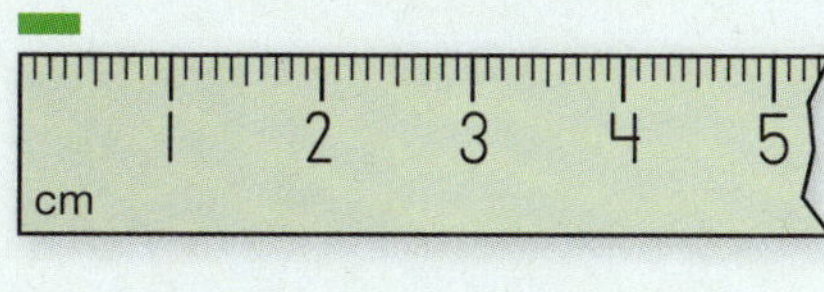

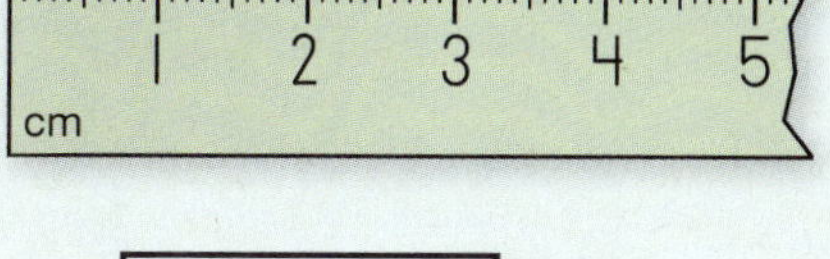

☐ cm

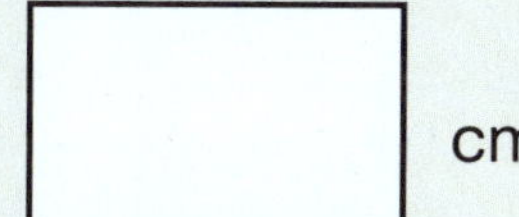

☐ cm

Unit Wrap-Up

Choose the more sensible unit for each item.

Perimeter of a sticky note

20 cm	20 m

Perimeter of a window

18 in.	18 ft.

Perimeter of a garden

14 m	14 km

Area of a sticky note

25 sq. cm	25 sq. m

Area of a window

20 sq. in.	20 sq. ft.

Area of a garden

10 sq. m	10 sq. km

Find the perimeter of each shape. Include the correct unit in your answer.

15 m

7 m

Perimeter: ____________

All sides are equal.

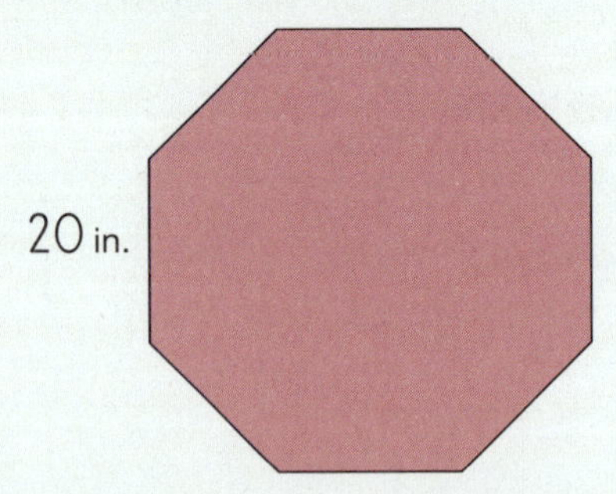

20 in.

Perimeter: ____________

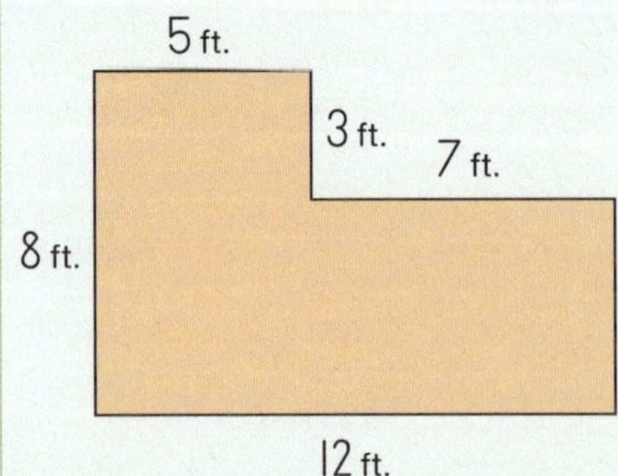

5 ft.

3 ft.

7 ft.

8 ft.

12 ft.

Perimeter: ____________

Unit Wrap-Up

**Find the area of each shape.
Include the correct unit in your answer.**

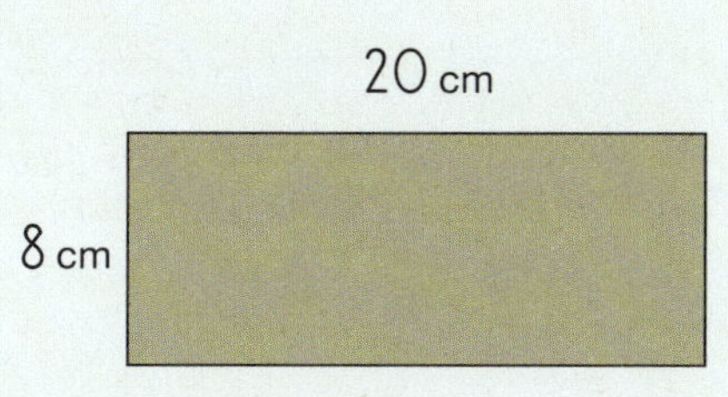

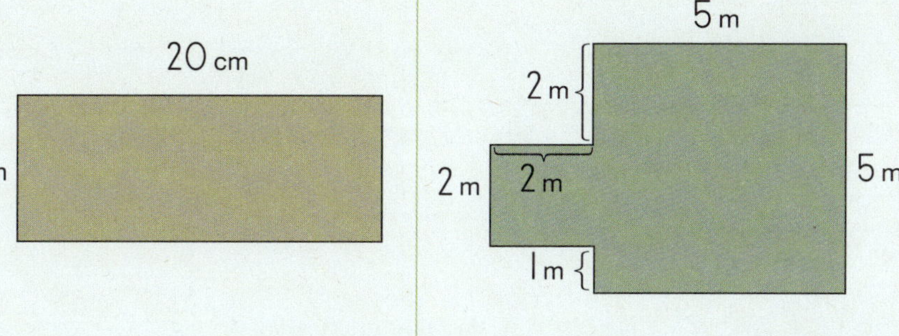

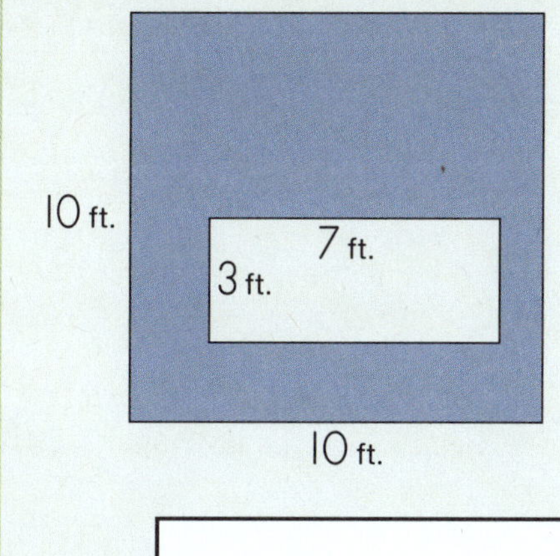

Area: ____________

Area: ____________

Area: ____________

Find the length of each missing side.

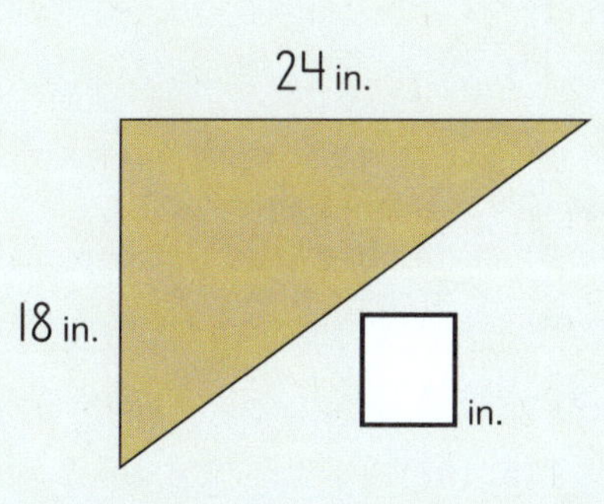

Perimeter: 72 in.

All sides are equal.

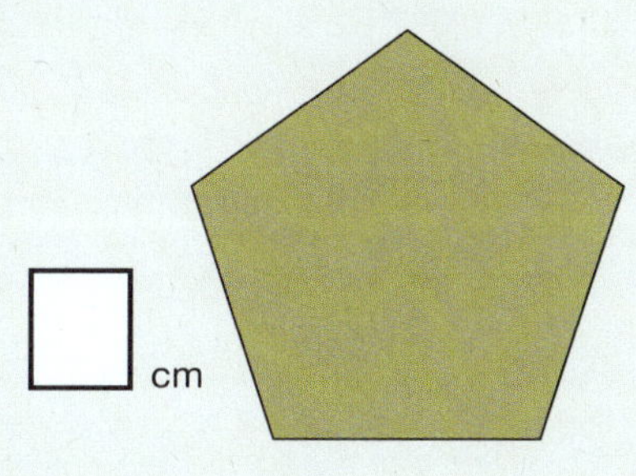

Perimeter: 40 cm

Area: 42 sq. m

Use the price list and diagram to answer the questions. Write the equations you use.

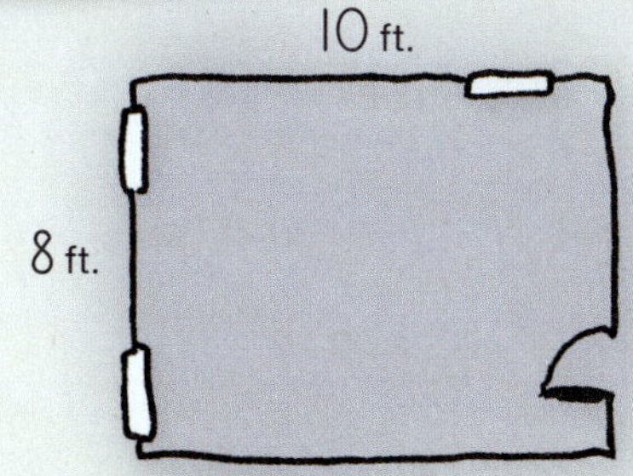

- How much will it cost to carpet the room?

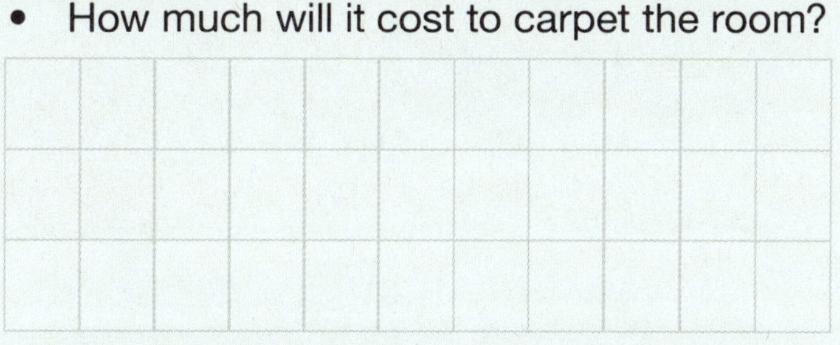

- How much will it cost to put ceiling trim around the edge of the room?

Lesson Activities 

Tickets to the concert cost $21.
How much do 3 tickets cost?

```
  2 1        2 1
  2 1      × 3
+ 2 1
```

```
  4 3        4 3
+ 4 3      ×   2
```

```
  3 2        3 2
  3 2      ×   4
  3 2
+ 3 2
```


Tickets to the game cost $24.
How much do 3 tickets cost?

```
  2 4        2 4
  2 4      ×   3
+ 2 4
```

```
  1 5        1 5
  1 5      ×   4
  1 5
+ 1 5
```

```
  3 5        3 5
  3 5      ×   3
+ 3 5
```

Practice 

Complete. Use the sample problem to help.

Solve. Write the equations you use.

Tickets to the hockey game cost $16.
How much does it cost to buy 6 tickets?

Khadija is 7 years old.
Her great-grandfather is 13 times her age.
How old is her great-grandfather?

Review

Find the perimeter of each shape.
All the sides of each shape are equal.

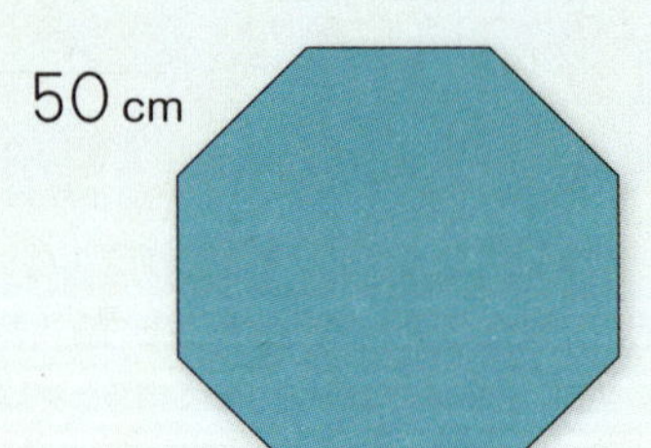
50 cm

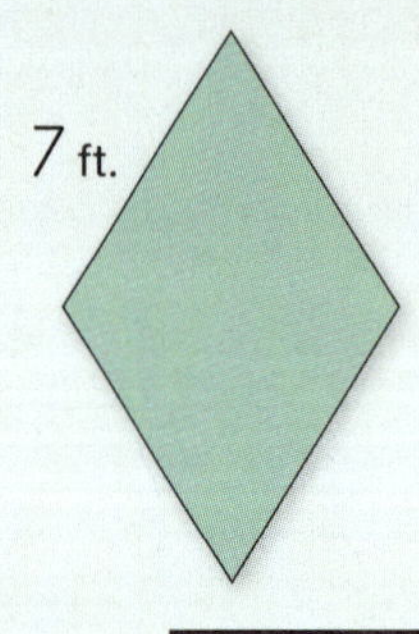
7 ft.

8 in.

Perimeter: ____________   Perimeter: ____________   Perimeter: ____________

Complete.

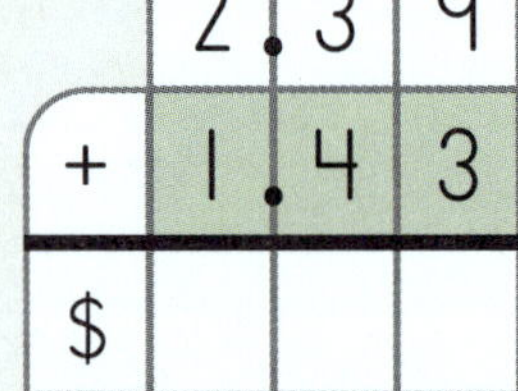

Draw a line to match.

$2\dfrac{3}{4}$ in.

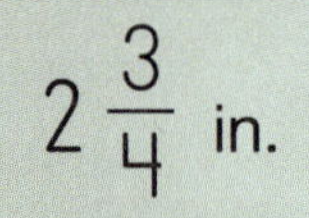

$3\dfrac{5}{10}$ cm

$4\dfrac{1}{10}$ cm

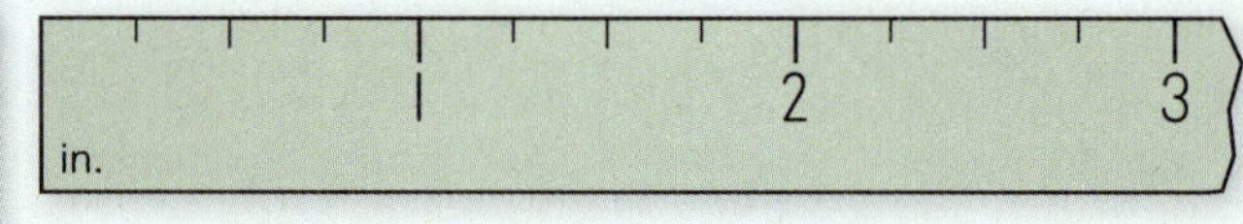

Complete.

$11 \times \boxed{} = 77$ $11 \times \boxed{} = 99$ $11 \times \boxed{} = 110$

$12 \times \boxed{} = 24$ $12 \times \boxed{} = 48$ $12 \times \boxed{} = 72$

$12 \times \boxed{} = 60$ $12 \times \boxed{} = 96$ $12 \times \boxed{} = 84$

Lesson Activities

Box Method

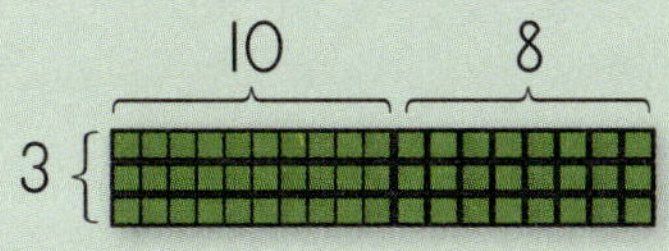

10   8

3

10   8

3

$3 \times 18 =$

30   5

7

$7 \times 35 =$

Algorithm

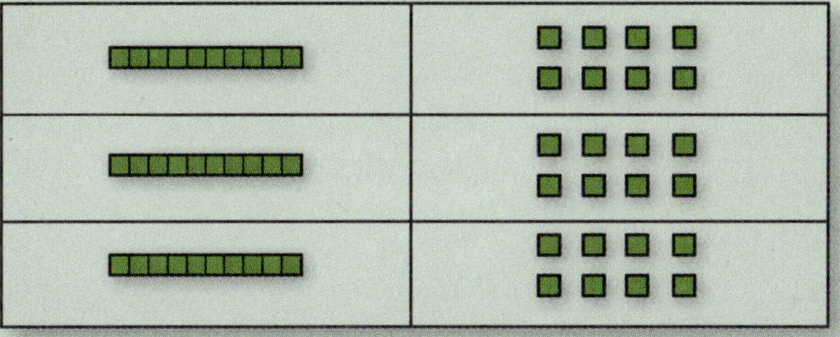

1   8
×   3

3   5
×   7

Roll and Multiply

	Player 1			

Player 1

2   8
×

3   9
×

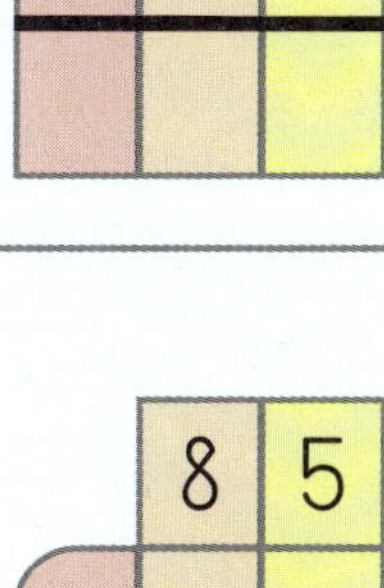
7   2
×

8   5
×

Player 2

2   8
×

3   9
×

7   2
×

8   5
×

Practice

Complete.

Example:

	4	5
×		4
		0

→

	4	5
×		4
1	8	0

	9	2
×		2

	4	8
×		5

	2	5
×		8

	8	0
×		4

	5	1
×		6

	2	4
×		9

	7	1
×		8

	6	3
×		3

	7	5
×		4

	1	9
×		7

Find the missing digits.

	3	6
×		5
1		0

	7	4
×		7
5	1	

⭐

	3	7
×		
2	5	9

⭐

		6
×		6
2	7	

Solve. Write the equations you use.

The sea lions at the zoo eat 56 kilograms of fish each week. How much fish do they eat in 4 weeks?

The elephants eat 27 bales of hay each week. How many bales of hay do they eat in 6 weeks?

Review   **Find the length of the missing sides.**

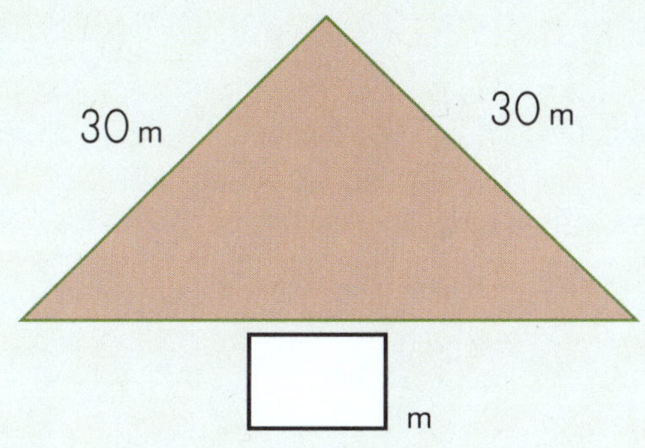

Perimeter: 102 m

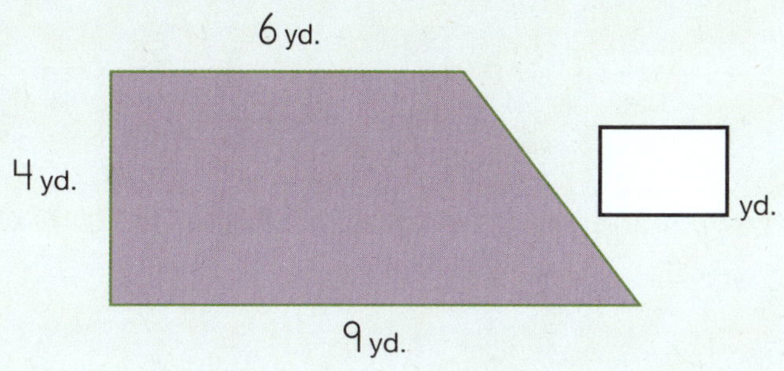

Perimeter: 24 yd.

Label the mixed numbers on the number line.

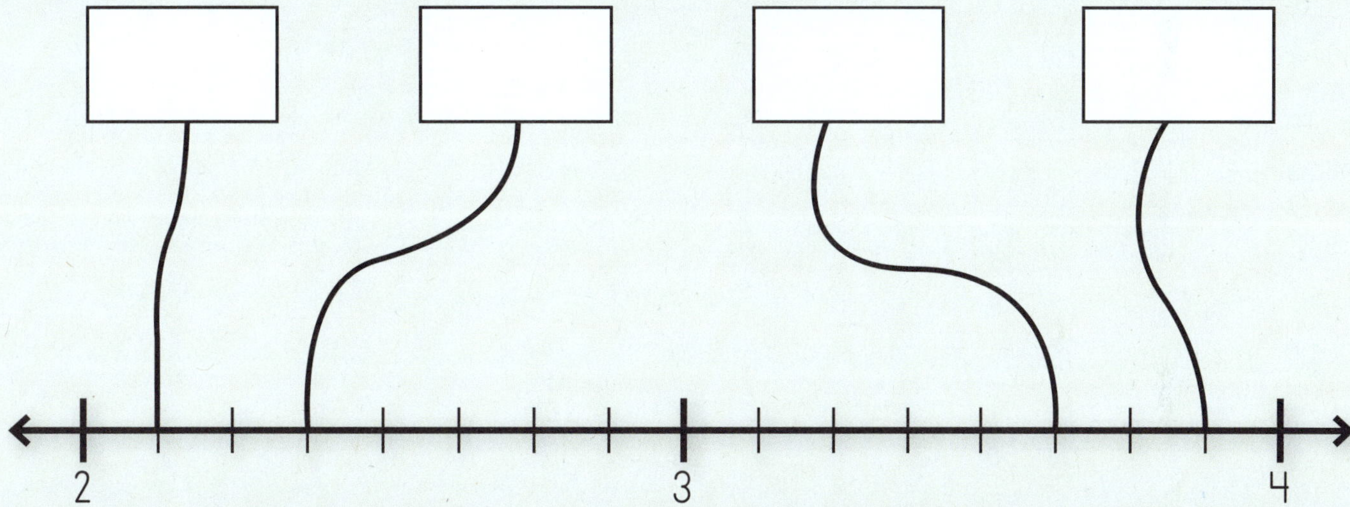

Solve. Write the equations you use.

Abram has 26 marshmallows.
He makes 6 cups of hot chocolate.
He puts 4 marshmallows in each cup.
How many marshmallows does he
have left?

Emery makes 8 cups of hot chocolate.
She puts 3 marshmallows in each cup,
and then she has 2 left.
How many marshmallows did she
start with?

Lesson Activities 👥

How much do 3 lamps cost?

	1	4	2
×			3

How much do
3 bookshelves cost?

$286

	2	8	6
×			3

How much do
2 armchairs cost?

$470

	4	7	0
×			2

How much do
8 chairs cost?

$153

	1	5	3
×			8

Snowball Fight

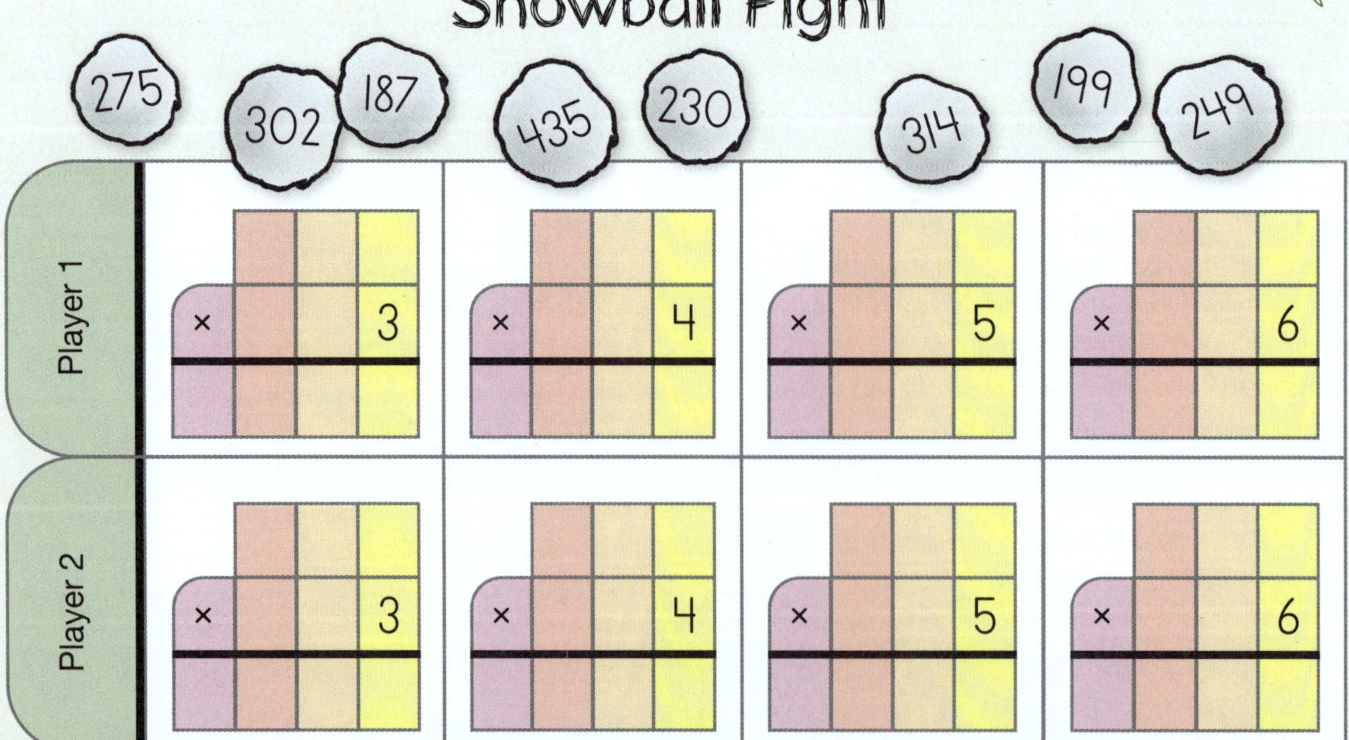

Practice

Complete.

Use the price list to solve. Write the equations you use.

How much do 4 small rugs cost?

How much do 3 large rugs cost?

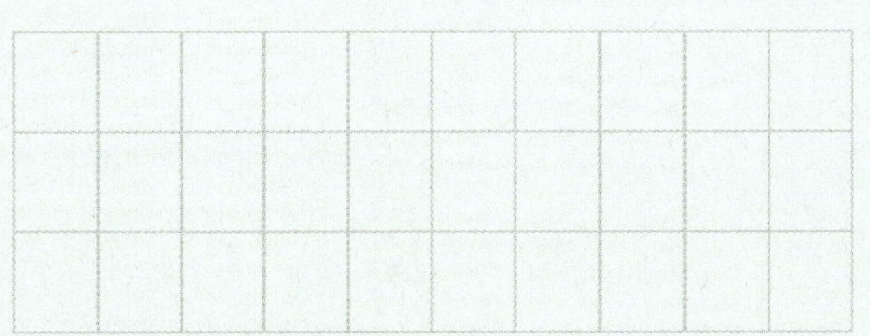

★ How much do 3 large rugs and 2 side tables cost?

Review

**Find the length of the missing sides.
All the sides of each shape are equal.**

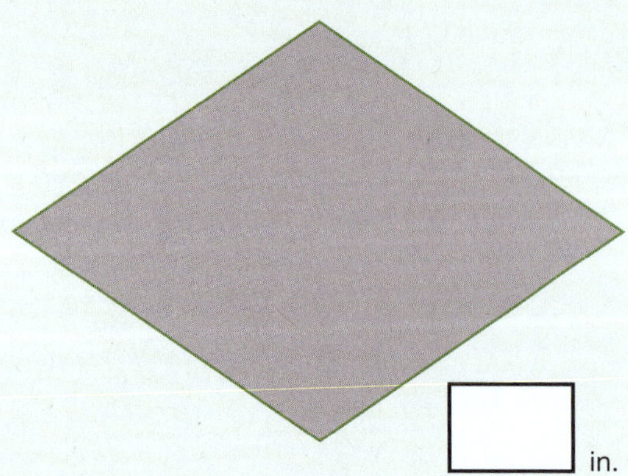

Perimeter: 120 in.

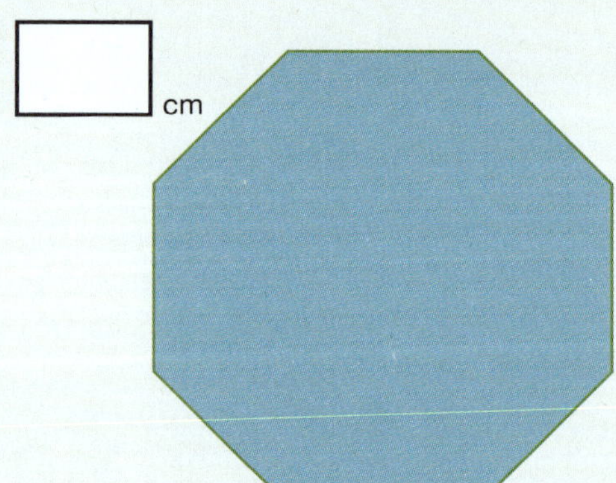

Perimeter: 400 cm

Complete.

$48 \div 6 =$ ☐

$480 \div 6 =$ ☐

$4,800 \div 6 =$ ☐

$48,000 \div 6 =$ ☐

Complete.

Round each number to the underlined place. Use the number line to help.

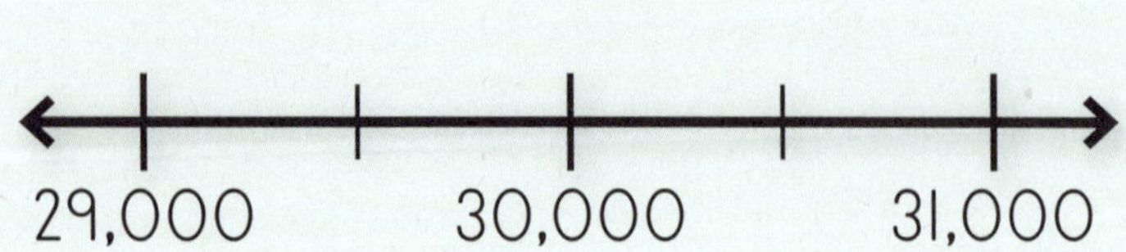

$30,572 \approx$ ☐

$30,371 \approx$ ☐

$29,865 \approx$ ☐

$29,099 \approx$ ☐

Lesson Activities

A

Estimate

| 1, | 8 | 4 | 6 |
| × | | | 3 |

Estimate

| 3, | 0 | 5 | 8 |
| × | | | 6 |

B

SPIN TO WIN!

Player 1

Player 2

2,387 2,980
1,439 1,706
2,531 1,235

2 6
4 5
7 3

Practice

Estimate the answer to each problem. Then, solve.

Estimate

$$6{,}453 \times 2$$

Estimate × ______

Estimate

$$1{,}741 \times 3$$

Estimate × ______

Estimate

$$2{,}069 \times 4$$

Estimate × ______

Estimate

$$1{,}340 \times 5$$

Estimate × ______

Estimate

$$2{,}301 \times 3$$

Estimate × ______

Estimate

$$5{,}138 \times 4$$

Estimate × ______

Solve. Write the equations you use.

The reptiles at the zoo eat 2,300 mealworms each day. How many mealworms do they eat each week?

The tigers and lions eat 1,475 pounds of meat each month. How much meat do they eat in 6 months?

Review

Match pairs whose sum is 90.

| 60 | 70 | 75 | 45 | 50 | 65 |

| 20 | 45 | 40 | 25 | 15 | 30 |

Copy the shapes.

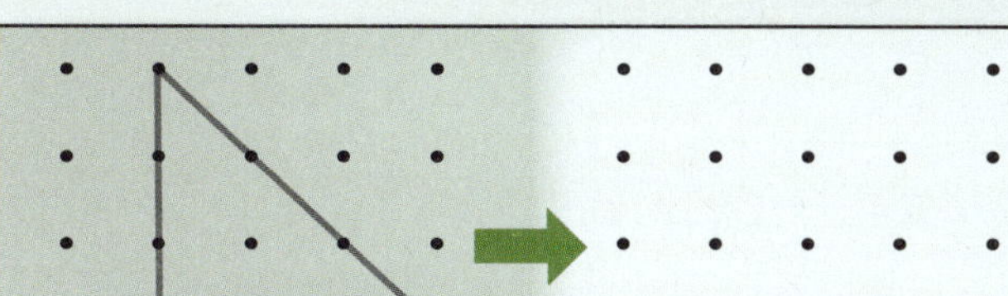

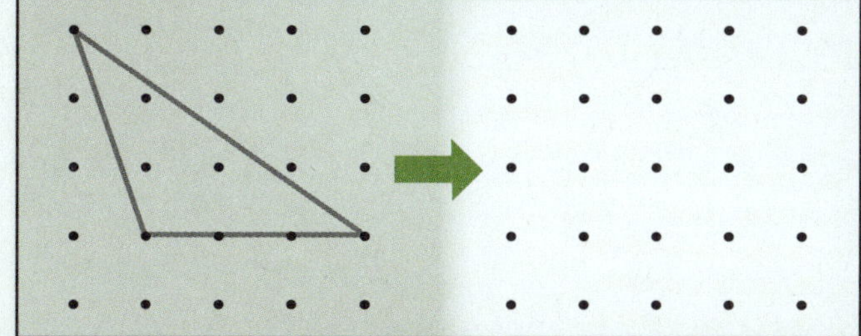

Find the perimeter and area of the shape.

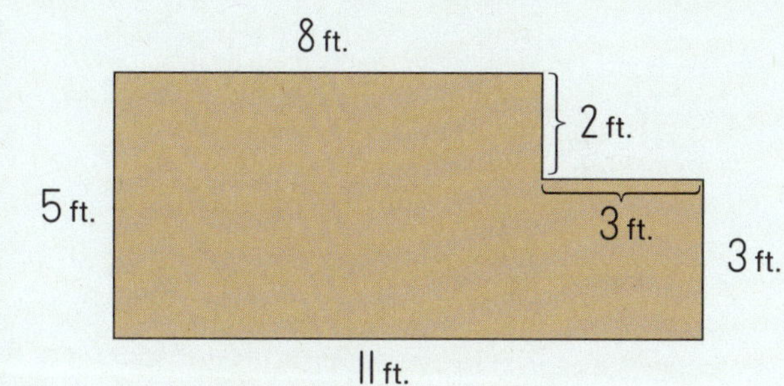

Perimeter:

Area:

Convert the mixed numbers to fractions.
Convert the fractions to mixed numbers or whole numbers.

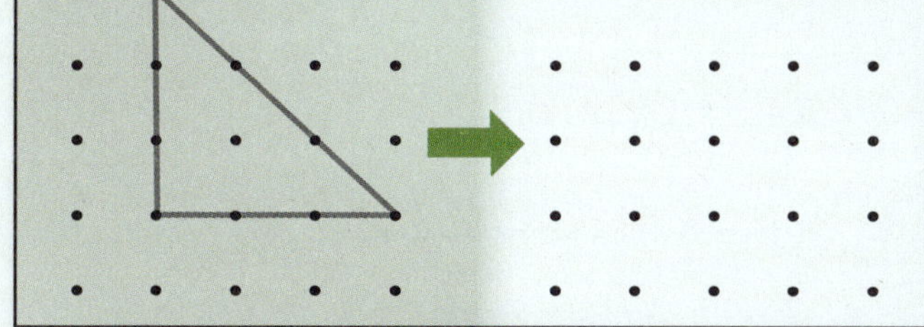

$5\dfrac{2}{3} = \dfrac{17}{3}$

$4\dfrac{7}{10} = \boxed{}$

$9\dfrac{1}{2} = \boxed{}$

$\dfrac{13}{6} = 2\dfrac{1}{6}$

$\dfrac{18}{5} = \boxed{}$

$\dfrac{32}{8} = \boxed{}$

Lesson Activities 

×	1,	5	3	2
				4

×	2,	6	3	0
				5

×	7,	2	9	4
				3

B

1,762 ft.

1,762 ft.   1,762 ft.

1,762 ft.

What is the perimeter?

×	1,	7	6	2
				4

38 cm

C

What is the area?

27 m

4 m

×	2	7
		4

38 ft.

9 ft.

Practice  Complete.

$$1,546 \times 3$$

$$9,090 \times 2$$

$$7,960 \times 4$$

$$3,333 \times 5$$

$$3,062 \times 7$$

$$2,495 \times 8$$

Use multiplication to solve. Write the equations you use.

Each side of the flag is 27 cm long. What is the perimeter of the flag?

The rose garden at the botanical garden is 9 feet wide and 137 feet long. What is its area?

Maryem helps her parents build this deck. Each square foot of decking costs $4. How much does it cost to buy enough decking to cover the whole deck?

Review

Match pairs whose sum is 180.

90	110	120	115	100	135

60	45	70	90	65	80

Copy the shapes.

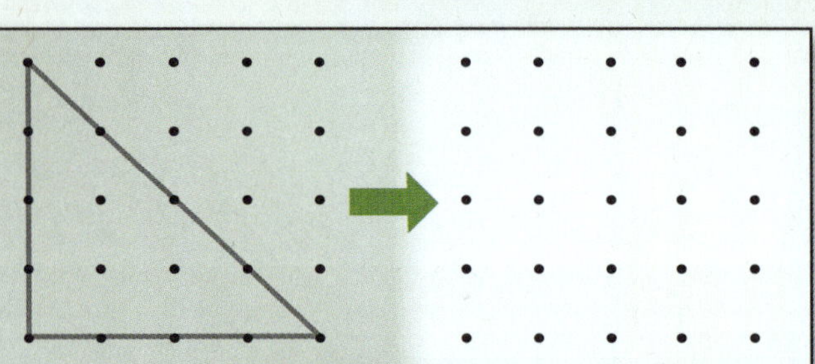

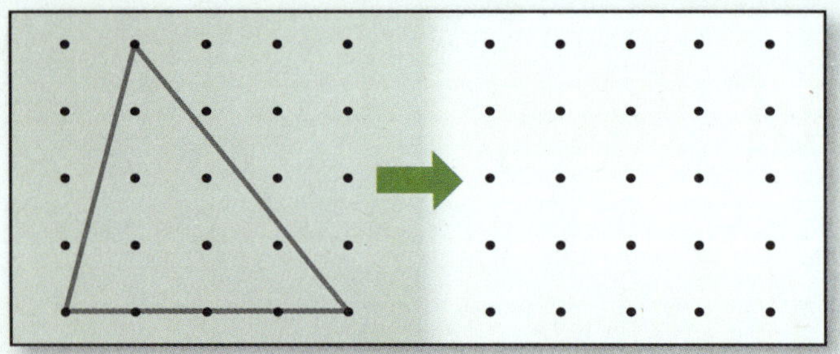

Find the shaded area.

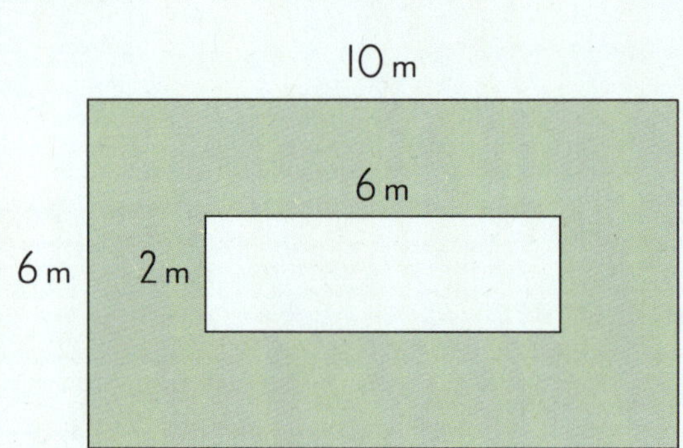

Area: __________________________

Use the words in the word bank to complete the blanks.

12, 24, 30, and 54 are _________________________ of 6.

1, 3, and 9 are _________________________ of 9.

15 is _________________________ by 1, 3, 5, and 15.

13 is a _________________________ number.

14 is a _________________________ number.

prime

composite

factors

multiples

divisible

Unit Wrap-Up 

Complete.

4	2
×	6

4	0	6
	×	5

1,	0	3	2
		×	8

7	8
×	5

3	1	2
	×	3

1,	3	7	0
		×	7

9	7
×	3

2	9	1
	×	4

1,	1	1	1
		×	9

Find the area or perimeter of each shape.

All sides are equal.

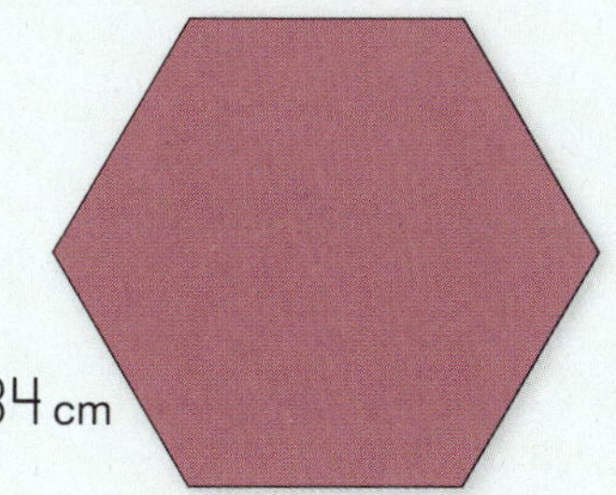

Perimeter: ☐

All sides are equal.

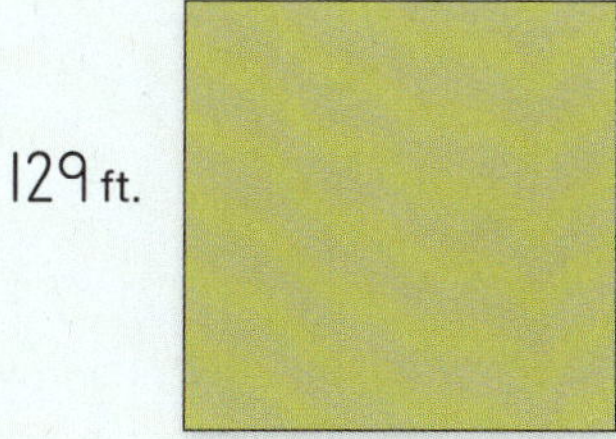

Perimeter: ☐

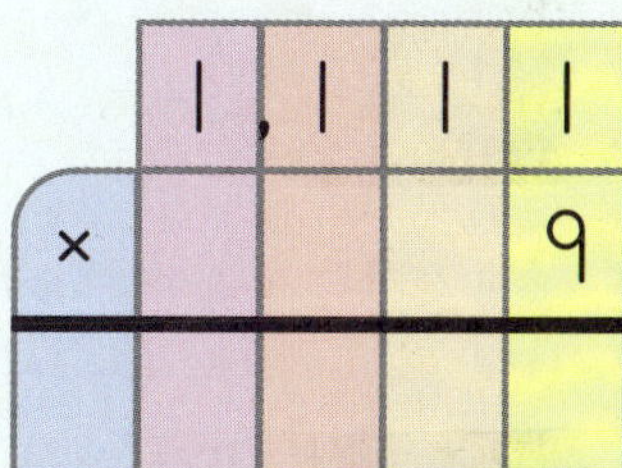

Area: ☐

Unit Wrap-Up

Use the price list to answer the questions. Write the equations you use.

Price per round-trip ticket

Greece	$880
Costa Rica	$704
South Africa	$912
India	$1,065
Australia	$2,143
Thailand	$1,539

How much do 2 tickets to Greece cost?

How much do 5 tickets to Costa Rica cost?

How much do 3 tickets to South Africa cost?

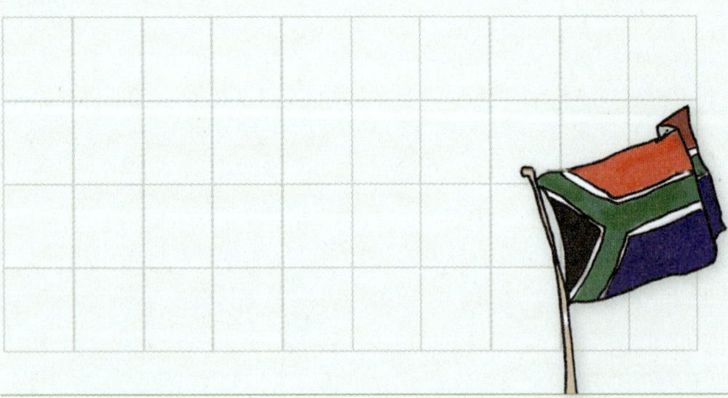

How much do 5 tickets to India cost?

How much do 6 tickets to Australia cost?

How much do 4 tickets to Thailand cost?

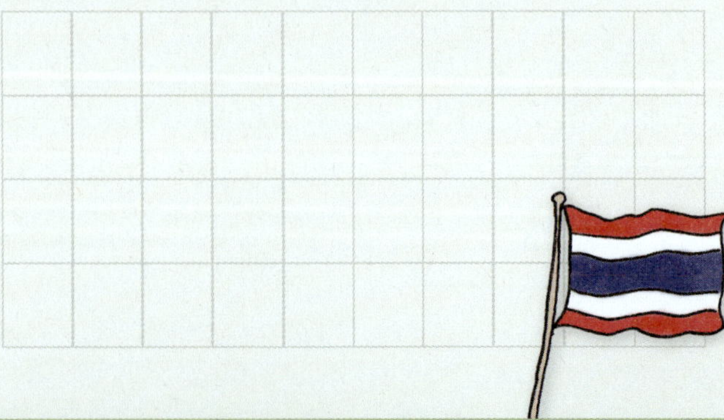

Lesson Activities

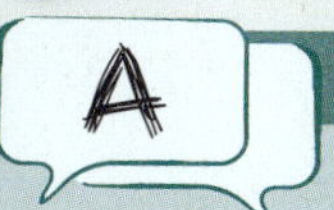

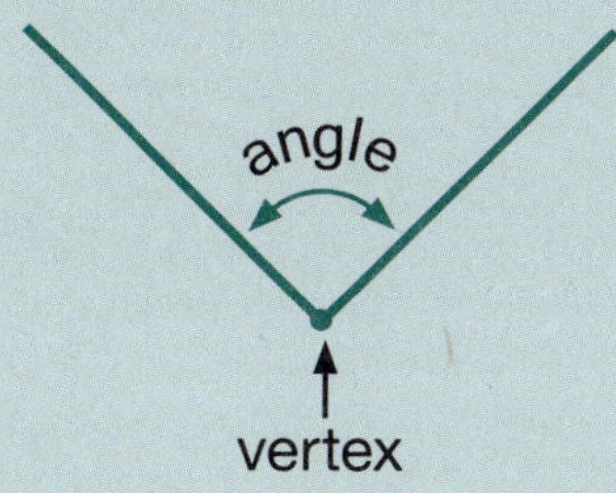

An **angle** is formed when two lines meet.

The point where the lines meet is the **vertex** of the angle.

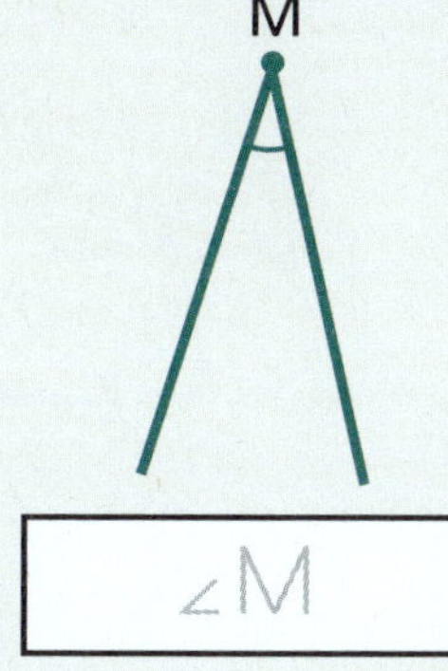

∠M

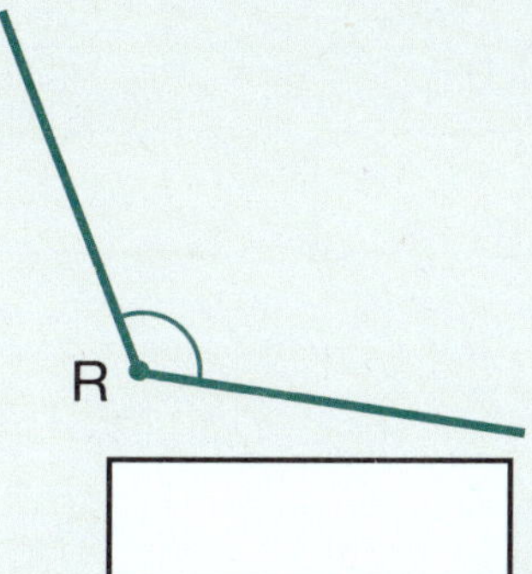

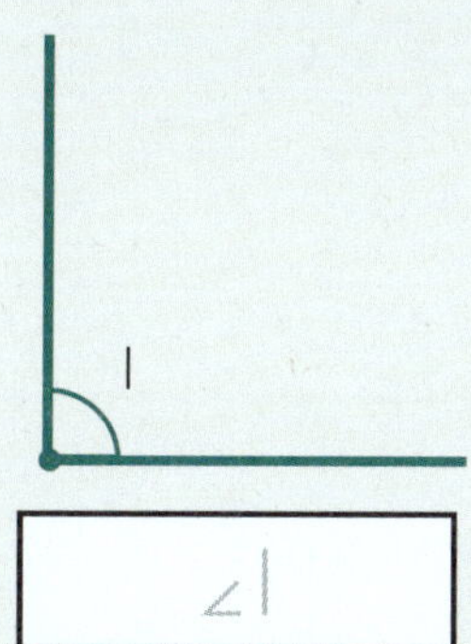

∠1

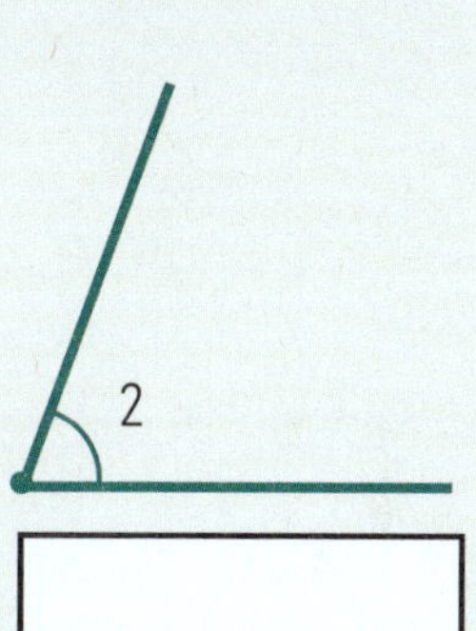

B

ANGLES IN MY NAME

Practice

Label the angles.
Then, write the angles in order from smallest to largest.

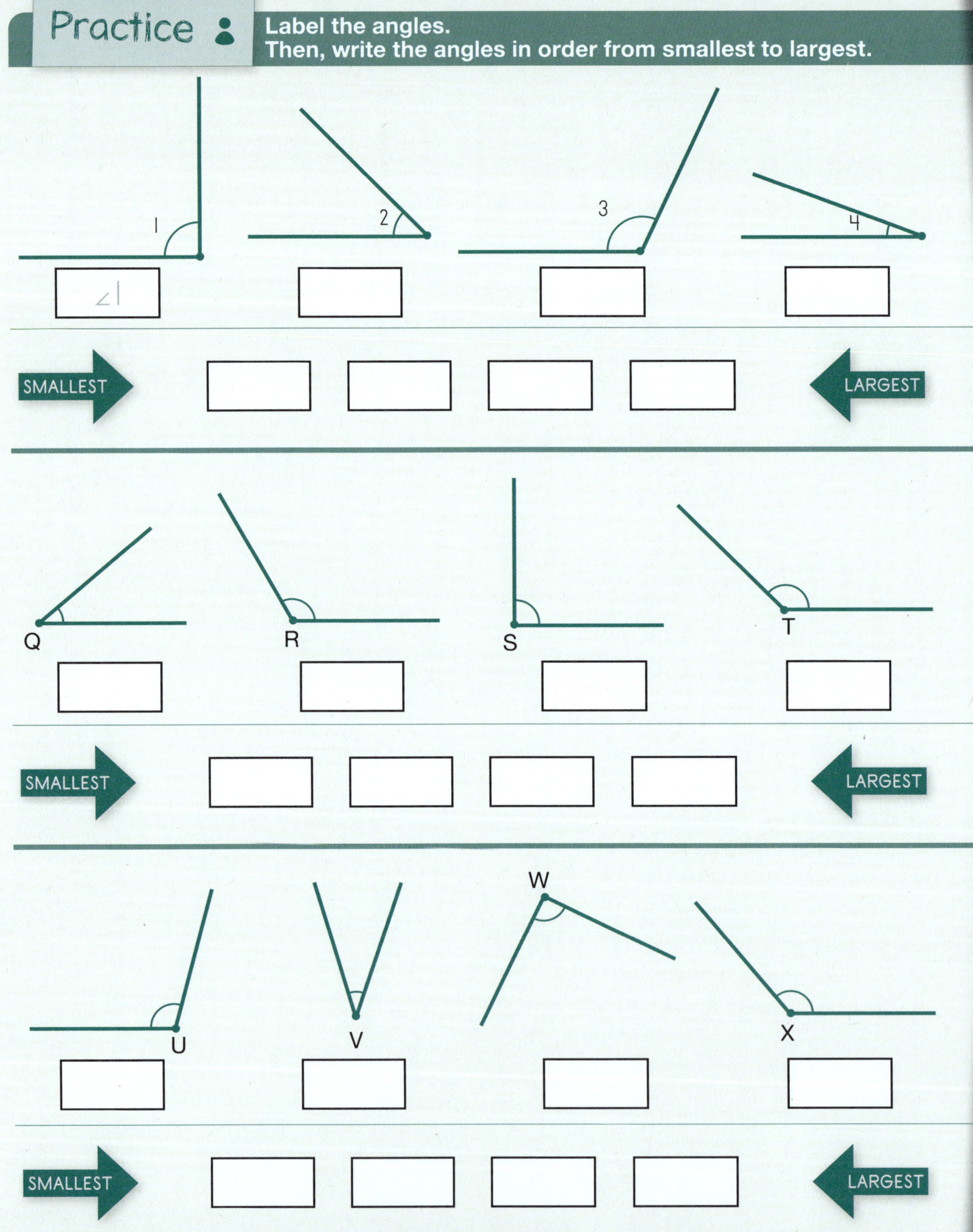

Lesson 8.1

Review 👤 Complete.

	3	,	2	9	4
×					7

	1	,	5	0	4
×					9

	2	,	1	8	5
×					6

Choose the more sensible unit for each measurement.

Height of a cup

10 cm	100 m

Weight of a cup

290 g	290 kg

Capacity of a cup

175 mL	175 L

Convert the mixed numbers to fractions.
Convert the fractions to mixed numbers or whole numbers.

$7\frac{2}{5} = \boxed{}$

$7\frac{2}{10} = \boxed{}$

$6\frac{2}{6} = \boxed{}$

$\frac{43}{6} = \boxed{}$

$\frac{43}{10} = \boxed{}$

$\frac{43}{8} = \boxed{}$

Solve. Write the equations you use.

Caleb has $10.00.
He buys a drink for $2.79
and a sandwich for $6.55.
How much money does
he have left?

Lesson Activities 👥

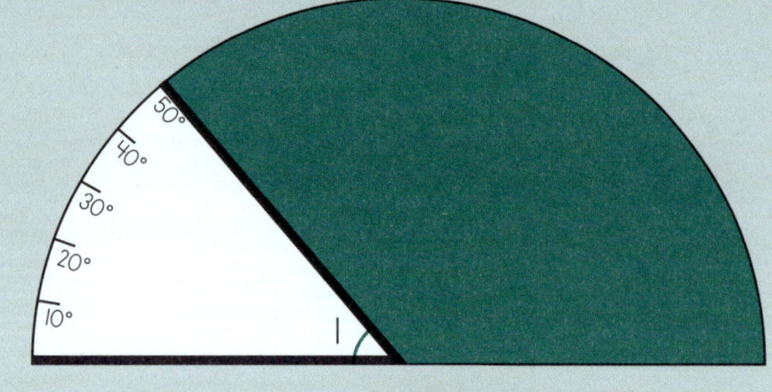

$m\angle 1 \ =\ \boxed{}\,°$

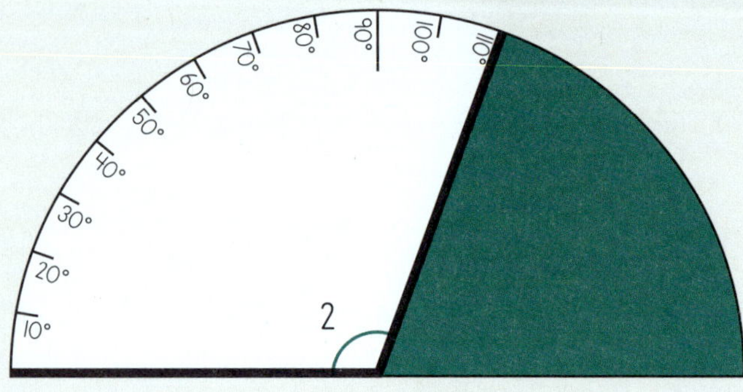

$m\angle 2\ =\ \boxed{}$

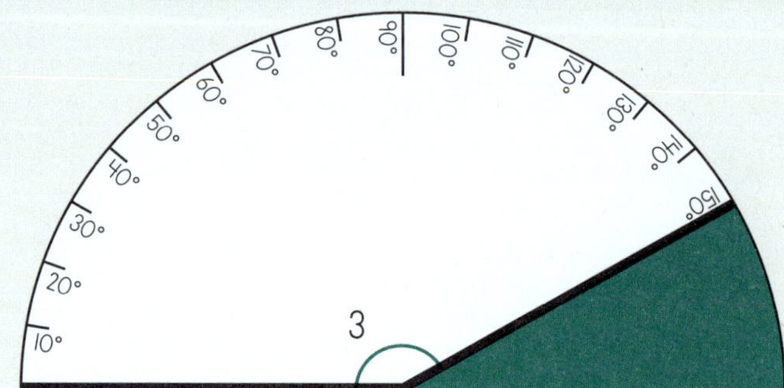

$m\angle 3\ =\ \boxed{}$

Angle	∠A	∠B	∠C	∠D	∠E	∠F
Estimate						

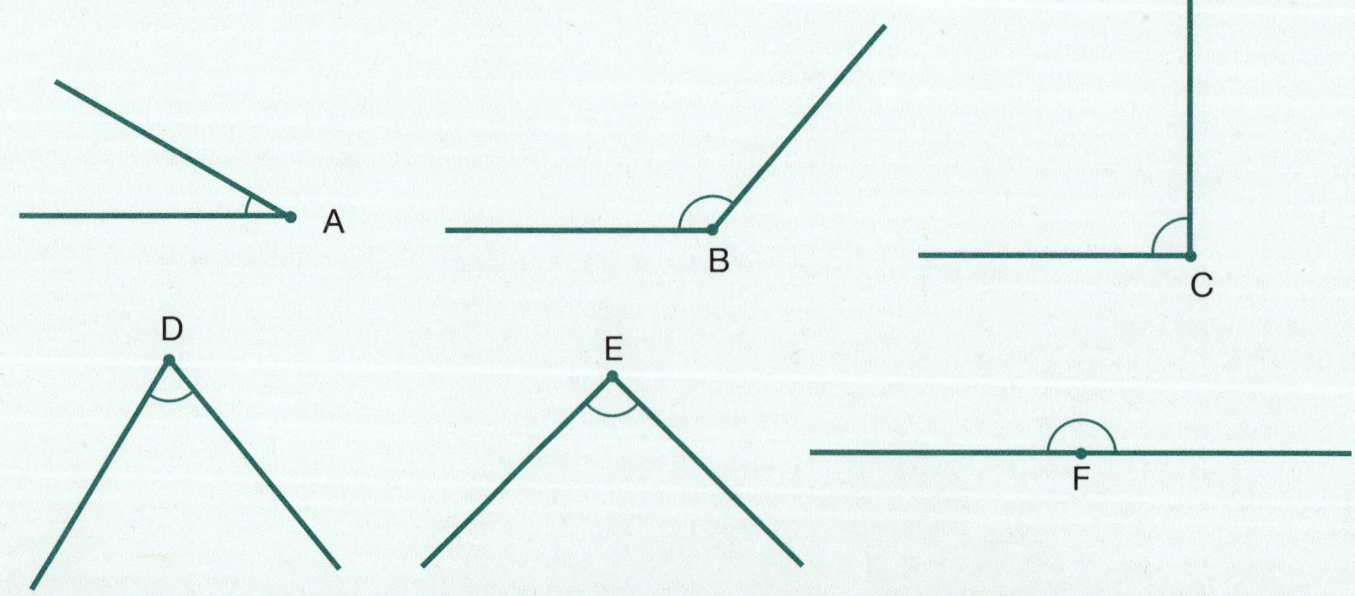

Practice

Find the measure of each angle.

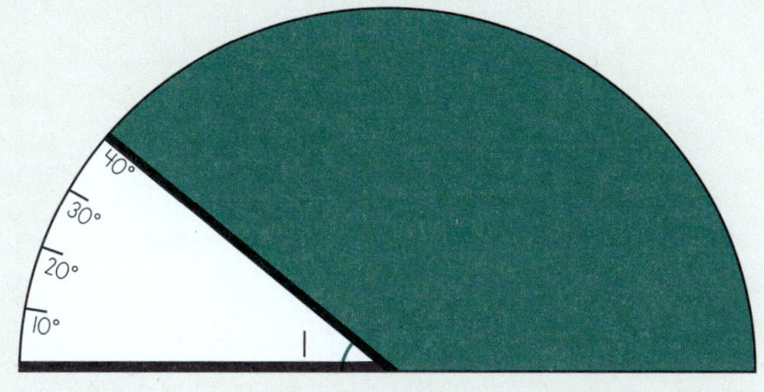

m∠1 = ☐

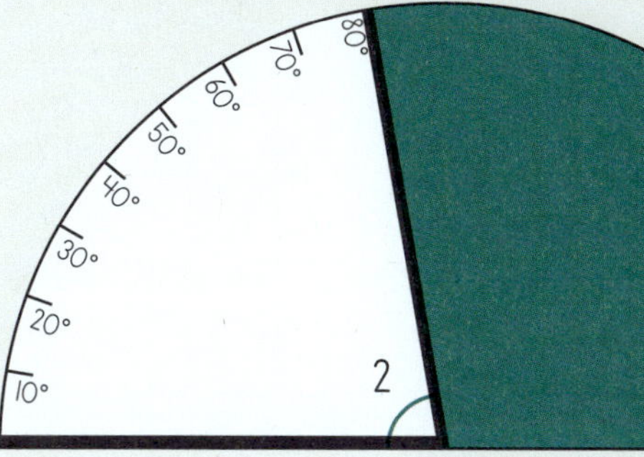

m∠2 = ☐

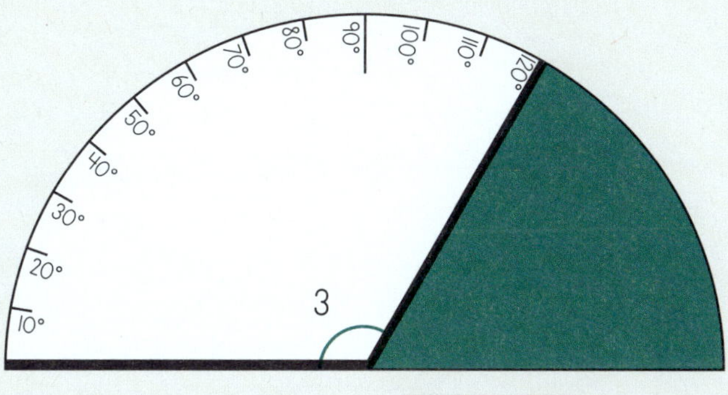

m∠3 = ☐

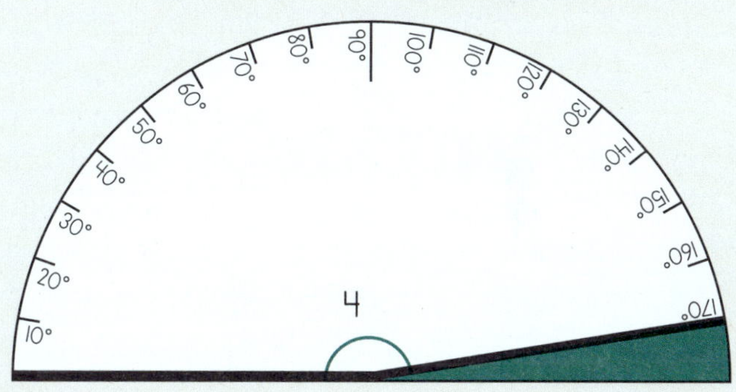

m∠4 = ☐

Choose the more reasonable measurement for each angle.

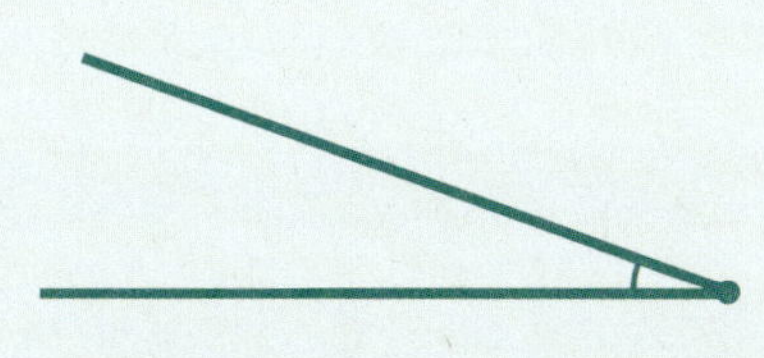

20°   120°

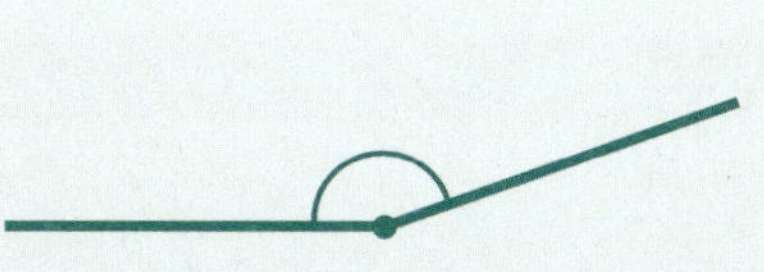

60°   160°

40°   90°

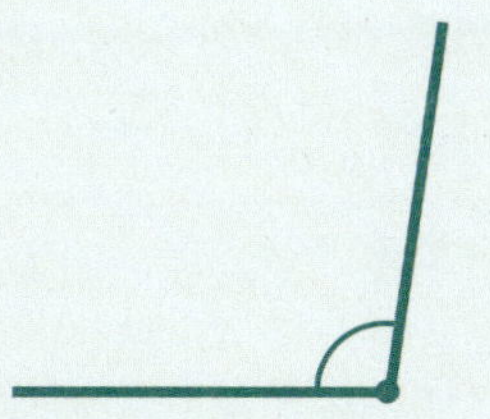

100°   80°

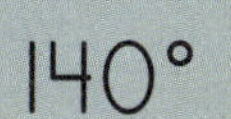

180°   140°

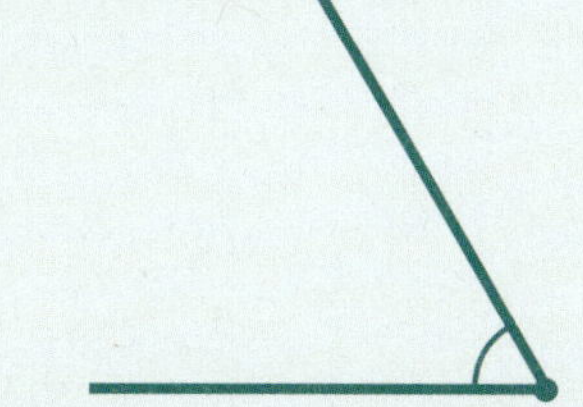

30°   60°

Review   Complete.

	2	9	6
×			4

	8	3	5
×			3

	3	0	5
×			7

	9	9	9
×			6

Complete. All times are a.m.

7:55 → 15 min. → ☐

8:40 → 40 min. → ☐

9:50 → ☐ min. → 10:10

☐ ← 35 min. ← 11:30

☐ ← 60 min. ← 11:55

Complete.

150 − 35 = ☐

275 − 50 = ☐

400 − 65 = ☐

510 − 40 = ☐

820 − 60 = ☐

900 − 150 = ☐

Solve. Write the equations you use.

Mihika uses the calendar to find there are 13 weeks until the first day of spring. How many days are there until the first day of spring?

Phoenix's karate lessons cost $28 per week. How much do 4 weeks of karate lessons cost?

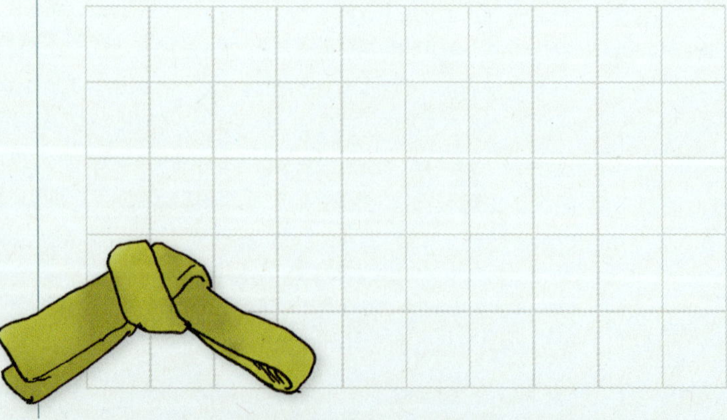

Lesson Activities

A

Right angles measure 90°.

Acute angles measure less than 90°.

Obtuse angles measure more than 90° and less than 180°.

Straight angles measure 180°.

B

Angle Four in a Row

Key

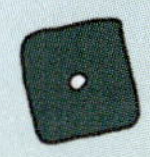 Acute 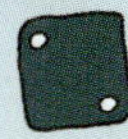 Right 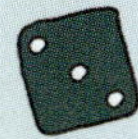 Obtuse  Straight  Wild  Remove one counter

Practice

Match.

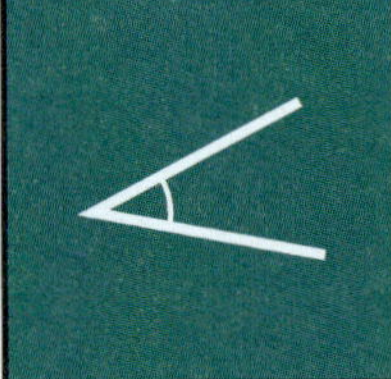

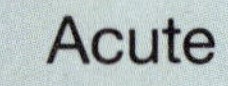
Acute

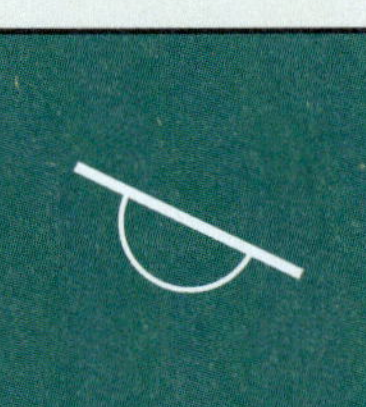

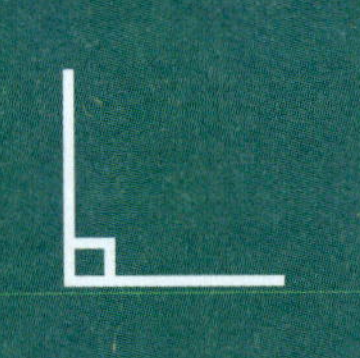

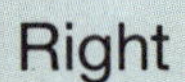
Right

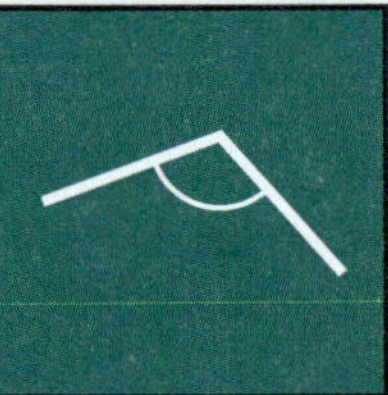

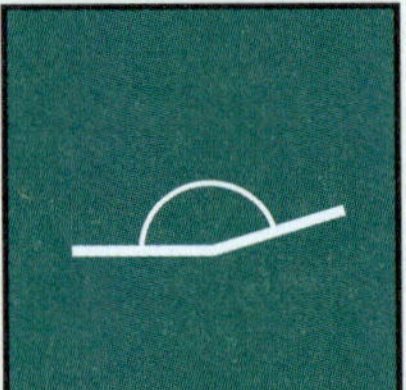

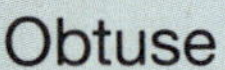
Obtuse

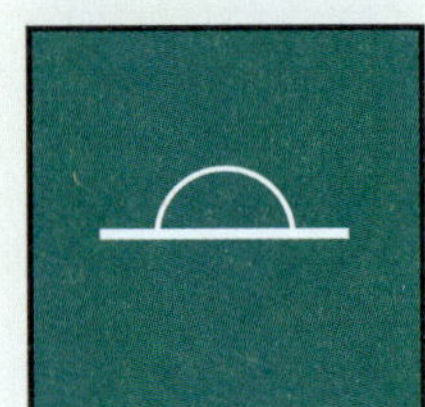

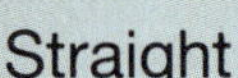
Straight

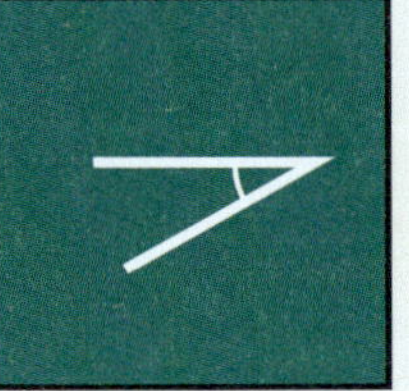

Copy the angle. Then, write whether it is acute, right, obtuse, or straight.

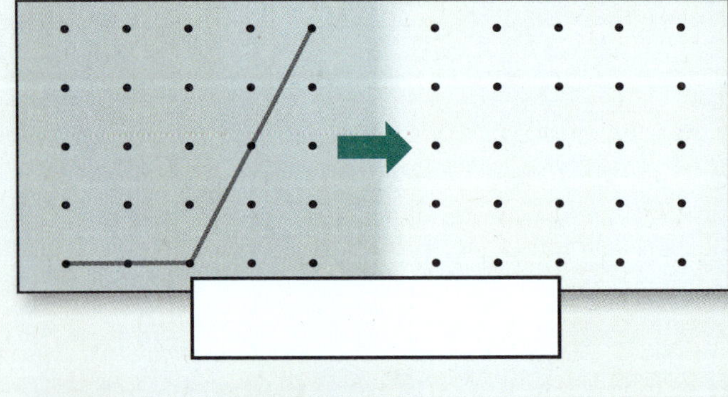

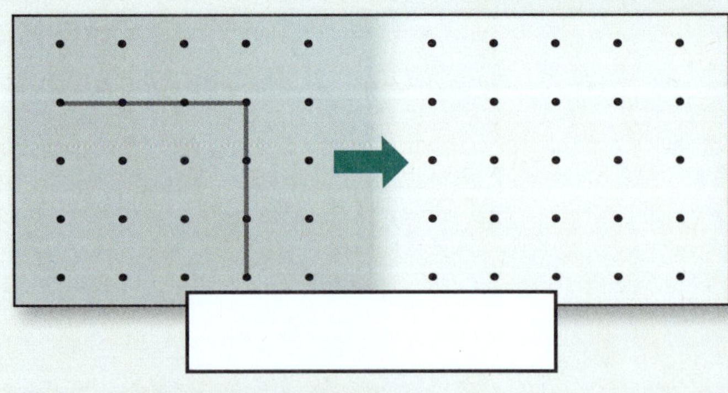

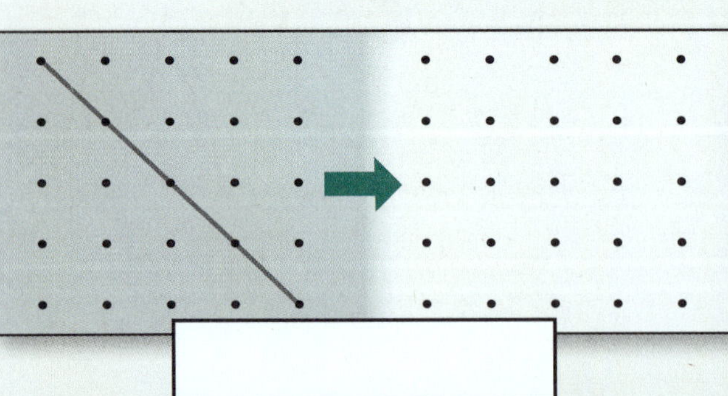

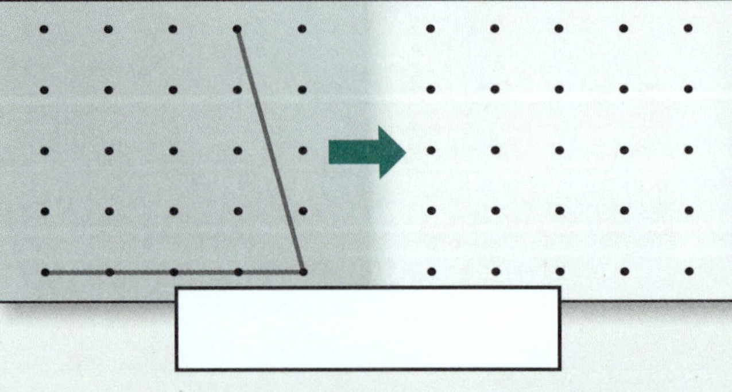

Review 👤 Complete.

<table>
<tr><td>

	7	3
×		6

</td><td>

	9	8
×		6

</td><td>

	5	5
×		9

</td><td>

	8	7
×		5

</td><td>

	6	3
×		7

</td></tr>
</table>

Complete. Convert your answer to a whole number or mixed number if possible.

$$\frac{7}{8} + \frac{4}{8} = \boxed{} = \boxed{}$$

$$\frac{15}{6} - \frac{4}{6} = \boxed{} = \boxed{}$$

$$10 \times \frac{1}{5} = \boxed{} = \boxed{}$$

$$8 \times \frac{3}{4} = \boxed{} = \boxed{}$$

Solve. Write the equations you use.

Samuel's family buys carpet for this room. Each square foot of carpet costs $4. How much does the carpet cost?

The area of this room is 96 square feet. One side of the room is 12 feet long. How long is the other side?

Lesson Activities 👥

How to Measure Angles with a Protractor

1. Line up the midpoint and vertex.
2. Line up the zero line and one side of the angle.
3. Choose the correct scale.
4. Find where the other side of the angle intersects the scale.

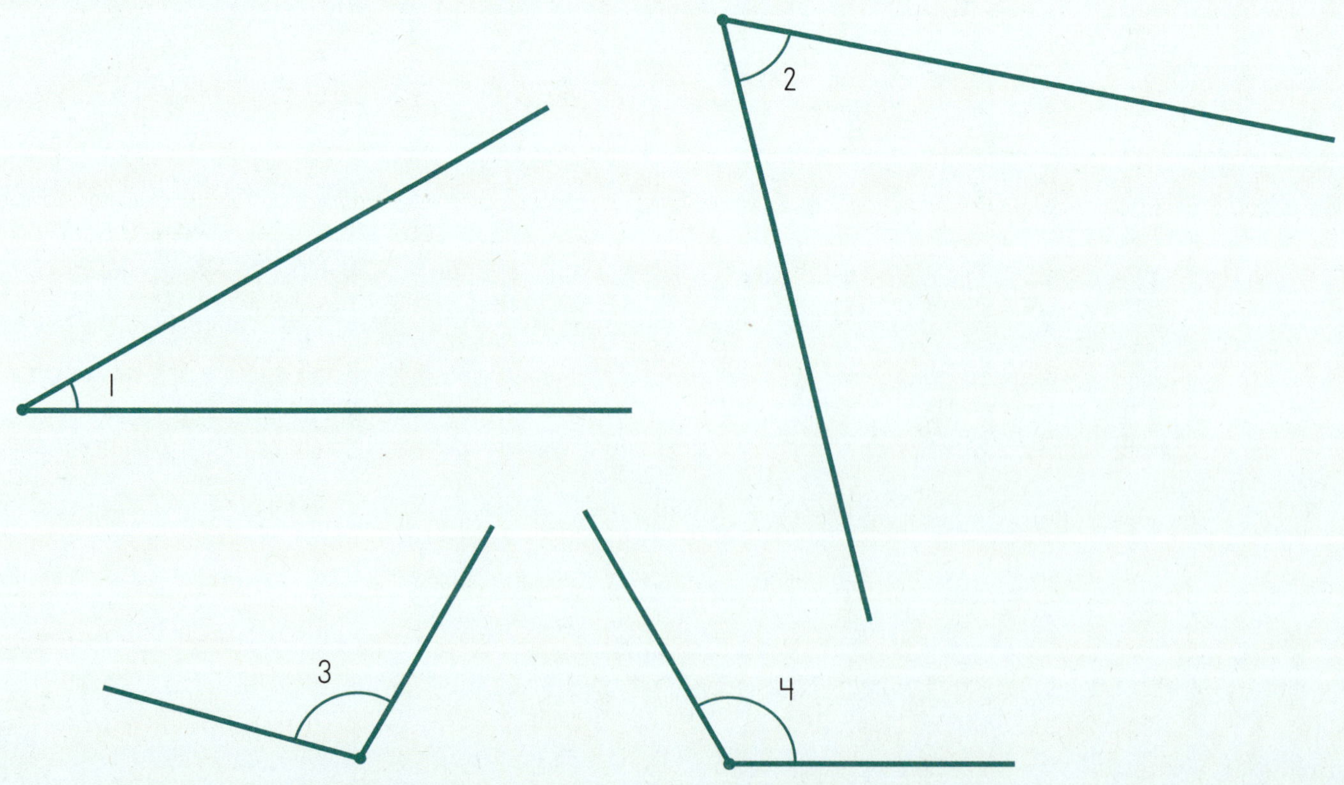

Practice

Use the printed protractor to measure the angles.

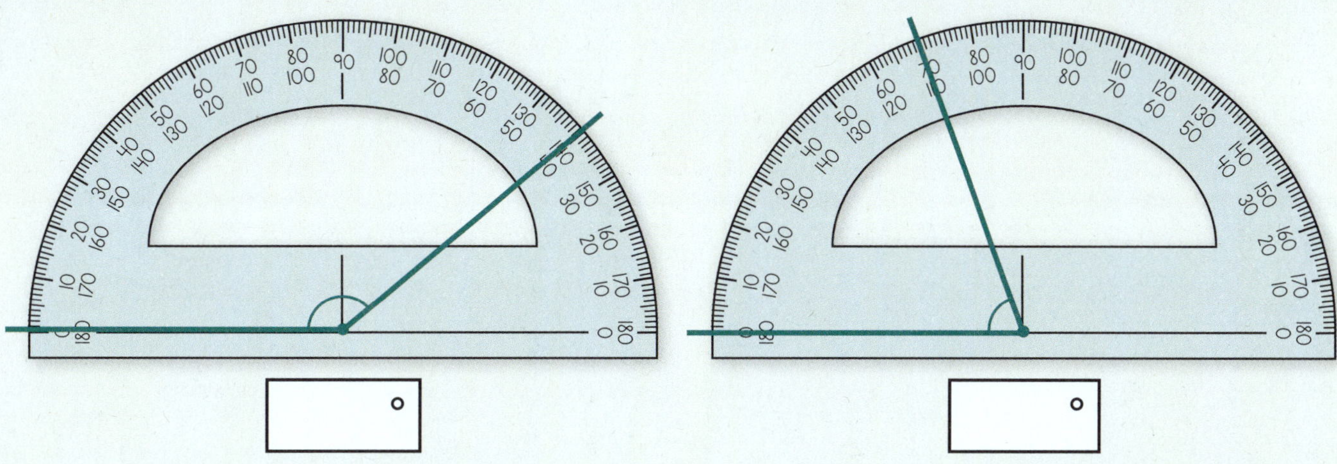

<table>
<tr><td></td><td>°</td><td></td><td>°</td></tr>
</table>

Use a real protractor to measure the angles. Extend the sides as needed.

Angle	Measure
∠L	
∠M	
∠N	
∠O	

Review

Complete.

<table>
<tr><td>3,0 7 8</td></tr>
<tr><td>×   6</td></tr>
</table>

<table>
<tr><td>4,2 9 0</td></tr>
<tr><td>×   5</td></tr>
</table>

<table>
<tr><td>6,7 0 8</td></tr>
<tr><td>×   9</td></tr>
</table>

Complete.

$(6 \times 10) - (6 \times 2) = \boxed{}$

$6 \times (10 - 2) = \boxed{}$

$(6 \times 5) + (6 \times 3) = \boxed{}$

$6 \times (5 + 3) = \boxed{}$

★ $6 \times (1 + \boxed{}) = 48$

Find the perimeter and area.

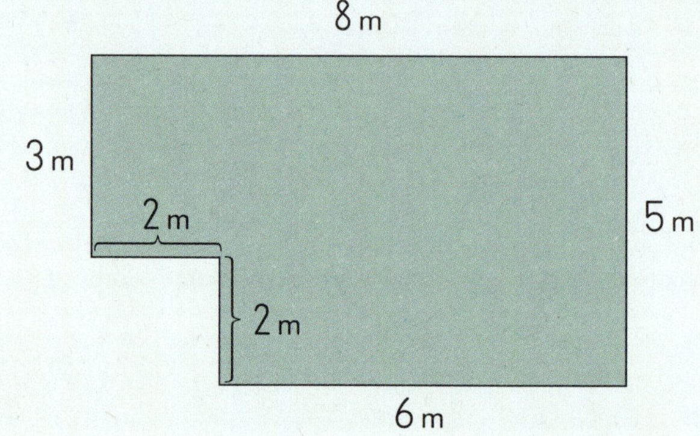

Perimeter: ______________

Area: ______________

Solve. Write the equations you use.

Apollos uses $\frac{2}{3}$ cup of brown sugar and $\frac{2}{3}$ cup of white sugar to make chocolate chip cookies.
How much sugar does he use in all?

Janessa's family has a 5 kg bag of potatoes. She helps her dad peel $2\frac{2}{10}$ kg to make a big batch of mashed potatoes.
How many kilograms of potatoes do they have left?

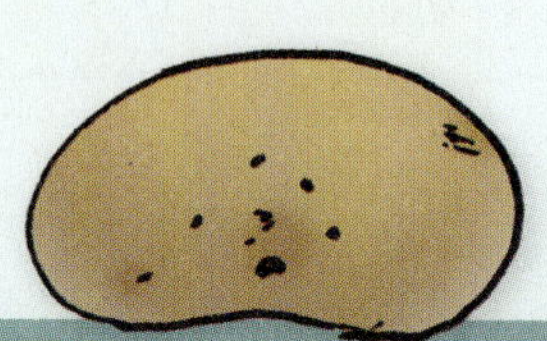

Lesson Activities 

A

B

C

Player 1	Player 2

Practice Use a protractor to draw an angle with the given measure. Use the printed line for one side. Use the dot for the vertex.

80° 35°

140° 105°

Review 

Complete. Follow the steps.

1. Divide
2. Multiply
3. Subtract

7⟌65   6⟌45   8⟌75   9⟌55

Color the problems that match the number in the star.

| 71 − 68 |
| 60 ÷ 30 |
| 36 ÷ 12 |

| 96 − 91 |
| 110 − 106 |
| 48 ÷ 12 |

| 63 − 56 |
| 77 ÷ 11 |
| 92 − 84 |

| 108 ÷ 12 |
| 81 − 72 |
| 270 ÷ 3 |

| 200 ÷ 4 |
| 210 ÷ 7 |
| 15 × 2 |

| 25 × 2 |
| 200 ÷ 5 |
| 360 ÷ 9 |

| 35 × 2 |
| 240 ÷ 3 |
| 210 ÷ 3 |

| 720 ÷ 8 |
| 55 × 2 |
| 45 × 2 |

Solve. Write the equations you use.

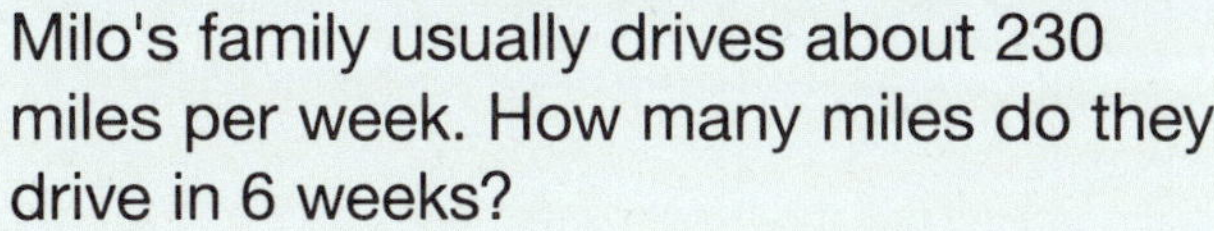

Aliya walks 5 km each day. How many kilometers does she walk in 31 days?

Milo's family usually drives about 230 miles per week. How many miles do they drive in 6 weeks?

A

Pattern Block Angles

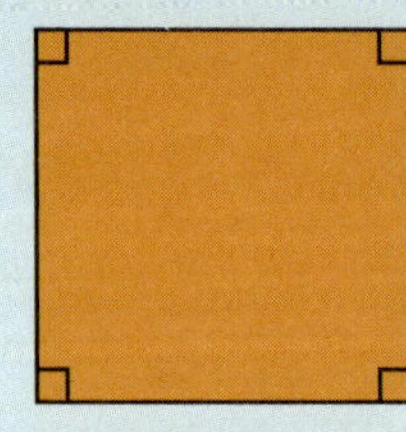

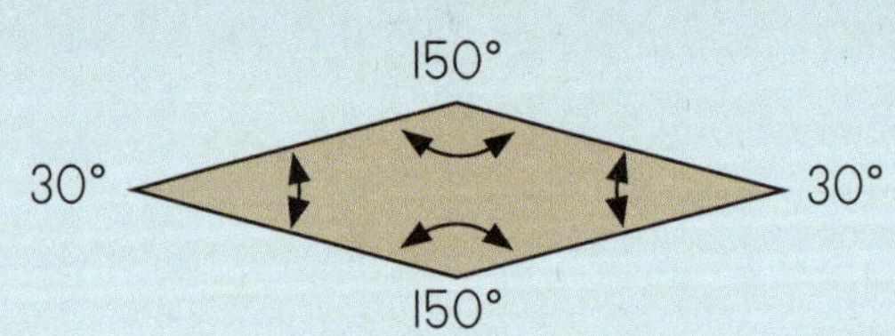

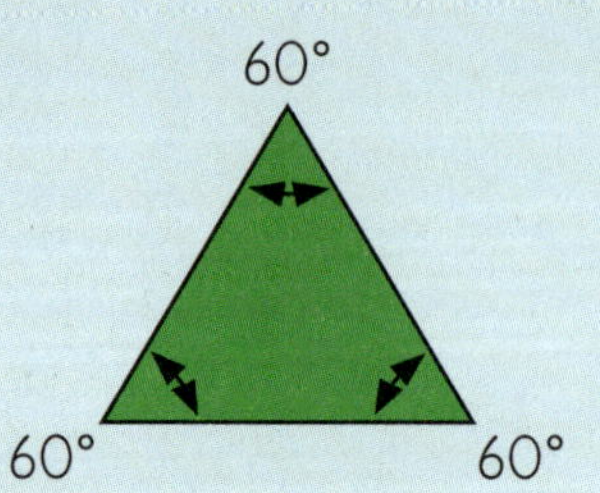

A

Equations

m∠ A =

B

Equations

m∠ B =

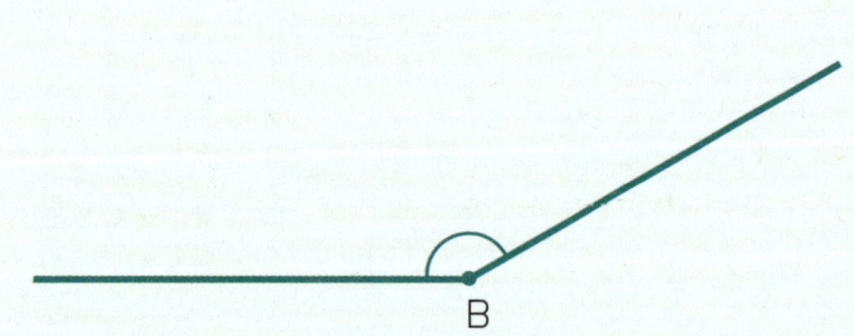

C

Equations

m∠ C =

Practice

Use the labeled angles to find the missing angle measures.

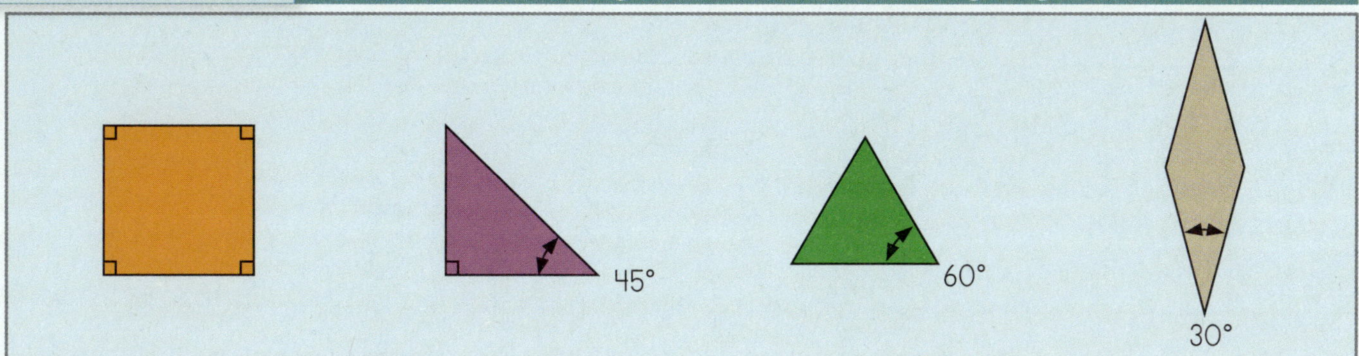

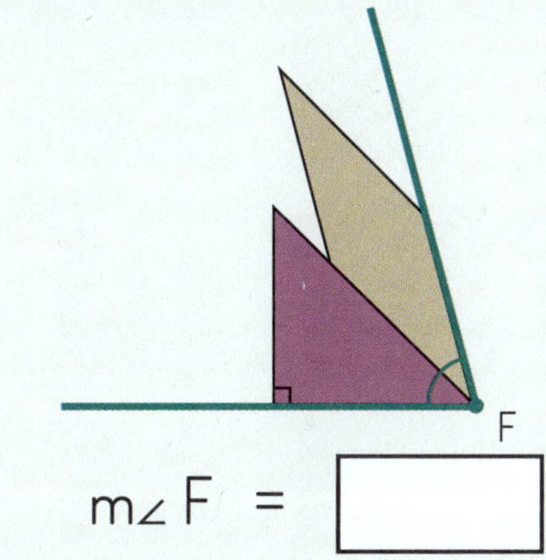

m∠ F = ________

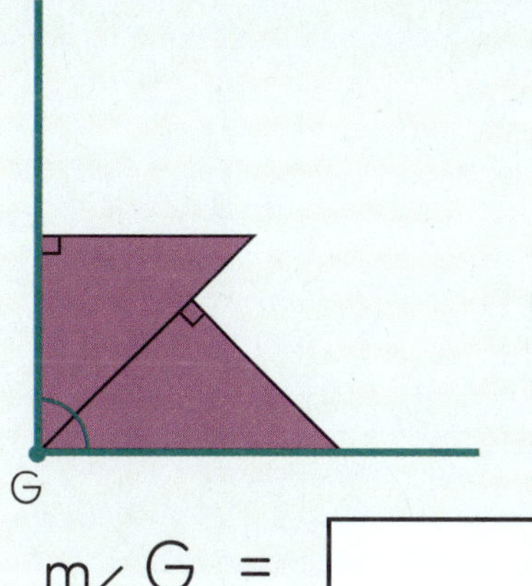

m∠ G = ________

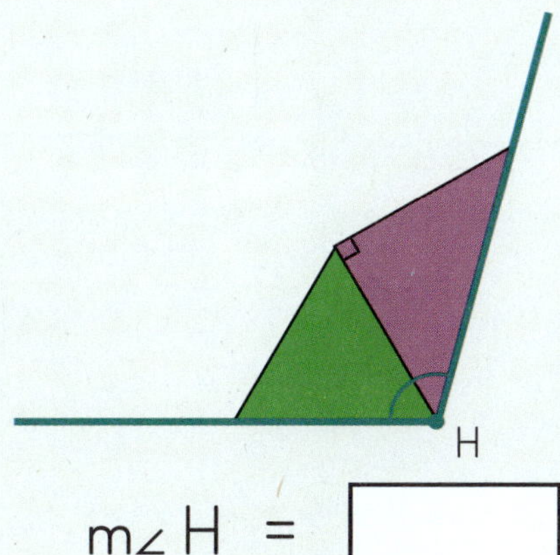

m∠ H = ________

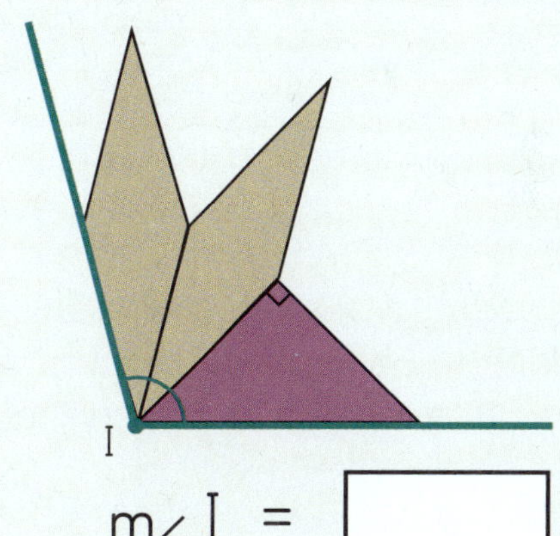

m∠ I = ________

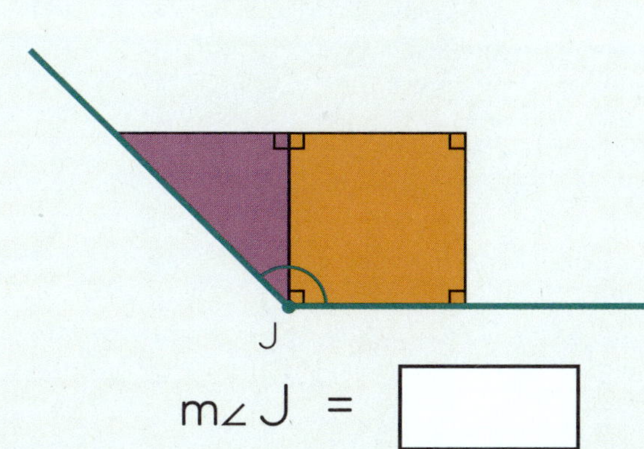

m∠ J = ________

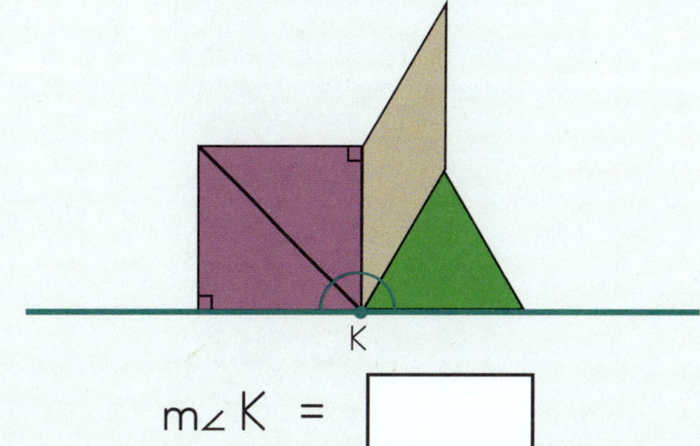

m∠ K = ________

Review · Complete.

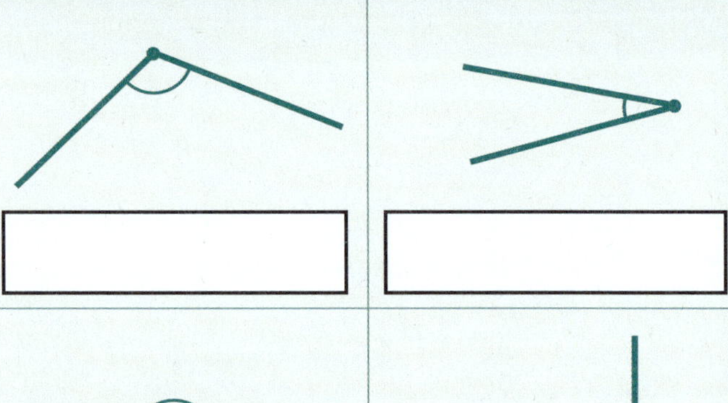

8	4	5
×		7

9	3	7
×		4

8	2	5
×		8

7	0	7
×		7

Write whether each angle is acute, right, obtuse, or straight.

Circle the prime numbers. X the composite numbers.

15	16	17	18
19	20	21	22
23	24	25	26
27	28	29	30

Solve. Write the equations you use.

Evie sews together 5 pieces of fabric to make a blanket. Each piece of fabric is 30 in. long and 8 in. wide. What is the total area of the blanket?

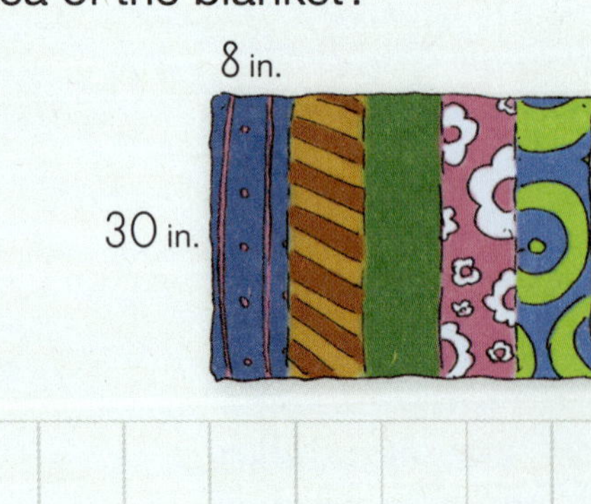

Eliana's backyard is shaped like a square. Each side is 76 feet long.
What is the perimeter of her yard?

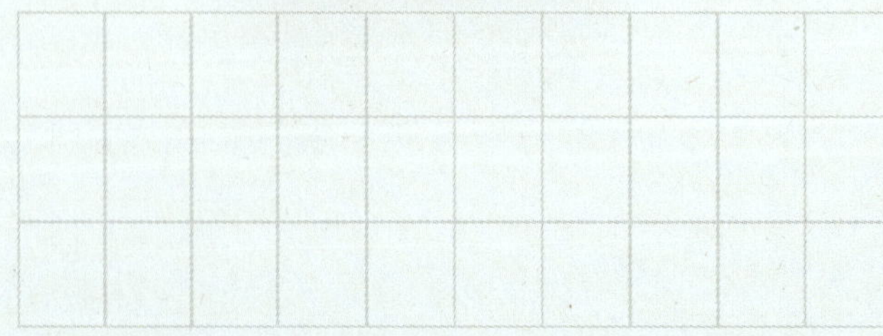

Lesson Activities

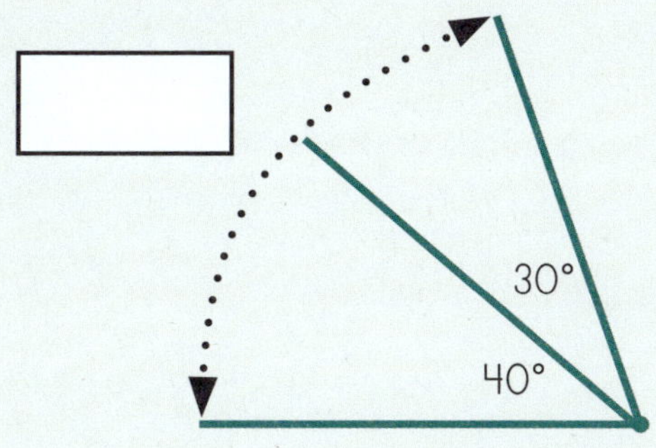

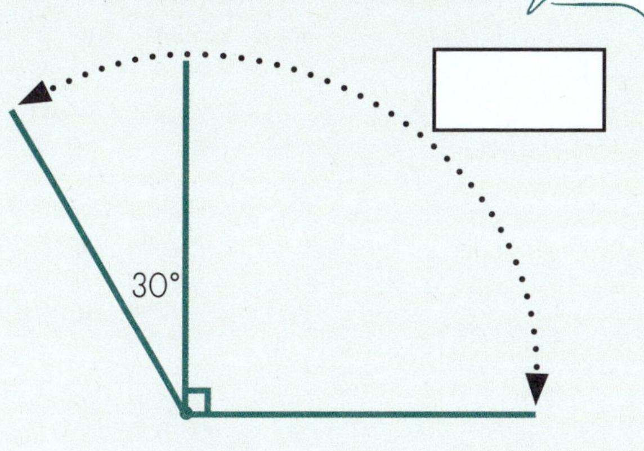

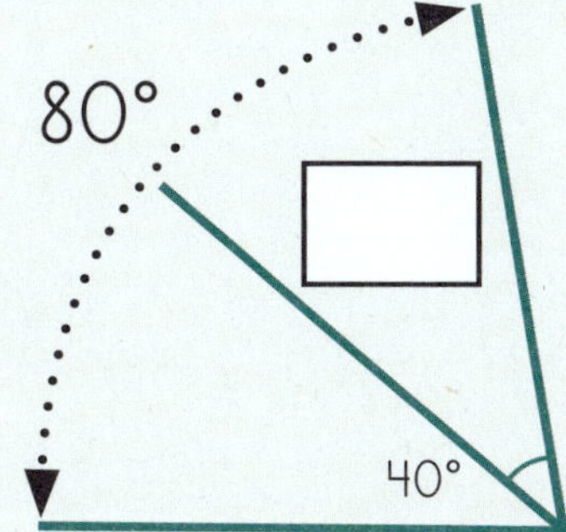

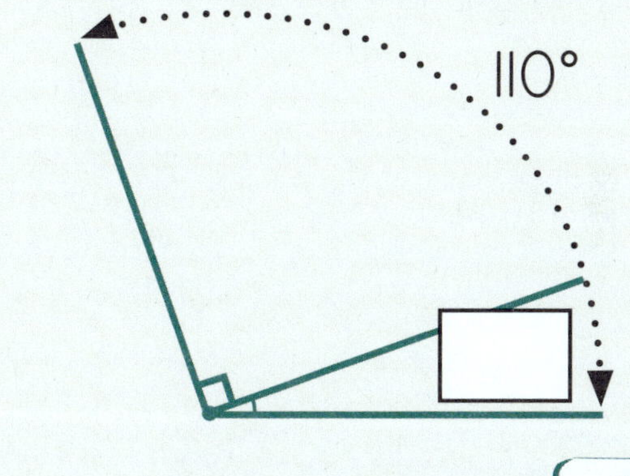

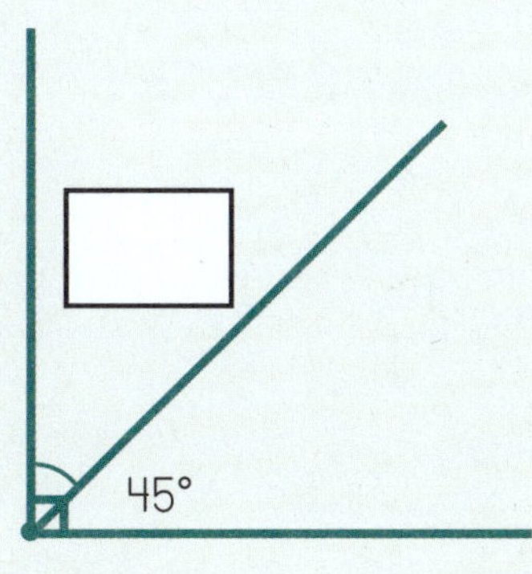

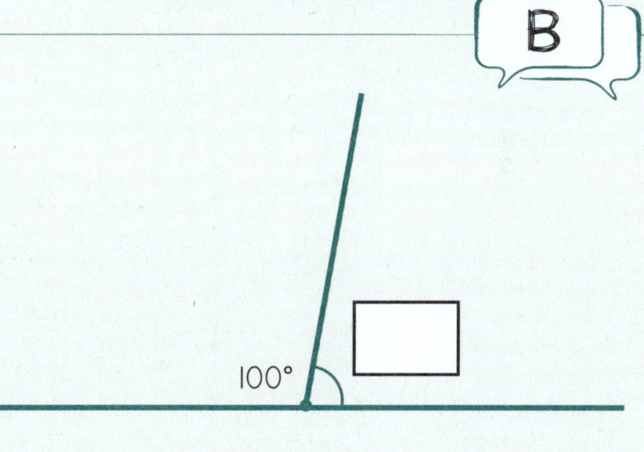

Practice   Find the missing angle measures.

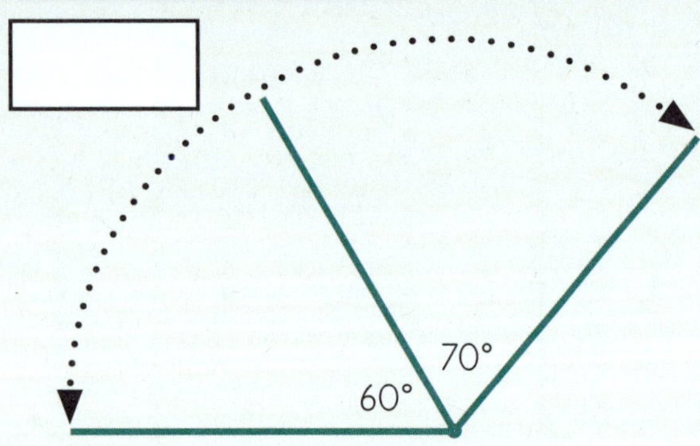

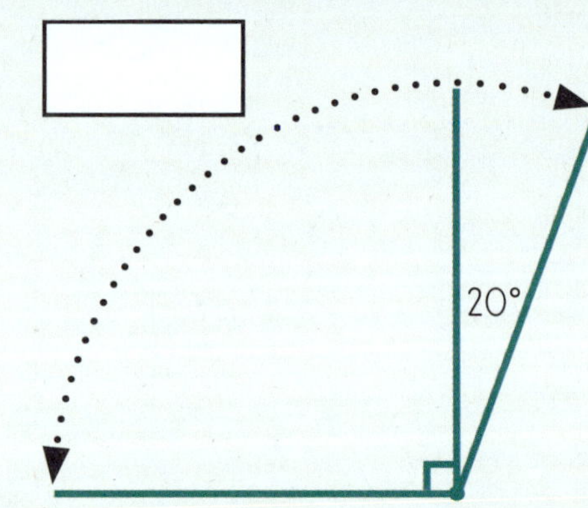

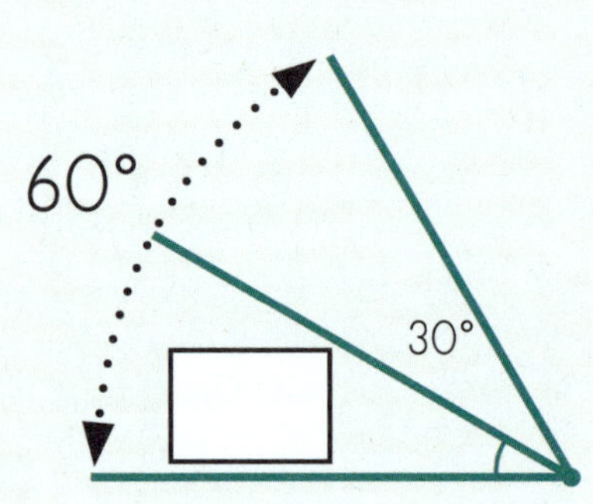

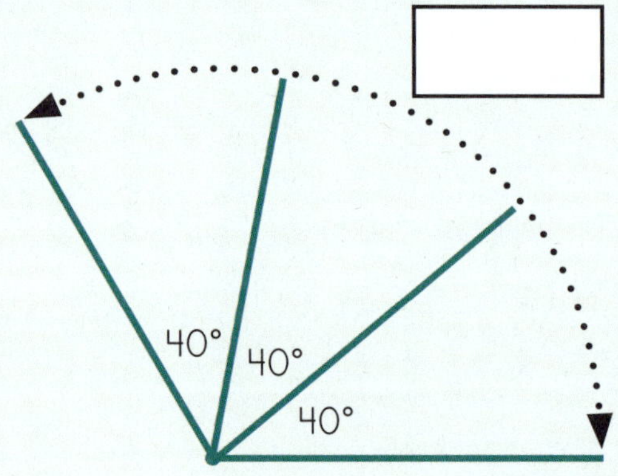

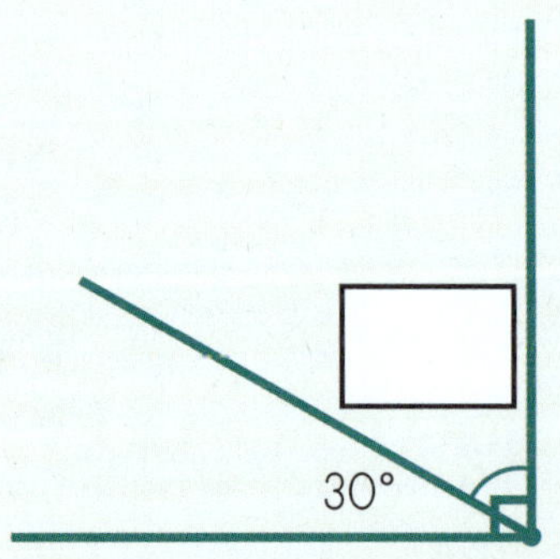

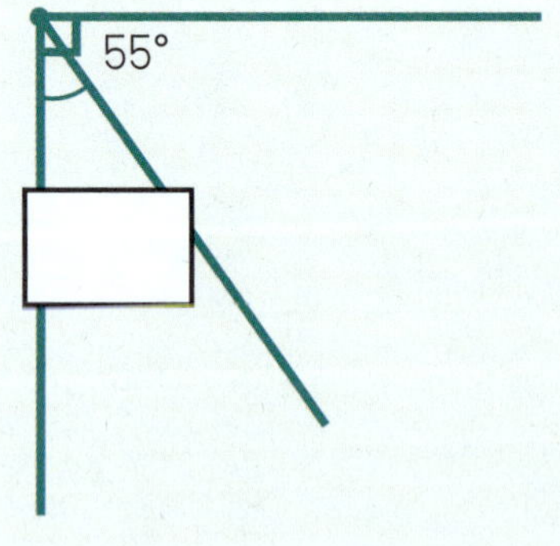

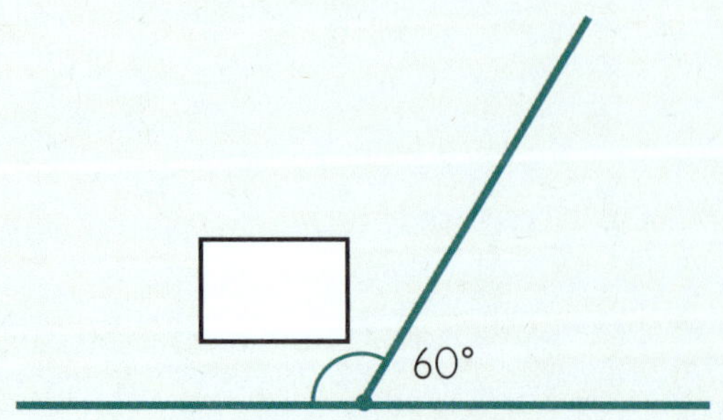

★
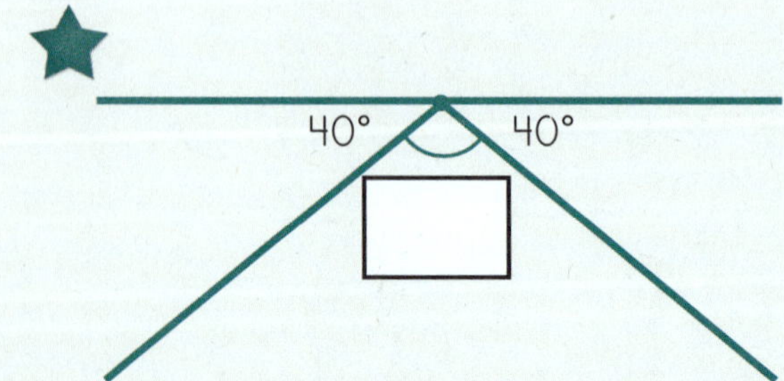

Review

Complete.

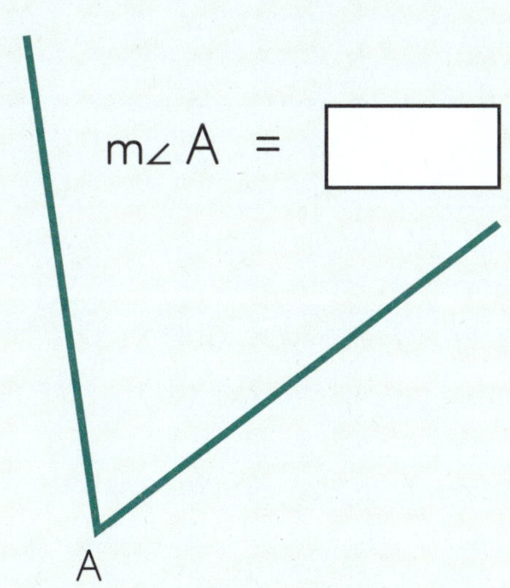

	3	$\frac{1}{5}$
+	2	$\frac{3}{5}$

	7	$\frac{1}{10}$
−	4	$\frac{6}{10}$

	4	$\frac{3}{8}$
+	2	$\frac{2}{8}$

	5	
−	2	$\frac{5}{6}$

Use a protractor to measure the angles. Extend the sides as needed.

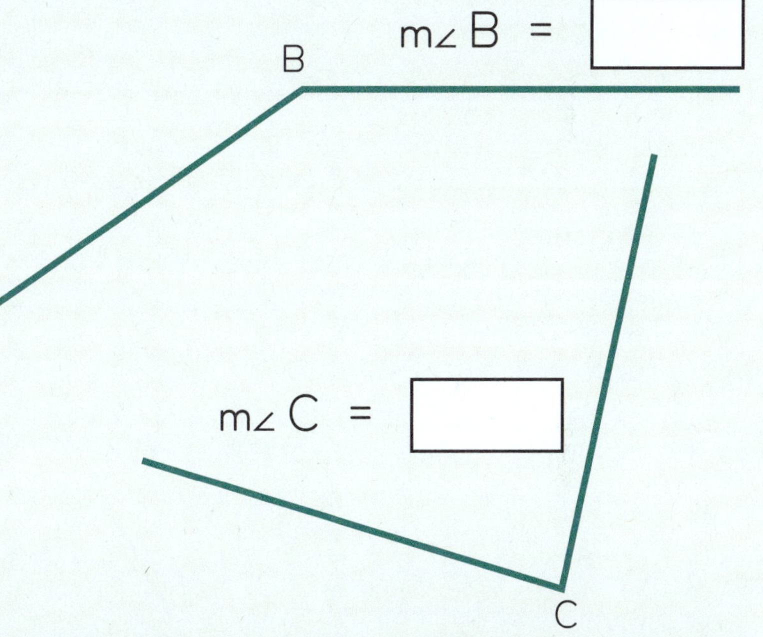

Solve. Write the equations you use.

Forge has 28 craft sticks.
He needs 3 sticks for each snowflake craft.
After he makes as many snowflakes
as possible, how many craft sticks will he
have left?

3 friends work together to earn $150.
They split the money equally.
How much does each friend get?

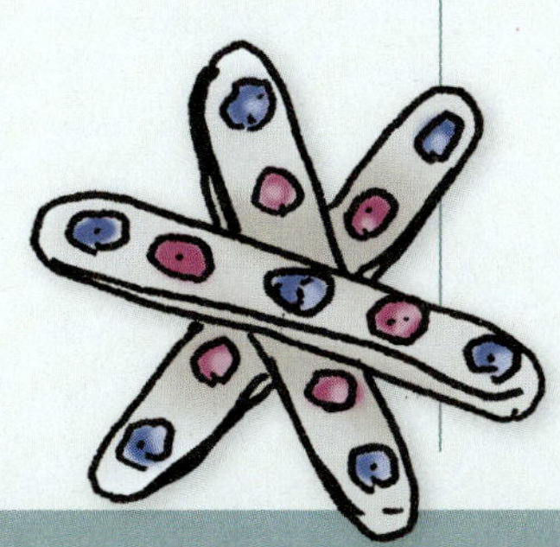

Unit Wrap-Up

Choose the more reasonable measurement for each angle.

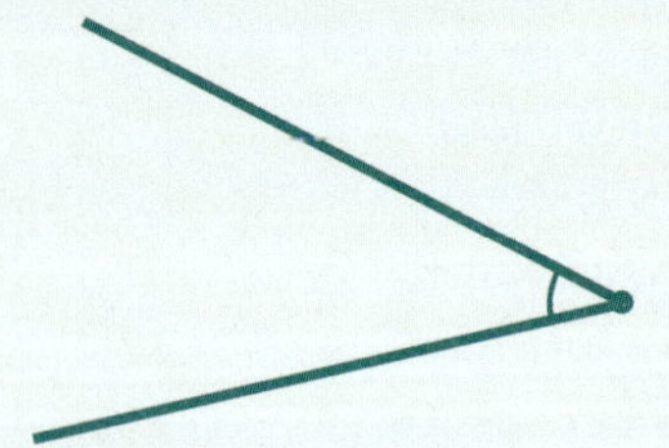

40°	80°

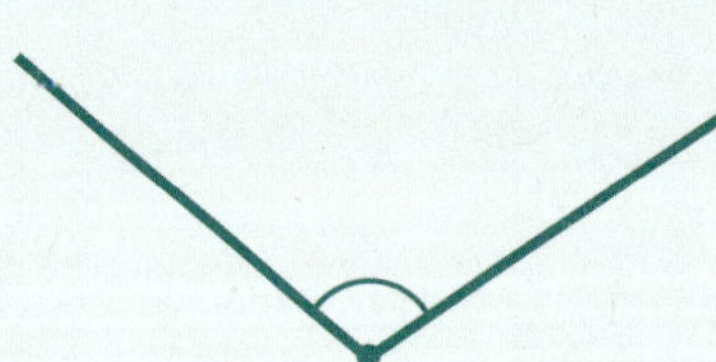

105°	150°

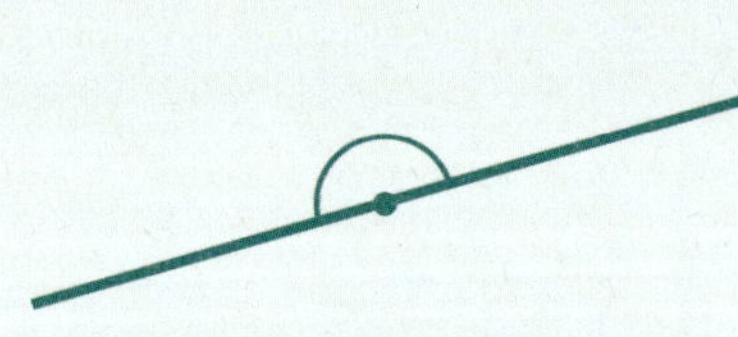

170°	180°

Write whether each angle is acute, right, obtuse, or straight. Then, use a protractor to measure each angle.

Angle	∠Q	∠R	∠S	∠T
Type				
Measure				

Unit Wrap-Up

Use a protractor to draw an angle with the given measure. Use the printed line for one side. Use the dot for the vertex.

| 25° | 125° |

Find the missing angle measures.

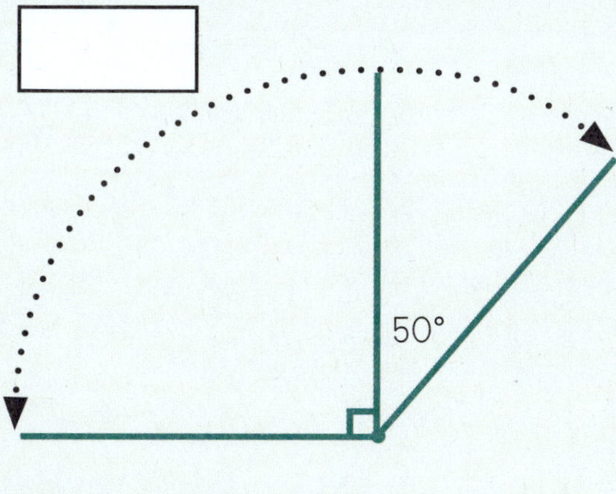

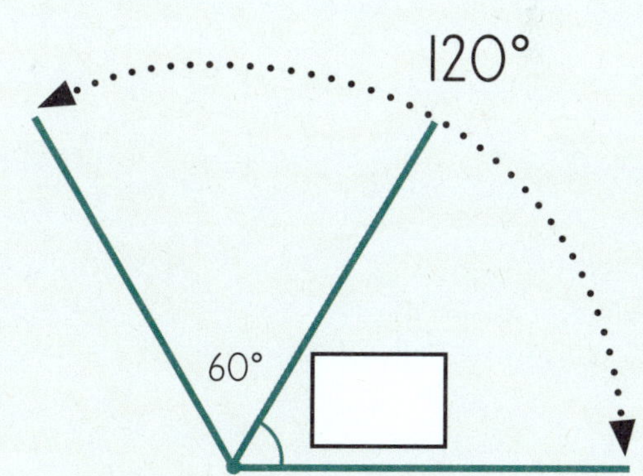

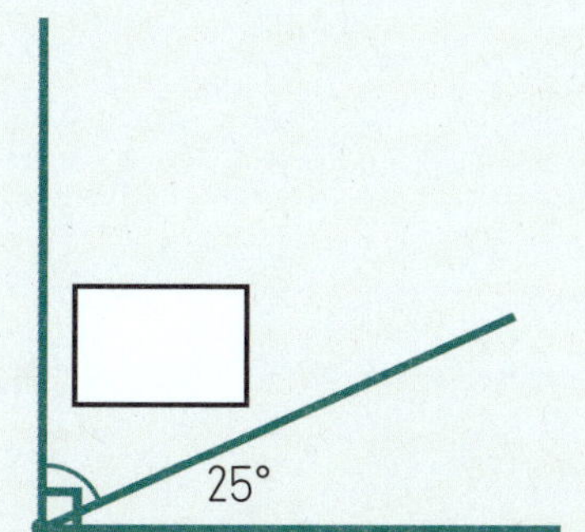

★

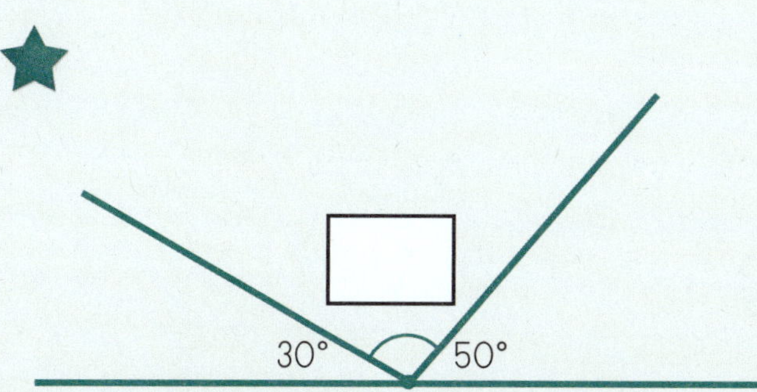